The fall of the Fre
1787–1792

The fall of the
French monarchy
1787–1792

MICHEL VOVELLE

Translated by

SUSAN BURKE

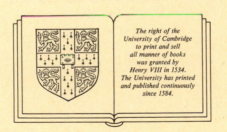

The right of the
University of Cambridge
to print and sell
all manner of books
was granted by
Henry VIII in 1534.
The University has printed
and published continuously
since 1584.

CAMBRIDGE UNIVERSITY PRESS

Cambridge

London   New York   New Rochelle   Melbourne   Sydney

EDITIONS DE LA MAISON DES SCIENCES DE L'HOMME

Paris

Published by the Press Syndicate of the University of Cambridge
The Pitt Building, Trumpington Street, Cambridge CB2 1RP
32 East 57th Street, New York, NY 10022, USA
10 Stamford Road, Oakleigh, Melbourne 3166, Australia
and Editions de la Maison des Sciences de l'Homme
54 Boulevard Raspail, 75270 Paris Cedex 06

Originally published in French as *La Chute de la monarchie 1787–1792*
by Editions du Seuil 1972
and © Editions du Seuil 1972
First published in English by Editions de la Maison des Sciences de l'Homme
and Cambridge University Press 1984 as *The fall of the French monarchy
1787–1792*
English translation © Maison des Sciences de l'Homme and
Cambridge University Press 1984
Reprinted 1986

Printed in Great Britain by the University Press, Cambridge

Library of Congress catalogue card number: 83-7800

British Library Cataloguing in Publication Data

Vovelle, Michel
The fall of the French monarchy 1787–1792.–(The French Revolution; 1)
1. France–Politics and government–Revolution, 1789–1799
I. Title   II. La chute de la monarchie
1787–1792. *English*   III. Series
944.04   DC155

ISBN 0 521 24723 3 hard covers
ISBN 0 521 28916 5 paperback
ISBN 2 7351 0032 4 hard covers (France only)
ISBN 2 7351 0033 2 paperback (France only)

Contents

Chronology   *page* ix
Preface   xv

1   The *ancien régime*   1

Feudalism   1
Fiefs and feudalism: a debate. The originality of the French
system. The network of seigneurial rights. Landed society:
distribution of property. Forms of cultivation. The world of
the peasants: collective life. Peasant society. A world ruled by
tradition? Technology and production. Tensions in rural
society.

A society of orders   13
A current controversy. The nobility. The noble reaction. The
clergy: structures and functions. The world of the clerics:
diversity. Crisis in the French clergy? Is the third estate an
order? Corporations. From fraternities to unions.

Absolutism   24
Controversies: absolutism French-style. The king and his
court. The royal government. Local administration. The army,
justice and taxation. Incoherence: the weight of the past.
Social limits: the world of privilege. The debate over
absolutism.

2   Conflict and change   38

The 'glorious' eighteenth century   38
The towns. The 'Atlantic' France of the merchants. The
structures of French industry. Change in the rural world.
Population growth. Price movements. The problem of French
economic 'take-off'. 'Prosperity Revolution' or 'poverty
Revolution'?

The bourgeoisie: myth or reality?   49
The controversy over the 'bourgeois' Revolution. Financiers,
businessmen, bosses. Mixed types: *rentiers* and professional
men. The other revolt. The multiplicity of urban society. The
'workshop' and the 'stall'.

An enlightened Revolution?   59
The diffusion of the Enlightenment. The culture of the
popular classes. Popular religious practice. Between illiterates
and élites. A debate over the élite. The culture and the
structures of the élite. A turning-point in sensibility. Was the
élite revolutionary?

3   Birth of a Revolution (1787 to May 1789)   73

Aristocratic revolt or pre-Revolution
(summer 1786 to summer 1788)   73
A mediocre monarch. Political crisis: the deficit. Calonne and
the notables. The Brienne ministry. The 'Revolution of the
notables'. The example of Dauphiné. Was a compromise
possible?

Crisis and revolution   83
An 'intercycle of recession'. The economic crisis. The social
crisis. Risings in the town and in the countryside.

From complaints to demands   89
New problems, old-fashioned spokesmen. 'Patriotic party' or
'national party'. The *cahiers de doléances*. Content of the
cahiers. The elections to the Estates General. The deputies.

4   The constitutional Revolution   99

Three Revolutions? Or one Revolution?
(5 May to 6 October 1789)   99
A single or multiple Revolution? The Revolution at the top
(May to July 1789). Disturbances in the towns. Paris, the
centre of the Revolution. The 'municipal Revolution'. Rural
risings. The Grande Peur. Reaction to the Grande Peur. The
night of 4 August. The difficulties of the Revolution of the
parlements. The 'days' of October 1789.

The false respite   118
Was there a 'fortunate year'? The organisation of political life.
The Constituent Assembly: factions and individuals. La
Fayette: a new Caesar? The Festival of the Federation. The
geography of the counter-revolution. The attempt to regain

control. The financial crisis and the birth of the *assignat*. The
religious problem.

The hardening of political attitudes
(*summer 1790 to summer 1791*)   131
Politics. Clashes at the base. The counter-revolution. The
religious schism. The Revolution and Europe. The *émigrés*. The
flight to Varennes and its aftermath. The Champ-de-Mars
massacre.

5 Revolutionary France (1789–92)   146

A new France: institutions in 1791–2   146
Revolutionary proclamations. Equality. Liberty. Property and
economic freedom. France reconstructed. The constitutional
monarchy. The legislative power. Local government. The
judicial system and the army. Financial reforms. The Church
and the State. The consequences of the schism.

A new equilibrium or a boiling point?   162
Economic pressures. Population movements. A redistribution
of roles? Redistribution of the *biens*?

The revolutionary dynamic   171
The Assembly and its deputies. Local political life.
Revolutionary practice. The revolutionary 'days'. The
revolutionary crowds and action in the countryside. Ideas and
actions. The sociology of the participants. The clubs. The
national guards. The birth of the section movement. Public
opinion. The revolutionary press. The revolutionary festival.
Revolutionary symbols. A new aesthetic sensibility.

Obstacles: an ignorant or hostile France   199
Ignorance. A map of rejection. Who are the aristocrats? The
ideas of the counter-revolutionaries. New revolutionary
proclamations.

6 The second Revolution   210

From the crisis at home to the foreign war
(*October 1791 to April 1792*)   211
The Legislative Assembly. The counter-revolutionary peril. An
economic and social crisis. The *sans-culottes*. The coming of
war. The Jacobin ministry.

From war to the fall of the monarchy
(*20 April to 10 August 1792*)   223
The period of setbacks. The failure of the Girondins. The

'day' of 20 June. The eve of 10 August. Patriotic and democratic movements. The fall of the monarchy.

Glossary   233
Bibliography   238
Index of names   244

Chronology

1787

22 February	Meeting of the Assembly of Notables
8 April	Dismissal of Calonne, replaced by Loménie de Brienne
25 May	Dismissal of the Assembly of Notables
June	Brienne's reforming edicts
16 July	The Parlement of Paris appeals against them to the Estates General
14 August	Exile of the Parlement
4 September	Recall of the Parlement

1788

5 May	Arrest of d'Eprémesnil and Montsabert, leaders of the Parlement
8 May	Lamoignon's reform of justice
7 June	'Day of Tiles' in Grenoble
21 July	Assembly of Vizille
8 August	Estates General summoned for 1 May 1789
24–26 August	Dismissal and recall of Necker
5 October	Second Assembly of Notables

1789

24 January	Letter of summons and electoral regulations for the Estates General
March	Elections to the Estates General
March–May	Peasant revolts in Provence, Cambrésis and Picardy
27–28 April	Riots in the Faubourg Saint-Antoine against Réveillon
5 May	Formal opening of the Estates General
6 May	The third estate takes the name of 'Commons' and demands the verification of powers

ix

17 June	The Commons call themselves the 'National Assembly'
20 June	The oath of the Jeu de Paume
23 June	The king visits the Assembly and refuses the demands of the deputies
27 June	The king persuades the clergy and the nobility to join the third estate
9 July	The National Assembly calls itself the 'Constituent Assembly'
11 July	Dismissal of Necker
12 July	Riots in the Palais-Royal in Paris; charge of the Royal German dragoons
14 July	THE TAKING OF THE BASTILLE
16 July	Recall of Necker
17–19 July	Rising in the Normandy *bocage* begins
15–31 July	'Municipal revolt'
20 July	Beginning of the Grande Peur
22 July	Bertier de Sauvigny, *intendant* of Paris, hanged by the people
22–26 July	Risings in Alsace and Franche-Comté begin
4 August	NIGHT OF 4 AUGUST: privileges relinquished
26 August	Declaration of the Rights of Man
28 August–	
11 September	Debates on the royal veto
1 October	Banquet of the lifeguards and the Flanders regiment
5–6 October	The march on Versailles; the king is taken back to Paris
15 October	Secret correspondence between Mirabeau and the king begins
21 October	Martial law decreed
2 November	Secularisation of Church property
29 November	Confederation of the national guard at Etoile near Valence

1790

January	Peasant revolts in Quercy, Périgord and Brittany
2 February	Claude Dansart founds the first Fraternal society for both sexes
13 February	Monastic vows for life prohibited
19 February	The Marquis de Favras, a royalist conspirator, is hanged
April–June	Trouble in the south-east (Nîmes, 6 April–13 June; Montauban, 10 May)

17 April	*Assignats* issued
27 April	Cordelier club founded
15–22 May	Discussion of rights to declare war and make peace
31 May	Discussion of Civil Constitution of the clergy begins
10–12 June	Rising in Avignon in favour of union with France
12 July	Civil Constitution of the clergy voted
14 July	Festival of the Federation in Paris
22 July	Civil Constitution of the clergy receives the royal assent
18 August	First counter-revolutionary assembly at the Jalès camp in the Vivarais
26 August	Constituent Assembly repudiates the 'family arrangement' with Spain
31 August	Massacre of the Swiss guards of Châteauvieux at Nancy
4 September	Dismissal of Necker, followed by the dismissal of the other ministers and the formation of a pro-La Fayette government (20 October)
28 October	Affair of the *princes possessionnés* of Alsace
27 November	Civil servants obliged to take an oath 'to the Nation, the Law and the King'
3 December	Letter of Louis XVI to the king of Prussia to demand a Congress of the European Powers

1791

3 January	Civil servants obliged to take an oath to support the Civil Constitution of the clergy
February	Formation of the constitutional clergy
19 February	The king's aunts emigrate
21 February	Debate on *émigrés* at the Assembly
28 February	'Conspiracy' of the 'knights of the dagger'
2 March	'Allarde' law suppresses corporate bodies
11 March	Pope condemns Civil Constitution of the clergy (brief *Quod aliquantum*)
2 April	Death of Mirabeau
4 April	Body of Mirabeau taken to the Panthéon
13 April	Pope reiterates condemnation of the Civil Constitution of the clergy
18 April	King prevented from going to Saint-Cloud
7–15 May	Debate on the colonies and the rights of non-whites
30 May and 14 June	First and second 'Le Chapelier' laws proscribe craft unions
11 June	Voltaire's ashes transferred to the Panthéon

20–21 June	Flight of the royal family and their arrest at Varennes
end of June	Campaign to abolish the monarchy
13–16 July	Debate in the Assembly on the flight of the king and decrees on his reinstatement
16 July	Feuillants separate themselves from the Jacobins
17 July	Massacre of the Champ-de-Mars
end of July	Repression of the democratic movement
4 August	First battalions of volunteers raised
5 August	'Declaration of world peace' by the Constituent Assembly
27 August	Declaration of Pillnitz
3 September	Constitutional act drafted
13 September	Constitutional act approved by the king
1 October	OPENING OF THE LEGISLATIVE ASSEMBLY
16 October	Trouble in Avignon (murder of Lécuyer, massacre of the Glacière)
31 October	Decree of the Assembly enjoining the king's brother to return to France
9 November	Decree of Assembly on *émigrés*
11 November	King vetoes last two decrees
14 November	Jérôme Pétion becomes mayor of Paris
29 November	Decree of Assembly against non-juring priests
7 December	Formation of a Feuillant administration
12 December–	
2 January	Robespierre's speeches against the war
19 December	King vetoes decree on non-juring priests

1792

6 January	Elector of Trier 'disperses' the *émigrés*
23 January	Sugar and coffee riots begin in Paris
February–March	Food riots and peasant revolt
end February– beginning March	Counter-revolutionary disturbances in Lozère and Dauphiné and La Rouairie's conspiracy in the west
15 March	'Jacobin' administration with Roland and Clavière
15 April	Festival of Liberty in honour of the Swiss guards of Châteauvieux
20 April	WAR DECLARED ON THE 'KING OF BOHEMIA AND HUNGARY'
28–29 April	First defeats at the frontier: General Dillon lynched by his troops
5 May	New levy of national volunteers

16 May	Secret talks between La Fayette and the Austrians and effective end to hostilities
20 May	Brissot denounces the 'Austrian committee'
27 May	Decree on the deportation of non-juring priests
8 June	Plan to levy 20,000 *fédérés*
11 June	King vetoes decrees on *fédérés* and non-juring priests
12 June	Roland's administration dismissed
20 June	The people of Paris invade the Tuileries and ask the king, without success, to sanction the decrees
27 June	La Fayette tries to intimidate the Assembly
27 June	Petition against the monarchy by the general council of Marseilles
11 July	Assembly declares 'the fatherland in danger' (decree proclaimed 21 July)
15 July	Cordelier club demands a 'Convention'
17 July	In Paris, the *fédérés* demand the suspension of the king
20 July	Frightened by the popular movement, the followers of Brissot make moves towards the king
25 July	'Brunswick manifesto' menaces Paris with reprisals and 'total upheaval'
3 August	47 out of 48 Paris sections demand the dismissal of the king
10 August	THE TAKING OF THE TUILERIES AND THE FALL OF THE MONARCHY

Preface

Because it is a constant source of new questions, the French Revolution has not ceased to be controversial. Fifty years ago there was a conflict – substantive and methodological – between supporters of Robespierre and of Danton. Today there is an opposition between adherents of the Jacobin tradition and the 'republican catechism' and those who want to 'reread' the Revolution without ideological blinkers.

Confrontations such as these are not without consequences. They force historians to be precise and to define their terms, and help them – even those who do not accept the current heterodoxy – to leave the beaten track of conventional wisdom.

It seems to us that a truly new approach cannot be confined to a new interpretation of old material. True innovation involves the attempt to draw on the most recent research and to emphasise new discoveries, though without trying to conceal the gaps in our knowledge and the problems which remain.

This is in fact what we are trying to do here. We might have asked ourselves whether the Revolution constantly progressed or whether it would be better to avoid the constrictions of a teleological interpretation and end on 14 July 1790, the culmination of the bourgeois Revolution and the 'fortunate year'. However, we have chosen to begin each chapter with a report on the current state of affairs: the problems, the debates, the controversies. After this introduction, we have emphasised the aspects of the Revolution which are most relevant to our own time and on which new research has concentrated: the social history and the history of collective feelings or sentiments.

1

The 'ancien régime'

Is it anachronistic to speak of the *ancien régime*? Is it not to take too seriously a concept unknown to contemporaries? It is obvious that the Revolution was necessary before the economic, social and political system could be seen as a whole regime, and of course before it could be seen as *ancien*. We plead guilty, but we are unrepentant. Such 'anachronisms' are indispensable if we wish to do more than blindly accept the 'illusion of the epoch'. What is more, we are going to commit a further sin because to describe this system we shall have immediate recourse to the three notions of 'feudalism', 'society of orders' and 'absolutism', any one of which, in its own way, may shock the purist. The main thing is to make ourselves clear.

FEUDALISM

Fiefs and feudalism: a debate

To characterise the socio-economic structure dominant on the eve of the Revolution as 'feudal' is, we are told, to misuse language: historians of the Middle Ages remind us that this label can legitimately be applied only to a very precise set of relations which obtained at only one period. A number of historians of the early modern period, or of the Revolution, accept this restriction (for example Roland Mousnier, Georges Lefebvre himself). In practice, though, this fine distinction has not been observed. From the beginning of the Revolution the term has been employed unquestioningly: it has been legitimised by usage provided that one asks oneself what Frenchmen of 1789 understood by 'feudal' and 'feudalism'. The jurists of the Constituent Assembly were clear about this. Under the heading of what they called 'complexum feudale' in their legal jargon they identified the main elements of the

I

social and legal system: not only what was, in the strict sense, dependent on the fief, but also everything which brought about the subjection of one individual to another, and all that was concerned with the payment of dues, whether in labour, in kind, or in cash. Part of this definition, which was in use until 1792, was subsequently dropped, while another part acquired pejorative overtones and became much more widespread. The expression 'feudal system' (*féodalité*) was to become associated, or synonymous, with tyrannical regimes, oppressive governments and even the monarchy.[1] From a precise relationship of dominance and subordination it came to refer to the whole economic, social and institutional system of the *ancien régime*.

At this point we are not far from what is now called 'feudalism', or the feudal system as defined by a recent conference with some precision: 'All historians present...agreed that one should continue to use the expression "feudal regime" to designate the system characterised by a particular type of property, often by servitude and always by the payment of dues known as "feudal" and "seigneurial"',[2] but also, more widely, all the socio-economic, and even political, institutions associated with this mode of production.

The originality of the French system

In the sense in which we have just defined it the feudal system in the France of 1789 was certainly under threat, if not in its last agony. To understand it better we may compare the French system with two other models of an agrarian regime described by Henri Sée and later by Georges Lefebvre.[3]

On the one hand we have the example of England, which was already emancipated. There the peasants – those who were left – were free and worked within the framework of an agricultural system which was already capitalist in structure. On the other hand, we have the model of the seigneurial regime which covered the whole of central and eastern Europe, where, far from declining, feudalism sometimes gained a stronger hold (in the Russia of Catherine II). Here, the estates of the great aristocratic landowners – boyars, Polish magnates, Junkers – represented the dominant form of land tenure and these estates were exploited by the forced labour of serfs.

[1] Mazauric (18), pp. 119–34. (Figures in brackets refer to the bibliography, pp. 238–43.)
[2] Toulouse conference on *The Abolition of Feudalism*, 1968.
[3] H. Sée, *Histoire du régime agraire en Europe*; Lefebvre (74, 12).

The French system was strikingly different from these two models. It was less advanced than the English regime: the peasant usually had personal freedom but he was still liable to pay seigneurial dues. The lesser and middle peasantry were more independent than their counterparts in England. But the French system was also unlike the seigneurial regime: the peasant owned a not insignificant proportion of the land, so that he no longer experienced forced labour (the *corvée*) as a crushing obligation. This intermediate position is reflected in the legal terms applied to the various forms of land ownership. There were no longer many 'servile tenures' (*tenures serviles*), but, on the other hand, the *alleu* (freehold land involving no duties or restrictions) was still not a common form of tenure, except in certain regions: the axiom *nulle terre sans seigneur* still applied. As far as the seigneurs' estates were concerned, after the breakdown of the medieval system, a distinction emerged between the *domaine proche* or *réserve* which the seigneur exploited himself and over which he retained total control, and the *domaine utile* or *mouvances*, the rest of the estate, over which he only retained a distant interest. This token right was sanctioned by the payment of dues, but the true ownership of the land had passed to another – peasant or otherwise – who could sell it or pass it on as an inheritance. The French system differs from the seigneurial regime in that in France the seigneurial *réserves* represented only a small proportion of the estates, perhaps a quarter, as we shall see.

The legal status of the peasantry confirms this: 95% of French peasants had personal liberty. There remained perhaps a million serfs and *mainmortables*. The *serf de corps*, who could be brought back by force if he escaped, as a function of *droit de suite*, had almost disappeared. But in certain areas of central and eastern France (Franche-Comté) there were still peasants who were *mainmortables*: they had greater personal liberty but their goods could be forfeited if they left the land.

The network of seigneurial rights

So the essential feature of the seigneurial and feudal regimes – the 'complexum feudale' of the jurists – was simply the payment of certain dues, which is not to say that the burden was a light one.

Under the feudal regime in the strict sense, we should distinguish the dues liable to be paid on noble holdings or fiefs from those paid on the holdings of commoners. The first group were a continuation of the ancient obligations of a vassal to his overlord: even though the 'vassal' might by now be a bourgeois, or even a peasant. If this vassal were to sell his holdings, or leave them as a legacy, transfer duties had to be paid — *relief, rachat, quint* — which brought in a substantial revenue for the overlord. These were the *fiefs de profit*, as opposed to the *fiefs d'honneur*, the overlord of which had a right to homage. The *aveu et dénombrement* made his presence felt from time to time.

Non-noble lands (*terres roturières*) had their own specific obligations. Some recurred at regular intervals: the *cens* was collected in cash, and thus its value was often much reduced as a result of fluctuations in prices. This was not true for dues paid in kind, which were calculated on the harvest: the *champart*, for example (elsewhere known as the *carpot*, *terrage*, *agrier*, or, in the Midi, the *tasque*), varied between one-twentieth and one-fifth of the harvest in different regions. In addition to these recurrent dues, there were others collected when tenures changed hands: those *lods et ventes* which the tenants claimed were excessive.

Amongst the rights associated with this regime we must include those which derived from past usurpations of public authority. This is particularly true of rights of jurisdiction which were divided into three categories: upper, middle and lower. The highest court — authorised to inflict the death penalty and symbolised by the right to erect a gallows — had become rare, but in certain regions the lowest courts were still common, and were jealously defended as a source of income. It is tempting to pass over the symbolic rights — coats of arms, a privileged place in processions, the special pew reserved for the seigneur in church — but this would be a mistake since these signs of domination were taken seriously and strongly resented. They were not insignificant, any more than the 'useful' dues (*droits utiles*) which complete the seigneurial system. Some of these dues, for example the right of protection (*droit de guet* or *de garde*), were dying out. Others, though relatively limited in scale, were none the less deeply resented — for example the *corvée*, which was assessed in various ways (on lands or on individuals) but which rarely exceeded twelve days a year — a paltry amount in comparison with the Russian peasant, but still too much for men aware of the arbitrary nature of this servitude. They also kicked against the absurd oppression of the *banalités*: the obligation to pay for the use of the seigneur's mill, oven or press. These rights worked in the seigneur's interest, since they gave him the power to decide on the date of the harvests, and priority in the sale of wine (the *banvin*). The payment of taxes to the seigneur had almost disappeared, but he still received dues from fairs and markets. Finally, the privileges of the seigneur with regard to hunting, fishing and the dovecot were bitterly resented, as we can tell from the theft of pigeons and the poaching on seigneurial hunting grounds.

In this tangle of rights, what we need to know is of course the burden they imposed on the peasantry, and this is the subject of current research.[4] The discontinuous data available reveal some marked contrasts. In the Midi, where the seigneurial regime was weak, it appears that the levy represented 3 to 4% of the gross product, sometimes less. On the other hand, in Brittany, in Burgundy and no doubt throughout the north-east it appears to have been extremely heavy. There were several different Frances, and in particular there was a marked contrast between the underprivileged zone which extended from Brittany to the Marche and to Franche-Comté, and the Midi, including the Auvergne, where freehold tenures (*alleux*) were common, which shows that this area was part of the Mediterranean world.

In addition to regional variations, there were changes over time. Let us acknowledge with Ernest Labrousse that the seigneurial levy was a particularly heavy burden in a year of a poor harvest.[5] The seigneurial levy, the main feature of the 'feudal system', the extent and limits of which have been measured by historians, has come to represent one of the most significant, but at the same time most misleading aspects of 'feudalism', a mode of production based on *rente* from land which was without doubt still dominant.

Landed society: distribution of property

Feudal and seigneurial dues were only a part of the system: the aristocrat was only one of those privileged to collect *rentes*. The tithe, a payment of, on average, a tenth of the harvest, was originally intended to cover Church expenses. However, it easily became incorporated into the network of taxes under the *ancien régime* since it was by no means always paid to those one would expect to benefit from it: the 'great tithe-owner' was very often not the parish priest but the chapter or abbey which appointed him. The tithe was sometimes transferred like other forms of revenue, and 'impropriated' (*inféodée*), often becoming an integral part of the income of the local seigneur. There were also numerous ancient and archaic forms of *rente*.

To whom did the land belong? We are far from having a precise answer to this question for every area, and the considerable regional

[4] *Sur le féodalisme* (46).   [5] Labrousse (66).

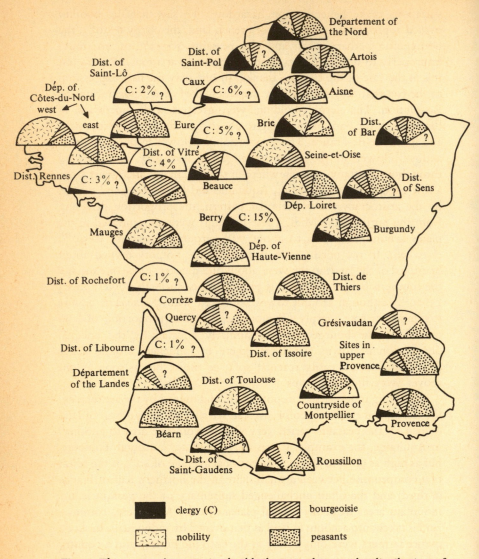

Fig. 1. The *ancien régime* on its deathbed: some data on the distribution of land in France at the end of the *ancien régime*. It should be noted that in certain areas there is only information concerning the percentage of land in clerical hands. In other places the sources do not distinguish between peasants and bourgeoisie. It goes without saying that this sample can offer only an impression of the relative amounts of land in the possession of different groups.

variations make generalisation hazardous. To say that the nobility owned approximately 20–25% of French land, the clergy 6–10%, the bourgeoisie perhaps 30% and the peasants 40–45% is no doubt improperly to disregard very marked regional variations. We can test this in the case of the clergy, 'thanks' (if one may use that expression) to the fact that they were totally dispossessed of their lands during the Revolution. The clergy's holdings were greatest in the north and in the plains of the Paris basin, rising to 20–40% in the plains of the north and in the Ile-de-France. This proportion was lower in the north-east, and still lower in the western *bocage*: it was very low (1–4%) throughout Brittany, and elsewhere in the mountains and (apart from a few exceptions) in the Midi, Aquitaine and Provence. Land owned by the aristocracy shows a similar pattern, the proportion declining from the north to the Midi. These holdings were concentrated in the plains around Paris: up to about 70% around Versailles, 30–40% elsewhere. In the north, as in Burgundy, the nobility owned about one-third of the land; in the west, about one-quarter. Once one reaches the southern half of France this proportion is distinctly lower, about 15–20%, although around towns associated with the *noblesse de robe* it sometimes rose sharply (Toulouse 45%). The proportion of land owned by the bourgeoisie was similarly affected by the unequal distribution of towns and their sphere of influence: around fairly important cities it easily reached 50% or more, but as soon as one moves away the level drops.

By adding together the proportion of land owned by the aristocracy, the clergy and the bourgeoisie, we can see that the proportion of land owned by the peasants varied very widely from one area to another: in Aquitaine, for example, it was only about 22% around Toulouse, but as high as 98% in Béarn. The national average of 40% is the result of a compromise between a small share in the northern half of France (a third) and the often unchallenged supremacy of the peasant in the mountain areas from the central plateau to the Alps: here, common land is taken into account as well as that owned by individuals. In short, owner farmers were only rarely in the extreme minority in a country where peasants owned a respectable proportion of the land. It goes without saying that we must take into account the proportion of the population in each social category.

Forms of cultivation

For that large part of the land from which the peasants were excluded the methods of cultivation played a decisive role. On the periphery of the old kingdom of France – Brittany, Aquitaine, the south-east – there was a mass of archaic tenures, representing an intermediate stage between the old forms of servitude and the modern system of indirect cultivation. There was *albergement* or perpetual leases in the south-east, *casement* in Gascony, *bordelage* in the Nivernais or the Bourbonnais, *tenure en quevaise* or *domaine congéable* in Brittany: numerous different forms of lease which discriminated unfairly in favour of the landlord and which often combined genuine security – the result of ancient links binding the peasant to the land – with heavy demands.

Whatever the importance of these archaic transitional forms, they were increasingly being replaced by modern forms of land tenure: tenant farming (*fermage*) and sharecropping (*métayage*). In rich areas, where the well-to-do farmer could afford to brave one or more lean years in order to profit fully from the good ones, the most common system was that of *fermage* or *arrentement*: the annual payment of a fixed sum, in cash or in kind, for the length of the lease. In poor areas with a precarious economy a sharecropping system was usually in operation (*métayage* or *mégerie*). Under this system, the landowner took a fixed percentage of the profits. These two systems of land tenure cut France in two: the rich areas of large-scale cultivation in the plains were areas of tenant farming; sharecropping, in various forms, was particularly common in the south-west. There were areas where the two systems coexisted, for example Provence, and there were also areas which fluctuated: for example in Lorraine the extent of tenant farming varied in direct response to changes in prosperity.

This observation of regional variations leads us to another question: how important were the *rentes* in terms of the total income of individuals and of communities? From every point of view they were dominant: seigneurial dues and the modern type of rent were associated with a whole network of additional, marginal but ever-present taxes. All the important estates were burdened with what the *ancien régime* called *rente foncière*, in other words, a perpetual obligation to pay a certain sum. For some areas we are in a position to assess the amount of landed capital: in Toulouse, for example, the aristocracy appears to have owned 71 % of the rural property, 68–85 % of the *rentes* and 63 %

of personal effects.[6] In the France of 1789 *rentes* were undoubtedly more
important than profits.

This enables us to understand the attraction of the aristocracy, or
more generally, of the land-owning classes, as a social model. For the
productive bourgeoisie, upward social mobility required investment in
land and a change to a *rentier* life-style. A new social type emerged:
that of the 'bourgeois' living nobly, i.e. essentially on income from
land. At the next social level, upward mobility involved the acquisition
of noble land and then access to the aristocracy through ennoblement.
On the eve of the Revolution, feudalism still had a powerful influence
on most forms of social behaviour, amongst the very groups which
were to launch an attack on it.

The world of the peasants: collective life

Defined in this broad sense, feudalism depended on the primacy of rural
society which still included the majority of the population. The world
of the subordinated simultaneously complemented and conflicted with
the world of their masters.

This rural society was a powerful demographic and economic force,
and it had a stable, long-established structure. At the end of the *ancien
régime* France had about 26 million inhabitants; 85% of them lived in
the country, and at least two-thirds of these were peasants.

This group was shaped by the routines and structures of the strictly
regulated collective life. The countryside itself dictated the rules, which
meant that life in the France of the plains in the north and in the Paris
basin with its open fields, strip system and intensive methods of
cultivation was very different from that in the *bocage* of the west,
marked by stock-breeding and individualism, or from life in the
Mediterranean Midi, with its irregular fields often planted with vines
and bushes, or from the mountain areas so often owned in common.
Despite these regional variations, the small farm (*manse* or *mas*,*
depending on the area) was disproportionately important, taken
together with its arable land and the surrounding wasteland (*terres vaines
et vagues*), grazing land, heathland, scrub and forests. In each case the
organisation of space required a precise, collective discipline at parish

---

[6] Sentou (40).
* The term *manse* or *mas* refers to the combination of the house and the rich enclosed
lands immediately surrounding it. [Trans.]

level. The parish was the unit of municipal life, especially in the Midi,
and it was everywhere a unit of spiritual life, centred on the Church.
It controlled farming and thus ensured the cohesion of the group,
especially in the open-field areas of northern France. The rotation of
crops within the framework of the three-field system, common grazing
on the fallow land and the care of the communal flock were all vital
preoccupations. There was also the collective administration of the
common land and the supervision of wood-cutting, which was a major
concern in mountain regions. The *bocage* in the west and the more
individualistic Midi shared these practices to a lesser extent, but here
one finds that it was the seigneur who fixed the date of the harvest.

Peasant society

The structure of peasant society, which at first sight seems homogeneous,
also varied considerably from region to region. If we are to give a brief
description of this rural society which was much less monolithic than
it appears, we could take as our point of reference the structure
common, with only slight variations, to the plains of large-scale
cultivation. Here, the crucial factor which created social divisions was
access to the essential means of production: the means of production
in this case being a pair of oxen and a plough, which were necessary
for a minimum level of productivity. This criterion, even more than
the ownership of land, was what characterised the *laboureur* (yeoman
farmer), who usually cultivated his own land side by side with the land
he leased. The *fermier*, a rich *laboureur*, did not need to own land himself
to establish his social superiority: he amassed land belonging to others.
Below this, the small-scale farmer, who often owned his land and was
known as a *personnier* or a *haricotier* or, most often, a *ménager*, formed
an intermediate social group, between the categories we have mentioned
and the *manouvriers* who owned small parcels of land and hired
themselves out to supplement their income. The lowest stratum of this
society were the farm-hands (*journaliers*) without land. These terms, like
the basic structure, are also to be found in the east of France and in
Burgundy, but in these areas the introduction of a sharecropping system
meant that new social types emerged, for example the *granger* or the
colon, sometimes with a *fermier* at their head. In Brittany, there were
the same transitional forms: the *laboureur* was at the top of a social
hierarchy of peasant proprietors or share-croppers which went from
closier through *bordager* and *méthivier* to the lowest levels of smallholder.

Thus we move slowly towards another type of rural hierarchy which was particularly widespread in Aquitaine. Sharecropping was at the core of this system. The *pagès* or the *bientenants* who owned and ran farms which were often small were less important than the major share-croppers (*bordiers*), who were at the top of a whole hierarchy of share-croppers (*faisandiers*), farm-hands who were part of a household (*méthiviers*) and casual labourers (*brassiers*). This complex and strictly hierarchical system can be found (with further variations) from the Pyrenees to the west of the Massif Central. Here, however, we find a different type of society, where small landowners were the dominant group and the commune was vitally important: a form of rural democracy which was to be found in the Alps as well as on the central plateau. In the Midi, in Languedoc and Provence, social stratification was apparently much less complex. The two social types involved here were the *ménager*, an independent farmer cultivating an average of 15 hectares of land, either wholly or partly owned by himself, and the *travailleur de terre*, who owned a much smaller amount of land and also hired out his labour.

Seen here in all its regional diversity, rural society, despite its colourful personalities (the *fermier* in northern France was often 'cock of the roost'), appears to have been isolated and governed by tradition. This is also the impression we gain when we look at agricultural production and techniques.

A world ruled by tradition? Technology and production

Agricultural techniques and methods were traditional, and so were the types of crop grown. Profits were low: it would be quite inappropriate to speak yet of an agricultural revolution. In 1760 the agronomist Duhamel du Monceau could write, with perhaps a little exaggeration: 'Almost half the land in this kingdom lies fallow, the other half is generally so badly cultivated that it would bring in at least twice as much if it were properly exploited.'

Was this true? Certainly agricultural tools remained traditional. The heavy plough (*charrue*) was used in the northern half of France but the light plough (*araire*) was used almost exclusively to the south, in Anjou, the Limousin, Berry and the Lyonnais. The most revealing controversy of this kind concerned the use of the scythe as opposed to the sickle. The scythe was sometimes used in the plains of large-scale cultivation, but if the *laboureurs* were in favour of it, the poor agricultural workers were not: they preferred to stick to the sickle which gave them more days' work and left more behind for their wives to glean. Such obstacles to progress, the result of economic, social and psychological factors, were to be found at every level. If we move from tools to production we find everywhere an obsession with corn, which meant that crops were restricted to the cultivation of cereals at a subsistence level. Because of this, new crops were only introduced slowly. There was certainly a 'maize revolution' in the south-west, and there was also a marked increase in the cultivation of vines, a commercial crop. The introduction of madder in Provence and in the Venaissin marked a first step towards a new style of agriculture, but the introduction of continuous cropping in the extensively cultivated plains (fodder crops and roots) remained localised and was viewed with suspicion. The low yields were the result of outdated techniques and of a lack of fertiliser, since stock-breeding remained in second place. There were many areas which achieved a yield of only two or three times the amount of grain sown!

The stagnation or, at least, very slow rate of growth of the rural economy was in keeping with the world of *rentes* and the feudal means of production which did not allow for a rapid accumulation of wealth. But was this not about to change?

Tensions in rural society

Changes there certainly were, but not always in the direction of progress and not always where one would have wanted them. The slow rate at which agricultural methods improved contrasted with the sudden appearance of tensions and problems new to the countryside. The land-owning nobility felt threatened by a relative impoverishment and in the second half of the century it inaugurated the movement which has been described as one of 'seigneurial reaction'. They were fighting a losing battle, but they fought all the more bitterly.

The attacks came from all sides. As far as the feudal dues were concerned, in the last decades of the century there was a general movement towards revising the documents in which the peasants' obligations were recorded. *Feudistes*, or land commissioners, made an effort to revive dues which had fallen into abeyance. So at the end of the *ancien régime* feudal and seigneurial dues were particularly onerous, and if there should then be a bad harvest, it was enough for them 'simply to exist' (Labrousse) to be bitterly resented.

The nobility were concerned about income and sometimes yields. They extended their attack from dues to property: there was an increase in the practice of *triage* and *cantonnement* (dividing) by which the seigneur compelled the community to divide up the common land, which was particularly precious to the poor. Whether he took his two-thirds or 'contented' himself with one-third, he appeared odious to his collective adversary, the group of peasants who were left with only the crumbs to share out.

There were also significant developments in the system of exploitation itself. In the rich France of the plains there was a movement towards the establishment of very big farms which were concentrated in the hands of wealthy tenant farmers. These men were regarded as valuable middlemen by the land-owning classes. The average *laboureur*, however, saw in this the destruction of his working environment, increasing the difficulty he would have finding jobs for his sons. In the poor areas of France where sharecropping was predominant the *fermier général* had a similar function. He took a lease entitling him to collect the annual income on behalf of the aristocratic absentee landlords. We hardly need to add that this inflexible, uncharitable intermediary was not generally popular. Far from receding, then, the feudal system seems to have become more deeply entrenched in the last decades of the *ancien régime*. What were the full implications of this rearguard action? To establish them, we must look at the seigneurial reaction in the wider context of a feudal backlash.

A SOCIETY OF ORDERS

We have been able to talk of feudalism and rural society in general without too much reference to a society of orders. This is simply because these formal distinctions, as Pierre Goubert points out, were irrelevant in the country, where everyone knew the difference between the *laboureur* (yeoman farmer) and the *ménager* (who hired out his labour). This is not to say that this second key concept which we are using to analyse the social structure of the *ancien régime* is not closely connected to the first: in what way we shall see.

A current controversy

This division of society into 'orders', which became increasingly controversial as the Revolution approached, only seems so important because it was the top of a whole pyramid of concepts which interpreted society as a hierarchical system which determined social standing, and in which the orders were themselves subdivided into 'estates'. This ladder of honours was by no means 'honorary': it conferred very real privileges, political or fiscal, and it was very keenly felt at the level of social relations as they were experienced.

It is easy to understand how, for certain contemporary writers (Mousnier),[7] this system of classification is better than any other at revealing the true state of a society as seen by itself. In his table of 'social hierarchies', Mousnier places the France of the *ancien régime* amongst the 'societies of orders', which he contrasts with class societies and caste societies. There is no shortage of documents to support this view: old, but not outdated, works like Loyseau's *Traité des ordres* describe the hierarchy of social esteem which structured this society.

This method aims to reject all dogmatism in order to get as close as possible to the reality experienced by the people of the time. However, some serious objections have been raised. Goubert has wondered whether one is not dealing with a 'traditional vision' rather than with 'profound realities'; whether this was not a traditional society which saw itself as divided into corporate bodies, while it was actually, as historians recognise, divided into classes.[8]

It is not to advocate a petit bourgeois compromise to think, like Régine Robin,[9] that somewhere between these two views there may be a more satisfactory interpretation: perhaps the 'estates', inegalitarian status groups, while not being totally identified with the classes of this feudal mode of production, nevertheless fulfilled a real and essential function since they guaranteed and shaped the hierarchies they produced.

It remains to say that during the period we are concerned with the old social structure – a *class* structure, but cast in the mould of a society of *orders* – came face to face with the pure class structure of the nascent capitalist system. It would be very imprecise and simplistic to imagine that this confrontation was straightforward: there were numerous common links between these two worlds, mixed statuses abounded, and the 'orders' of the *ancien régime* are revealed to us in all their ambiguity.

---

[7] Mousnier (50).   [8] Goubert (43).
[9] Robin (59).

The nobility

The nobility was in law the second order, after the clergy, but in fact
it was the first order, and perhaps the only one to have any real
homogeneity. It corresponded to a clearly defined socio-economic
group which formed the kernel of the *rentier* class and was the major
beneficiary of feudal rights. This *de facto* pre-eminence was backed up
by a whole range of political, fiscal and legal privileges: here, class and
order disclose a real complicity.

What proportion of the population did this dominant group
represent? Was it 80,000 or 400,000 strong? If we need to decide on
a figure, let us say 300,000 perhaps, or 1·5 % of the overall population.
In spite of appearances, it is not easy to define the nobility. It was
not that informally defined élite of wealth and power represented by
the 'gentry'. On the other hand, it could by no means be confined
to its narrow self-definition. The nobility which was incontestable was
that which was transmitted through the male line. 'There is in the seed
a certain strength and a certain principle which passes on to the children
the virtue of the parents.' They were a 'race' of nobles which sought
historical confirmation: were noblemen not descendants of the Frankish
warriors? In fact, only a small minority could trace their nobility back
to 1400 or even 1550: noble status was more often conferred by royal
patents, which were not sold as liberally as it has sometimes been
claimed, and still more frequently by the purchase of so-called
'ennobling' offices; certain administrative and judicial posts conferred
a form of nobility which was sometimes hereditary and sometimes
personal, in other words, for one life only. As one might have
suspected, this acquired form of nobility was not the most highly
respected and there was a certain amount of carping about the *noblesse
de cloche*: town councillors or aldermen. Then there was nobility
originally acquired by straightforward abuse and usurpation but
sanctioned by time immemorial. Noble status was forfeited if the
noblemen took part in 'ignoble' productive activity (this loss was called
dérogeance). Apart from careers in the army or in the service of the king,
only a few occupations did not result in 'loss of caste': ironmaster, or
master glassmaker for example, as well as activities connected with big
business. These distinctions resulted in a social group which was in some
ways homogeneous, in others, heterogeneous. Its leaders were the
'grandees', princes or great lords, the core of the court nobility which
was concentrated at Versailles and to which one had to be formally

'presented'. The fortunes of the most important were impressive: the
Duc d'Orléans had an annual income of 6,800,000 *livres*, and the Prince
de Conti 3,700,000. This great nobility had certain pretensions: it was
from amongst its ranks that the pressure group known as the 'court
party' was recruited, and it collected pensions, titles and gratuities at
source. It was perhaps this group that best lived up to the classic
description of the eighteenth century as the time of *douceur de vivre*.
It had a very free moral code, although the figure of rake was no longer
fashionable, but this freedom of demeanour was often only superficial.
The upper nobility was in a precarious position: it was living beyond
its means and running into debt. The very scale of its ill-considered
demands made it particularly dangerous for the declining *ancien régime*
to which it clung, and which it in fact helped to smother.

The *noblesse de robe* appear to have been much more solid, though
this group was more highly structured and its members were not as
rich individually as those of the traditional nobility. In the distant past
these people had been commoners, often engaged in trade. In general
their noble status could not be traced back as far as two centuries, but
it was very important to them and on the whole they had closed the
doors behind them: by this time one had to be noble to gain admittance
to most provincial *parlements* (law courts). We should also add that an
office was very expensive to purchase, and brought in relatively little
income. Amongst the members of this legal caste the sense of common
identity overrode local variations. They married within the caste, and
lived identical lives. They often owned considerable amounts of land
(for example the vineyards around Bordeaux and in Burgundy) which
guaranteed a high level of income. The security and easy conscience
of this 'caste' proved at times to be more than irritating: Voltaire,
Mirabeau and de Sade all denounced it. In spite of being a closed
society, this group was not uncultivated: Montesquieu in Bordeaux or
the *président* de Brosses in Dijon bear individual witness to the high
level of culture of this group. The analysis of the contents of libraries
and an examination of the numbers of its members belonging to learned
societies have shown that this section of the nobility was in the forefront
of scholarship.

As we descend the hierarchy of the nobility, we see numerous groups
of lower and middle nobility in the provinces. The existence of a noble
'proletariat' has rightly been emphasised: the noblemen of Poitou who
in 1789 turned up at the convocation of their order in overalls were
merely extreme examples of this. But statistically speaking the middle

nobility were more important. It is not difficult to describe the typical life-style of this group. They had no occupation (though in many cases the head of the household had served the king) and they owned at least 100 hectares of land, often more. They lived off income from their tenants, such as the feudal dues from one or more domains, and they owned a house in the country as well as one in the town.

The *noblesse de robe* and the *noblesse de cloche* (legal and municipal nobility) which we have discussed existed side by side with the traditional middle and lower nobility, without becoming merged with them. The life-style and income of these two groups were identical, but the legal and administrative nobility could perhaps be symbolised by the figure of the *conseiller secrétaire* to the king, several of whom were to be found in the smallest town of any significance.

The noble reaction

On the eve of the Revolution the contradictions in the position of the nobility were becoming more and more clear, but they remained more apparent than real. It is true that the order was to some extent open and the modes of upward social mobility discussed above show how it was possible to acquire noble status in three generations: the grandfather being a tradesman, the son *conseiller secrétaire*, and the grandson a magistrate in the *parlement*. At the same time, we should not ignore the fact that amongst the more dynamic sections of this order there was an increasing interest in new investments: speculation in property development in Paris, in shipbuilding in Nantes or Marseilles, and investment in mines and ironworks; all of which meant moving well outside the traditional world of income from land. But this was by no means widespread; the second half of the eighteenth century was more obviously characterised by what has been called the 'aristocratic reaction', an aggressive rejection of change. We have looked at the agrarian elements in this rejection: they were essential, but not the whole story.

The noble or aristocratic reaction began in the second half of the century and became stronger in its last decades. We can detect it through certain indicators. In the upper echelons of central government the 'long reign of the vile bourgeoisie' (as Saint-Simon described the age of Louis XIV) had come to an end: the Secretaries of State, the higher civil servants and the provincial *intendants* were increasingly drawn from the established nobility. In the Church, the last commoner to become a bishop (Abbé de Beauvais) was appointed during the 1770s, and commoners were no longer able to become canons in the great cathedral chapters.

In the army this trend was officially sanctioned. Until the middle of the century military service was a means of social climbing, but the orders of the Marshal of Belle-Ile (1758) and especially the edict of Ségur (1781) put an end to this: commoners no longer had direct access to the rank of officer, which conferred noble status. There was a great deal of tension in the army and in the navy between the noble officers of the *grand corps*, in red uniforms, and the commoners, more knowledgeable but subordinate, who wore blue. This closing of noble ranks resulted in a straightforward class conflict.

The clergy: structures and functions

Was the clergy the first order of the land, as it was described officially, or was it not an order at all, as claimed by those who emphasise the differences of status within it or who see it as merely exercising a function or public service? The case of the clergy is ambiguous, and at once illustrates and causes us to reconsider the whole notion of a society of orders.

The clergy is easy to define and to delimit. It had an articulated structure. In terms of numbers it comprised about 130,000 people, or perhaps 2% of the French population. About half of these were 'regular' clergy (members of religious orders), two-thirds of whom were women. The secular clergy were involved in the secular world and worked in the parishes. They were divided into two very unequal groups: the 'general staff' of bishops and canons of cathedral or collegiate chapters (perhaps about 8,000 in all) and the enormous rank and file of ecclesiastics, priests, vicars and chaplains, not to mention the host of non-beneficed priests who moved around gleaning masses without being attached to any particular parish.

Did the clergy constitute an order? It certainly fulfilled a function, of course, or rather several functions, a plurality which seems surprising only to a modern sensibility. The clergy watched over the salvation of souls, either by conducting services or through the contemplative life of the regular clergy. In this area, which seems straightforward, a turning-point came on the very eve of the Revolution with the 1787 edict of tolerance. This edict granted civil status to Protestants and sanctioned the hard-won acceptance they had gained since 1750. It opened the first breach in the privileged position of the Catholic Church as the established religion of the kingdom.

In the second place, the parish registers kept by the priests fulfilled the function of the modern Register Office. Teaching was virtually monopolised by clerics in the secondary sector, where the Jesuits had been replaced by Oratorians, and primary education, at least in towns, was also largely controlled by the Church. Finally, poor-relief and alms-giving were an integral part of the Church's responsibilities.

At this level we are speaking of the clergy not so much in terms of its 'function', but as an institution. The order had its independence and its privileges, which were very important. This independence may seem somewhat limited if we look at how the order was recruited. Since the concordat of 1516 which governed relations between the papacy, the king and the Gallican Church, appointments to the most important livings were ultimately made by the Pope, from a short list drawn up by the king and his advisers. This was an uneasy compromise which left scope for wrangling over the *annates* (first-fruits: a year's income from a new incumbent's diocese) or the *droit de régale* (the income from vacant sees). On the eve of the Revolution these old quarrels seem out of date, but other problems and other pressure groups had come to the forefront. As for the minor livings (those of vicars and curates), they were usually in the gift of the 'patron', the successor or descendant of the original founder, whether a cleric or a layman. The patron was often a cleric, abbey, or chapter. Parallel hierarchies were reinforced in the Church, especially since at the middle level (chapters, for example) new members were generally co-opted, thus accentuating the closed character of the milieu. The privileges of the order were real, whether legal or fiscal. The ecclesiastical courts (the *officialités*) dealt not only with clerics but also with certain cases involving the laity, especially in the area of morals. The clergy was exempt from most taxes paid by the non-privileged; it negotiated the annual subsidy it paid to the Crown (the 'free gift' or *don gratuit*), and assemblies of clergy held every five years decided how this sum was to be raised. The institution of the clergy, taken as a whole, can thus be seen to have had considerable power. It was rich, and enlightened opinion was on its side. Not only was the clergy exempt from most taxes, it also benefited from the product of the tithe which was supposed from time immemorial to cover the expenses of worship. No doubt this was sometimes alienated, to become the 'enfeoffed' tithe (*dîme inféodée*) taken by the seigneur. In any case it was not always the parish priests who benefited from the tithe: the 'great tithe-owner' often left the local clergy only a very small proportion of the product of the tithe, the *portion congrue*.

The Church was also, as we have seen, a great landowner. If, on a cautious estimate, we agree that 6–10% of French soil belonged to the clergy, this still represents enormous capital: country estates and property in towns made it the greatest landowner in the kingdom.

The world of the clerics: diversity

These generalisations apart, the clerical order was in fact heterogeneous, not to say deeply divided: the most obvious split was between the upper and the lower clergy. The upper clergy of prelates and canons was indeed a privileged body. Young men were sometimes accepted into the episcopate: Talleyrand became a bishop at 35, the Cardinal of Rohan at 26 and whole families (the La Rochefoucaulds, the Talleyrands and the Castellanes) monopolised these appointments. They were often very profitable: the see of Paris was worth 200,000 *livres* a year, that of Narbonne 160,000. On the other hand, the mini-bishoprics of the Midi did not even reach 10,000 *livres*. The image of the prelate of the *ancien régime* which is derived from these too exclusively economic data needs qualification. The court prelate, not resident in his diocese, arrogant as the result of his wealth and a sceptic in religious matters (Loménie de Brienne), co-existed with the bishop-pastor, charitable and devout (Monseigneur de la Marche, Bishop of Saint-Pol de Léon). In this period, at the end of the eighteenth century, many bishops took their pastoral responsibilities seriously, a practice which was equally in keeping with their vocation and with the times. The canons of cathedrals and collegiate churches were generally unpopular: their privileged position made them defensive and most parish priests lived in a very different world. The contrast between their poverty and the opulence of the upper clergy has often been emphasised. The image of the half-starved country priest, tragically reduced to his *portion congrue*, was not a false picture, but no doubt it needs qualifying. Recent research places less emphasis on the possibly exaggerated penury of the lower clergy. It concentrates instead on showing that the 'good shepherd' – whose image in the eighteenth century was no doubt derived from an excessively flattering view of his learning and of his exemplary behaviour – was most frequently of bourgeois origin, more urban than rural, and reasonably well off.[10]

Crisis in the French clergy?

The diversity and intensity of ideological differences amongst the clergy, as much, perhaps, as these social divisions, force us to reconsider the apparent monolithic structure of the order. On the eve of the Revolution the lower clergy appeared to have been moulded by a whole tradition of ideological clashes, which had crystallised around the Jansenist dispute. One might have thought that this was all over: did not Jansenism, scorned by the worldly, score an almost posthumous victory in 1763 when the Jesuits were expelled and the Society of Jesus dissolved? At a more fundamental level, that of attitudes, nothing was forgotten: a large section of the French clergy felt a renewed desire to defend the liberty of the Gallican Church, while the last phase of a certain form of Jansenism, or rather 'Richerism'* which had taken over from it, involved a defence of the priests of the second order rather in the manner of a trade union. The spirit of the controversy had changed, as well as its subject matter.

In the last analysis, an impression of crisis prevails. There were serious local clashes between the upper and the lower clergy, and a great many felt uncomfortable in this order which was not an order. To ask a naïve question: did all this have a harmful effect on religion? From this period on, we can detect unequivocal signs of disquiet. Nowhere was this more obvious than amongst the regular clergy, no doubt the most fragile sector. In a climate in which the contemplative life was no longer particularly respected, the decline in the monastic orders, especially the male ones, was marked. The 'commission for the regular clergy' met in 1766 to examine the problem and in 1768 an edict was issued closing or amalgamating empty religious houses. This precipitated a further decline and in 20 years (1770–90) the number of monks fell from 26,000 to 17,000. The order of the clergy was going through a period of internal change which in its own way reflected the crisis in the whole society of orders.

[10] See D. Julia's work, in progress, on the eighteenth-century parish clergy; and also T. Tackett, *Priest and Parish in Eighteenth-century France* (Princeton, 1977).

* Edmond Richer was a zealous seventeenth-century defender of the rights of the lower clergy. [Trans.]

Is the third estate an order?

As far as the third estate is concerned, we should not expect to find
as definite a structure as that of the nobility. By its very definition –
purely negative – the 'third estate' was not an order. This does not
mean that we do not find in it the same hierarchical structure of groups
or 'estates'; but, as Goubert has pointed out, the lower a group comes
in the social scale, the less rigid is its stratification.[11] In the towns, one
cannot seriously talk in terms of 'estates' about that part of the urban
population (approximately half) who came 'below the artisan'. In the
countryside there was certainly a very clear status hierarchy: in market
towns in Provence social distinctions separating the farmer from the
citizen and the workman were even reflected in the forms of their
festivities. Some danced to the drum, others to the violin. However,
this system of stratification concealed differences in social status which
could quite easily be described in terms of classes.

Corporations

It is in the plain setting of urban trades, the world of 'the stall and the
shop' – in other words, that of the guilds – that we find the clearest
example of a structure adapted to the ideal of a society of orders. These
'communities of trades and crafts', as they called themselves, were to
be found in most towns. The 'free trades' which were not organised
into guilds were no longer important, except in old-fashioned areas
(small market towns) or, on the contrary, very modern ones (large cities
like Nantes) where the role of the guild was limited. The guild provided
a rigid framework, established and confirmed by the royal and
municipal authorities. It comprised statutes governing admission to the
guild, relations between the masters and also the system of internal
management and control (*jurés* and *jurandes*). The system was very rigid.
It took years to rise from apprentice to journeyman (*compagnon*), while
access to master status – unless one was lucky enough to be the son
or son-in-law of a master – was dependent on making a 'masterpiece'.
The guild was a closed world, and had to defend its monopoly and
fight on many fronts. Adversaries included neighbouring guilds (pastry
cooks in competition with restaurateurs, drapers against haberdashers)
but trouble could also come from the free 'unincorporated' trades,
whether in the form of an unaffiliated merchant encroaching on guild

[11] Goubert (43).

territory, or, at the other end of the scale, the artisan working secretly at home (*chambrelan*). The masters also had to defend themselves against journeymen and their associations, against pressure from increasing tax demands, and, worst of all, against progress. In the name of an ideal which was not illusory — that of craftsmanship — there developed an increasing hostility towards mechanical inventions, which were perceived as competing unfairly with manual labour: in 1736 the manufacture of stockings on a loom was again forbidden. This endless struggle was exhausting and disastrously expensive: the guilds had made progress throughout the seventeenth century, but in the eighteenth century they declined. They turned in on themselves: admission fees became increasingly high, the masterpiece increasingly difficult to achieve, while at the same time the guilds ran into debt; also the Crown, whose tax demands were partly responsible for this situation, began to detach itself from the system. Economists (for example Gournay) encouraged this detachment and they were followed by statesmen: Bertin and especially Turgot, who inspired the 1776 edict on the suppression of the guilds in the name of that 'right to work [which] belongs to all men'. The fall of Turgot led to a partial reorganisation of the guilds, on what should have been a simplified basis; but this retrograde step could not conceal the extent of the crisis.

From fraternities to unions

The guild, with its rigid structure, is the archetypal example of human groups in this urban society of orders. In the space separating the master craftsman from the casual worker it would not be difficult to find other forms of association; these systems, moreover, intersected or overlapped. There were, for example, the professional fraternities (*confréries*), which were at once close to, but distinct from, the guilds. They had a similar policy of mutual aid, but they also catered, to a limited extent, for those of journeyman status. The journeymen in certain traditional crafts formed their own specific associations (which were actually quite illegal), known as *compagnons du devoir* or *du devoir de liberté*, and they had a sense of solidarity created by the practice of the 'tour de France', the travels of the apprentices. Similarly other groups, half-way between the independent producers and the wage-earners — of which the best examples are the dockers and market porters — also tended to form closed associations which jealously defended their monopoly of jobs.

These associations were specific to manual workers. We are quite familiar with them; more, no doubt because of their strict organisation, than with those 'bodies' or 'companies' which were their counterparts in the upper echelons of urban society: officers of the Crown, magistrates, barristers, notaries and attorneys. However, here too we find a very pronounced *esprit de corps* and a very strict hierarchy of status which we can measure by examining who tried to marry whom or who was refused by whom.

What are we to conclude? This society of orders appears to have been flourishing at the end of the *ancien régime*. This central idea had not lost its power in the interplay of attraction and repulsion which we call 'social change'. It inspired that defensive attack known as the aristocratic reaction and we find it again in the grievances of the guilds. However, it was not exclusively defensive. The typical pattern of upward social mobility of the bourgeois took three stages or three generations, the last involving access to the nobility. This process reveals the continuing attraction of this social model. Titles continued to be bought eagerly by commoners.

However, the spell was broken because a new society was emerging, a society which postulated a 'free contract' which was incompatible with the fine divisions and the hierarchical structures of a society of orders. We are not saying that a society of orders was being replaced by a class society: classes had always existed.[12] But the balance between orders and classes changed; the old scheme was no longer capable of representing social reality.

ABSOLUTISM

Controversies: absolutism French-style

Who could deny that absolutism was one of the major features of the *ancien régime*? This would be to deny the facts: was it not absolutism that the Revolution sought to defeat? But how far was it an integral part of the socio-economic complex we have symbolised by the two key words 'feudalism' and 'society of orders'? One might say, with some truth, that the king was no longer the suzerain, the head of the aristocracy (once fighters, then landlords), which was at the top of the feudal system: he stood aloof from the whole society of orders. Let us listen to Louis XV addressing the Parlement of Paris on 6 March

[12] Mazauric (18), pp. 112–13.

1766, the famous 'Flagellation' session: 'I will not tolerate the formation of an association in my kingdom...the magistrates do not form a separate body or order...sovereign power resides in my person alone...the power of legislation belongs to *me alone* – it is not dependent on or shared with anyone else.' The facts seem to confirm these declarations of intention: didn't the French Revolution begin with a 'revolt of the nobility' against absolutism?

To formulate the problem correctly we must listen briefly to the debates of their time as well as ours. In the eighteenth century the king himself gives us his view in the person of Louis XV: there could be no question of an absolute monarchy admitting any form of dependence, or even support. The king was the father of his subjects, a notion which – all things considered – was egalitarian, even if the king actually underwrote the inegalitarian system of the orders. We remember the dramatic gesture of Louis XVI in the revolutionary fray refusing to abandon 'his' nobility; weren't they, at least, conscious of this compromising solidarity? Here too, however, we must keep a sense of proportion. The aristocracy were nostalgic for their former liberties and lost power: from Saint-Simon and Boulainvilliers to Montesquieu, they did not cease to complain. But Montesquieu himself, in *L'Esprit des lois*, came to consider the monarchy as an autonomous power in the same way as the nobility (the upper house) or the people (the lower house). He was thus upholding the idea of the king as arbiter, an idea which was not peculiar to the aristocracy but was to permeate the whole *philosophe* movement, in which the word 'despot' was detestable but the most desirable solution remained an enlightened monarch. The odd man out was Barnave, whose *Introduction à la Révolution française* anticipated later emphasis on the importance of 'the distribution of wealth', but in spite of everything he allowed the 'royal power', so long 'oppressed by the aristocracy', its autonomy.

Many historians agree with this conclusion. The tradition of the State as arbiter has scarcely lost ground since Lavisse. However, the rise or renewed awareness of problems in neighbouring fields leads us to re-examine this view. A comparative approach encourages us to ask why France did not have an 'enlightened despotism', and whether this phenomenon was limited to the states of central and eastern Europe where in the absence of a true bourgeoisie there was no countervailing power to set against autocracy.[13] Others qualify the original thesis by

[13] See D. Richet's introduction to the French translation (Paris, 1966) of Leo Gershoy's *Enlightened Despotism*.

asking whether it is possible to detect in reform attempts of the later
eighteenth century the 'legal despotism' which might have been the
French model of political reform. But this does not tackle the problem
of accounting for the failure of these attempts at reform. Traditional
historians had their answers, which are not completely out of date, in
terms of technical factors or personal ones, such as the character of
individual monarchs. On the other hand, one may wonder whether
royal absolutism was not so integral a part of the traditional system
as to make half-hearted attempts to reform or rationalise it impossible.
This interpretation put absolutism back into the context of a general
crisis and it allows for qualification. Furet and Richet, for example,
argue that the 'reforming vocation of absolutism' was lost in the second
half of the eighteenth century, and suggest that certain individuals and
groups should bear responsibility for this.[14] This question leads to
others, regarding the future this time, not the past: why was there a
Revolution? Was it inevitable? Can we imagine an 'enlightened
despotism' or a 'bourgeois compromise' with the aristocracy which
would have achieved painlessly the results which were in fact brought
about by violence, leaving the monarchy its role as arbiter? Reformula-
tions go to show that there are still problems in describing the French
form of absolutism.

The king and his court

The system revolved around one man, the king: 'The whole state is
contained in him and the people's will is encompassed by his.' 'The
sovereign power in the kingdom belongs to the king alone...he is
accountable only to God.' A living law, God's viceroy on earth –
descriptions justified by tradition and evoked by rituals. Consecrated
at his coronation, the king was still a healer who touched for the 'king's
evil'. 'The king touches you, God cures you.' Even if, as in 1789, he
had the commonplace features of Louis XVI, the king, a father-figure,
retained a genuine power to fascinate.

The setting measured up to the role. Before we describe the king
in council, we should place him in his court at Versailles. His
surroundings began with the royal family, from Queen Marie-
Antoinette to the princes and princesses of the blood, and included the
horde of nobility who had been presented at court; the nobility were
at once domesticated, insatiable, unconditionally faithful and a terrible
liability. This world, ruled by a ritual which had not really relaxed since

[14] Furet and Richet (9), pp. 8–9.

the age of Louis XIV, may be divided roughly into the following: the King's household (civil and military), and the household of the queen, the princes and the 'children of France'. At the end of the *ancien régime* the court was seen primarily as an extremely expensive status symbol, which swallowed a twelfth of the revenue of the kingdom. In fact it was more, and one might say, worse, than that: a 'brand image' which associated the system (despite the simple honesty of Louis XVI himself) with that world of notorious immorality where intrigue, gaming and speculation were the other side of the *douceur de vivre*. It was also a pressure group of undeniable political importance. At one time an instrument for the taming of the nobility, the court now recovered political weight. People spoke of the 'court party'. Before the first rumbles of discontent made them huddle together more closely, what was most striking about the courtiers was their division into coteries. The combination of these diverse pressures reinforced the rejection of innovation and the defence and consolidation of privilege.

The royal government

Did the king play a part in government? Royal centralisation had gone a long way. The king's council, the decrees of which were expressions of his will, was divided into sections. There was the Council of State (*conseil d'Etat* or *Conseil d'en haut*), which was very exclusive and dealt with foreign affairs and major policy decisions; the Council of Dispatches (*conseil des dépêches*), which was concerned with local government; the Council of Finance, which absorbed the Council of Commerce in 1787; and finally the Privy Council (*conseil privé* or *des parties*), an extra-ordinary court for cases which the king reserved for himself, a controversial 'watch-dog of the executive power'. This centralised organisation grew stronger and larger in the course of the century. Departments multiplied. The example was set by the department of trade and that of roads and bridges. They sought efficiency and even a kind of technocracy. The dominant character was that of the 'commissioner' (*commis*) including those chief commissioners who assisted each Secretary of State. These Secretaries of State, the equivalent of modern ministers, remained five in number. The Chancellor (the only one of the great medieval officers of State to have retained a political function), who was appointed for life and had no superior but the king, paid a price for his excessive potential powers. When in disgrace, as Maupeou was after 1774, his judicial functions were exercised by the Keeper of the Seals, one of the Secretaries of State. The chief of these Secretaries had added to his functions the Controller-Generalship of Finance which made him, in effect, first minister. The Secretary of State for the Royal Household was in charge of the police and religious affairs; the Secretaries for War, the Navy and Foreign Affairs shared provincial administration with him, although the lion's share fell to the Secretaries for War and for the Royal Household. This does not seem to have been a system of ministries of the modern type in the sense that it did not possess a collective personality which would have asserted its authority in relation to the king. All the same, the 'committees of ministers' of the previous reign which, together with the first minister, prepared business for the councils, were ceasing to be a temporary expedient and were becoming an institution.[15]

Local administration

In the course of more than a century the absolute monarchy had succeeded in placing its men in local administration: not *officiers* but commissioners, agents of the king who could be dismissed by him.* These men were the *intendants* of 'police, justice and finance' or, as Lavisse described them, 'the king present in the provinces'.[16] There were 32 of them to administer the 34 *généralités* of the kingdom (two of these *intendants* administering two *généralités* each). Their title is an accurate description of the extent of their powers. 'Police', as understood by the *ancien régime*, was administration in the widest sense: enforcement of the laws, public order, religion, public works, industry, commerce and communications. In theory nothing escaped them. If the *intendant* of 'justice' was limited by the other forms of royal justice and acted essentially as an overseer or arbitrator, his colleague in finance was essential. It was his task to set the tax quotas for the *élections* (tax districts) in northern France and to argue about them with the estates in the rest of the kingdom. These were heavy responsibilities yet the *intendant* often had only an astonishingly small staff. He had his assistants, known as *subdélégués*, generally chosen from the local *noblesse de robe*. The often-quoted case of Turgot, who was *intendant* of Limousin before he was a minister, is exemplary but not unique. He

[15] Méthivier (52).

* The *officiers*, unlike the *commissaires*, bought their offices and so could not be dismissed. [Trans.]

[16] There are now some important monographs on the subject, such as M. Fréville, *L'Intendance de Bretagne* (Paris, 1953).

encouraged the local agricultural society, increased potato production, stimulated manufacture, improved roads and canals, reformed the system of compulsory labour on road construction and took an interest in poverty and public health.

Who were the *intendants*? They were recruited, often young, from the *maîtres des requêtes*. They generally held their posts for a long time and sometimes handed them down from father to son. They tended to come from the same social milieu. Whether they were old or new nobles they tended to come from the 'State élite' at the frontier between the magistrates of the towns and those of the *parlements*. A notable among notables, subject to local pressures, the *intendant* was shedding the image of the militant bureaucrat which had been his under Louis XIV. He would sometimes defend his region at the expense of central power. He got little thanks for it. These agents of royal absolutism, generally active, and often openly so, were made the scapegoats of the system they stood for and the 'despotism of the *intendants*' was condemned.

The army, justice and taxation

In the mature absolute monarchy of the classical period there were a number of key posts by which the progress of the regime and the power of the State can be measured. These posts were located mainly in the army, the judiciary and the administration of finance. We shall have little to say here about the army, possibly because it had not been called into action on land for more than twenty years, and also because of all these 'instruments' of royal power, the army was the one which was most amenable to modernisation. Thanks to reforming ministers, the French army (200,000 men divided into 175 regiments) appears to have been an efficient instrument. At the technical level, distinct advances were made in armaments (the Gribeauval cannon), in tactics (Guibert's adaptation of the innovations of Frederick the Great), in the training of officers and in organisation. If, however, one looks beyond the institution at the human reality, there remained the problem of the conditions of the regular soldier, who was maltreated and harshly trained, and there was also the crisis in the commissioning of officers which resulted from the edict of Ségur.

Gaining control of the judiciary had been one of the main preoccupations of the monarchy. The sovereign as judge and 'peace-maker' had usually managed to impose his rulings: it only remained to accomplish this without restrictions. In any case, the courts outside the control of the Crown had only a limited, and secondary, function: these were the seigneurial courts, the Church tribunals and the *officialités* (ecclesiastical courts where the bishop delegated his power to an *official*). There was a hierarchy of royal courts. At the bottom came the courts of the *bailliages* or *sénéchaussées*, then the *présidaux*, which judged the more important cases. Finally, the upper level – apart from the king's council, of course – was composed of the thirteen *parlements* and four 'sovereign courts'.[17] These were very powerful bodies, and they no doubt deserve their reputation, though they were not all equally important. The Paris Parlement with its 'Great Chamber' (Grande Chambre) and five lesser ones (three *chambres des enquêtes*, the *chambre des requêtes* and the *chambre des Tournelles*) was an exceptional example of these great institutions which were the embodiment of royal justice at its highest level. The Parlement was a court of appeal for cases heard in a lower court. It was both magistrate's court and appeal court for certain privileged cases, but it was much more than this. It considered itself the guardian of the unwritten Constitution derived from what it saw as the 'fundamental laws of the kingdom'. This involved invoking the *droit d'enregistrement*, by which royal edicts, to be enforceable, had to be inscribed in the registers of the Parlement; remonstrating against royal policy; and yielding only in the face of royal authority solemnly exercised at a *lit de justice*. These inordinate claims would have been impossible had there not been an autonomous magistracy which owned its offices and passed them on through inheritance: a condition favourable to the establishment of those 'intermediary bodies' discussed by Montesquieu. This was a classic example of the consequences of the sale of offices. In theory, the royal judiciary was an instrument of absolutism, but as a result of its own structures, it not only became uncontrollable but also came to represent a serious element of opposition to the monarchy.

What can be said about the administration of finance? It was one of the most important elements in the absolutist system. The French Crown had accumulated a whole arsenal of taxes. The main forms of direct taxation were the *taille*, essentially a land tax on communities, and the *capitation*, a tax on the individual assessed according to his income. Then there were the *vingtièmes*, related to putative income and a legacy from Louis XIV's *dixièmes*: these were periodically abolished, reintroduced and sometimes doubled. Indirect taxation also took many

[17] See Fig. 4, p. 34.

forms, from the *aides*, levied on drinks and on certain manufactured goods, to the *traites*, real internal customs tariffs. These indirect taxes were unpopular, but not as unpopular as certain state monopolies, for example tobacco and especially salt: the hated *gabelle*. The very multiplicity of these taxes suggests how unwieldy the system had become. We need say no more about the way the taxes were levied, or, in particular, about the way they were utilised in a State which did not estimate future expenditure. This brings us to the other side of this absolutist system: to its limits and its failures.

Incoherence: the weight of the past

These limits were first of all technical. The reduction in the staff of the provincial *intendants* is no doubt best illustrated by the example of the administration of finance. The monarchy was in no position to collect its taxes itself, and it had not managed to set up an administration specialising in this task, so it had recourse to the 'farm' system, under which the powerful group of *fermiers généraux* took out a lease, every six years, on the indirect taxes, essentially the *gabelle* (since the *aides* were brought under direct administration in 1778). The system was cumbersome and odious: the brutality of the agents of the *fermiers généraux*, the searches conducted by the *gabelous* (collectors of the salt tax), the way in which consumption was at once compulsory and restricted: these abuses of the system were in inverse proportion to its profitability.

The mechanism was crude and unsatisfactory. If we shared the optimism of the Enlightenment, we could see these problems as teething troubles, faults which would be progressively eliminated under an enlightened regime. But this diagnosis takes no account of the weight of tradition. The monarchy constantly patched up the system, and at each stage of development allowed earlier institutions to continue.

Each of the key sectors of the administration illustrates this point. The *intendant* was the king's agent in his own *généralité*. This was true, but the provincial *gouvernements* which had previously been administered by governors from the upper nobility still remained in being. By appointing lieutenants-general in addition, the monarchy had rendered this system redundant, though the Crown did occasionally draw on the still effective local influence of certain of these grandees. The *intendant* may no longer have had the *gouverneur* as a rival, but in certain areas at least he still had to take into account the existence

of the provinces. In most of France the term 'province' no longer had
an official meaning, but there were the *pays d'états* – generally those
regions most recently incorporated into the kingdom – which had their
'provincial estates'. These were assemblies of the three orders which
played an often essential role in financial matters and in administration.
However, with the exception of Brittany, Languedoc and, to a lesser
extent, Provence, the estates no longer had any political significance
and in some cases (such as Dauphiné) they no longer even met. All
the same, the provincial assemblies summoned on the eve of the
Revolution would do more than simply revive memories: they were
still very much a reality. All these overlapping jurisdictions defined the
'historic' limits and the geographical boundaries of absolutism.

The tax system distinguished between the *pays d'état*, where
taxpayers were better able to protect themselves and where the so-called
'real' *taille* was levied on lands, and what were known as the *pays
d'élection*, where an *élu* was responsible for assessing the 'personal' *taille*
on individuals. As far as indirect taxes were concerned, there were
differences between the areas of the 'great *gabelle*', the areas of the 'lesser
gabelle', the provinces which had bought themselves off, and the regions
with salt-works. We must add that the map of the distribution of the
gabelle did not correspond to that of the internal customs tariffs.

The judicial system was just as complicated: the different *parlements*
varied widely in their powers, and there was not even one single code
of law: the southern part of France, from Guyenne to Dauphiné, was
under Roman law, while the rest of the country was subject to a
multiplicity of regional customs.

This confused patchwork seems to confirm the idea held by many
contemporaries that the unity of the kingdom was no more than a
myth: an 'aggregate of divided people' as Mirabeau was to remark.
There is much evidence for this view, such as the local grievances
expressed in the *cahiers de doléances* in which everyone defended the
privileges of their own province or small town and put forward their
claims to be treated as a special case.

Social limits: the world of privilege

We should not exaggerate the undoubted importance of these factors.
There were other divisions which, although not very obvious on the
map, were perhaps even more serious: for example the essential contrast
between the towns and the countryside with regard to taxation. The

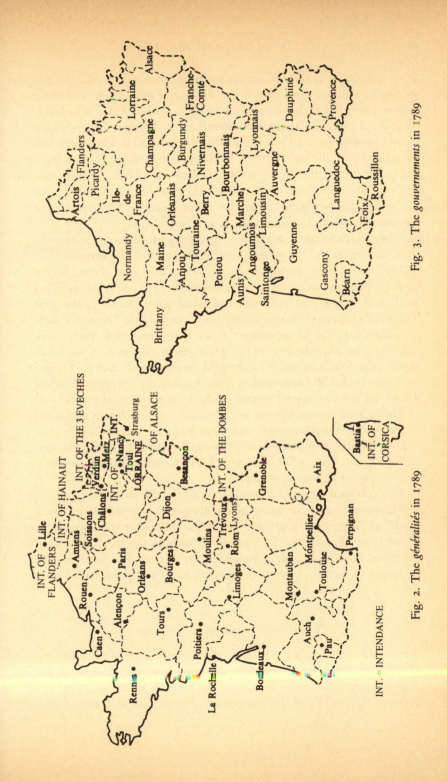

Fig. 3. The *gouvernements* in 1789

Fig. 2. The *généralités* in 1789

INT. = INTENDANCE

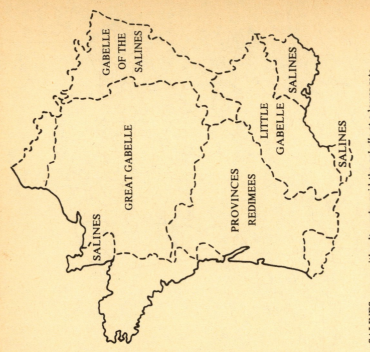
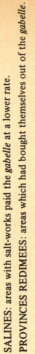

Shaded: area subject to Roman law

Fig. 4. The *parlements* in 1789

SALINES: areas with salt-works paid the *gabelle* at a lower rate.
PROVINCES REDIMEES: areas which had bought themselves out of the *gabelle*.

Fig. 5. Inequality of taxation: the unpopular *gabelle*

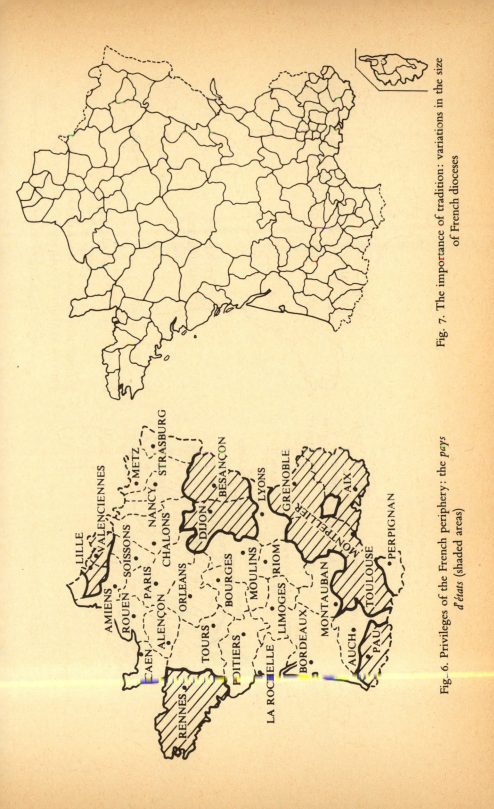

Fig. 6. Privileges of the French periphery: the *pays d'états* (shaded areas)

LILLE
VALENCIENNES
METZ
AMIENS
SOISSONS
NANCY
STRASBURG
ROUEN
PARIS
CHALONS
BESANÇON
CAEN
ALENÇON
DIJON
ORLEANS
LYONS
RENNES
TOURS
BOURGES
MOULINS
GRENOBLE
POITIERS
LIMOGES
RIOM
MONTPELLIER
AIX
LA ROCHELLE
MONTAUBAN
BORDEAUX
AUCH
TOULOUSE
PAU
PERPIGNAN

Fig. 7. The importance of tradition: variations in the size of French dioceses

main curb on royal absolutism was in fact a social one. The monarchy was the prisoner of those who were supposed to be its most loyal servants. This was the essential contradiction in an absolute monarchy which was structurally incapable of rationalising itself into an 'enlightened despotism' because of its class basis, which presupposed the defence of privilege.

We have encountered these privileges everywhere, though we have not encountered them all. No doubt the most important ones were those enjoyed by the nobility and the clergy. They were related above all to taxation, but there were also political and social privileges which were ratified and strengthened as a result of the movement of reaction in the second half of the eighteenth century. There were other forms of privilege, often less obvious. There was that enormous monopoly of royal offices which resulted from the fact that they could be purchased. By agreeing, for financial reasons, to the sale of offices which could be resold or inherited, the monarchy lost some of its authority and allowed the formation of one of those 'intermediary bodies' the theorists speak of: the 'caste' of the magistrates of the *parlements* is the most complete example of these bodies.

Another even more insidious aspect of this loss of power was the development of what we would now call pressure groups: informal coalitions which became effective as a result of the structural weaknesses of the absolutist system. Financiers, who were indispensable to the monarchy – the *fermiers généraux*, for example – came under attack, and so did the court party and the political coteries. Resentments against these groups were as old as the monarchy, but in a climate of crisis they came out into the open.

The debate over absolutism

To conclude, we should regard absolutism not as something fixed but as an ever-changing entity, as the eighteenth century itself regarded it. There is a risk of being confused by an impression of contradiction. On the one hand there is the image of a system at its zenith. A century of innovations confirms this view and the figure of the enlightened *intendant* is its symbol. On the other hand, there is the overwhelming opposition to the system, and the fact that its abuses were repeatedly condemned. Even certain executives of the system were uneasy about it (Malesherbes, the protector of Diderot and the *philosophes*).

It is no doubt only an apparent contradiction. Some historians believe that a turning-point occurred during the century: that the 'increasingly enlightened ministerial despotism' advanced, or was successfully defended, up to a certain point, but that in 1749 there was an attack on the privileged orders led by the *contrôleur* (Controller) Machaut, while in 1770 there was a second attack on the enlightened despotism of the ministers Maupeou and Terray.[18] In the end, in spite of some last-ditch efforts, of which Turgot's ministry was a typical example, the monarchy steadily retreated in the face of this ossified system of privilege. It was no doubt this feeling which enabled Furet and Richet to write: 'Reforms? This was the heart of the matter. For this was the period when the absolute monarchy lost its vocation for reforms.'[19]

Whether there really was a turning-point, and how far the absolute monarchy was able to hold a balance is open to discussion. But we can at least note, together with these authors, that the State was taken over, or more accurately steadily infiltrated by privileged groups, who then used it as an instrument to serve their class interests; the 'intermediary bodies' – in other words, the *parlements* – successfully defended their privileges. From this time on, aristocratic liberalism, nostalgic for its 'liberties', as outlined by Montesquieu, was quietly replaced by another attacker: bourgeois ideology, beginning to fight for its rights.

These two attacks converged, but were in fact radically opposed. Could the monarchy not have re-established itself as arbiter? Could it not have abandoned despotism (enlightened or not) to reconcile these two élites – that of the past and that of the future – within the framework of a 'gentry' system, itself evolving into an English-style constitutional monarchy? This is to impute to the absolute monarchy an independence it simply did not have. It is to underestimate the importance of the attack (spearheaded by the growing forces of the bourgeoisie) on the social and political aspects of the *ancien régime*.

[18] Méthivier (52).   [19] Furet and Richet (9), p. 8.

2

Conflict and change

The *ancien régime* did not die by accident. One might have guessed this from the internal contradictions of the system. The crisis and hardening of the 'feudal' system, the cracks in the edifice of the 'society of orders', the imperfections of the absolute monarchy and the opposition to it: all these factors were so important only because the development of the forces of production and the relations of production were creating a new France. This new France 'still second but not secondary', as Goubert puts it, was becoming mature at the end of the 'glorious' eighteenth century.[1]

THE 'GLORIOUS' EIGHTEENTH CENTURY

The towns

It was the towns which were in the forefront of innovation. We must not expect to find them triumphant. In a society where 85% of the population lived in the countryside, the world of the towns was a limited one. Thirty-eight or thirty-nine towns with more than 30,000 inhabitants apiece, and some fifteen more with 15,000 to 30,000 inhabitants did not make up a particularly dense urban network. Paris with some 550,000 inhabitants appears a metropolis by comparison. This urban France bore the marks of the world which had given birth to it. It was essentially peripheral and concentrated to a great extent along the coasts. A quarter of the towns with more than 20,000 inhabitants were ports, notably the centres of long-distance trade: Marseilles, Bordeaux, Nantes, Rouen. Industrial towns were not absent from the list, whether they were old textile towns (Lille, Amiens, Troyes and of course Lyons), or, more rarely, metal-working (Saint-

[1] Goubert (43).

38

Etienne). As far as dominant functions were concerned, however, pride of place must still go to the regional capitals: seats of *parlements* or political towns like Toulouse, Rennes, Montpellier, Dijon or Versailles. From Orléans to Caen, on the other hand, or from Metz to Strasburg we find towns which were not really dominant, except, perhaps, in the sense of being a place where the land-owning class lived, or a centre of inter-regional trade, or the capital of a *généralité*. This bird's-eye view of concentrations of population shows us where to look for bourgeois France.

The 'Atlantic' France of the merchants

We should start with Atlantic France, though we are tempted to extend it as far as Marseilles. Against the dull background of the small towns, with more than half of their collective capital still invested in land, the ports offer a shining example of a different form of prosperity which was becoming widespread in the eighteenth century. Here could be found merchants and ship-owners who made their fortunes from long-distance commerce such as – to take a simple example – the 'triangular trade' with the Antilles. A cargo of shoddy goods would be taken on board at Nantes or Bordeaux and exchanged in the Gulf of Guinea for a cargo of 'ebony' (in other words, slaves) who would be traded in the Antilles for the exotic products of the tropical plantations: sugar, molasses, coffee, cocoa, cotton or vegetable dyes. Daring but profitable, this was one of the surest ways for a middle class who rejected the mediocre security of income from land to enrich themselves.

Qualifications have to be made, of course. Marseilles does not fit the Atlantic paradigm. It was a port which had formerly been satisfied with its monopoly of the Levant trade but went further afield in the course of the eighteenth century. Despite qualifications like these, the men were the same. Whether he was called Montaudouin in Nantes, or Seymandy, Tarteiron or Audibert in Marseilles, the merchant illustrates the importance of commercial capital in this changing France.

This was all the more true because it was the merchant who encouraged and shaped the rise of industrial France. The industry was largely traditional, but innovations were coming in. Despite the oversimplification involved, it may be useful to compare Morazé's maps of English and French industry about 1789.[2]

2 C. Morazé, *Les Bourgeois conquérants* (Paris, 1957).

The structures of French industry

On the English side, the pattern already reveals industrial concentrations of coal and cotton. French industry, on the other hand, was rather dispersed. In the case of metallurgy, for example, which was essentially fuelled by wood, furnaces and workshops followed a diagonal line from north-east to south-west, from the Ardennes to Quercy and Périgord, but there was another line from lower Normandy to the Pyrenees (Ariège and Roussillon) and to Dauphiné. The same dispersal can be found in textiles; for if there were sectors of relative geographical concentration (cotton or silk), the woollen cloth industry, which was still preponderant, was spread throughout the countryside from the north of the Paris basin to Languedoc. And what region was totally without it?

The cartographical approach leads us to the description of structures. Geographical dispersal reveals lack of economic concentration. In towns small workshops were the rule, while in the countryside the work was done at home, often by peasants. This distribution corresponds to a system of production which was essentially by hand and to a hierarchy of the sectors of production very different from the one to which the nineteenth-century industrial revolution has accustomed us. The difference was that the textile industry was predominant, in terms of the number of people it employed, its place in overall production, and lastly the dynamism of certain sectors, such as linen and calico.

The lack of heavy industry is obviously related to the slow start of the technological revolution. Only 700,000 metric tonnes of coal were mined a year – a total well below that of Great Britain – and the mines of the Loire, Carmaux and Anzin were the leading sectors in a metal industry fuelled essentially by wood. The textile industry was assimilating the technical discoveries from across the Channel only little by little. As far as the spinning and weaving of cotton was concerned, the 'jenny' was rare, and the improved 'mule jenny' was unknown. No doubt this view of the archaism of French industry on the eve of the Revolution is in need of qualification. In Dauphiné, in Lorraine or even near Paris (in the case of the printed cloth business started by the self-made man Oberkampf at Jouy-en-Josas) a new type of entrepreneur and enterprise was coming into existence. We shall return to this point. However, it remains true that under the system of 'commercial capitalism' the merchant was still dominant. A few examples should make this plain. The merchant of Conches or Rugles who commercialised nail-making in the forests of Normandy and the Orléans businessman who put out socks and bonnets to be knitted by thousands of peasant women each illustrate in their own way the hold of urban merchant capital on the surrounding countryside. At Nîmes or Lyons, the silk merchants took strict control of the industry from the previously independent master craftsmen, like the *canuts** in the silk industry of Lyons. As some of the textile industries moved into the countryside and this countryside became more dependent on the towns, the world of the crafts and the guilds was being eroded by commercial capitalism.

Change in the rural world

The *ancien régime* of French society was threatened by the world of the towns, the world of long-distance trade, and the world of industry. However, we should not let ourselves be deceived by the apparently monolithic quality of the French countryside, which we have presented – too simply no doubt – as the great support of the old regime. The countryside too had its bourgeoisie and its innovations. We do not want to use words loosely; people have been too quick to speak of 'agrarian capitalism' or of the 'agricultural revolution' which we are still waiting for. All the same, the rural world on the eve of the Revolution was becoming a sharply differentiated world, incompatible with the survival of a traditional economy and society.

If we return to the map we will find that the area of *fermage* (subleasing) as it has been defined above coincides with that of a more developed form of agriculture and of a more socially differentiated peasantry. The *fermier*, or land agent, was a big businessman even if he was a small landowner, and he leads us to the 'cock of the village' and those rural notables who opposed the homogeneity of traditional rural society and had no respect for the seigneurial regime. They were the people responsible for the concentration of farms and the modification of traditional practices associated with the rise of agrarian individualism.[3] Thus there was progress from below, thanks to this 'conquering' rural bourgeoisie. There was also, somewhat earlier, progress from above: the work of a land-owning class which, whether noble or not, was acquiring bourgeois values and seeking profitability and improvements.

However, we should not confine ourselves within these frontiers.

---

* Silk weavers. [Trans.]

[3] See G. Lefebvre, *Questions agraires au temps de la Terreur* (Paris, 1952).

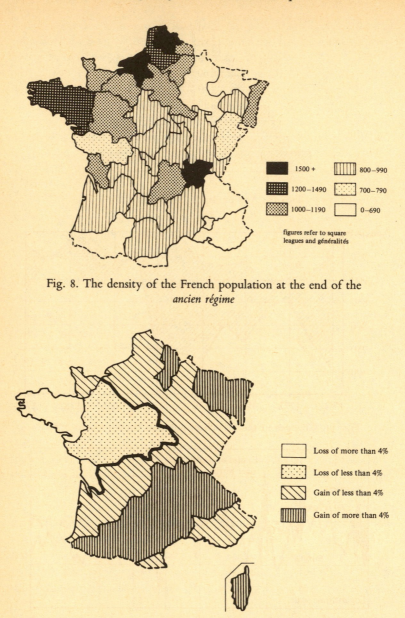

Fig. 8. The density of the French population at the end of the
ancien régime

Fig. 9. Gains and losses in population

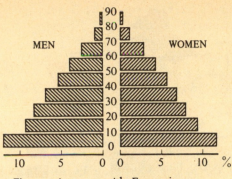

Fig. 10. Age pyramid: France in 1775

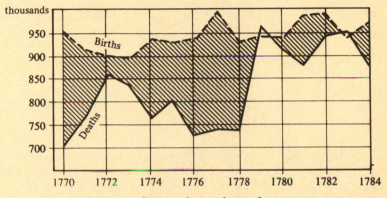

Fig. 11. Changes in the French population from 1770 to 1784

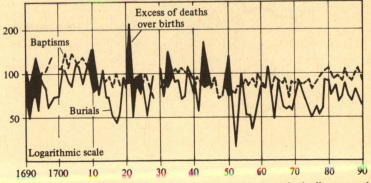

Fig. 12. Saint-Lambert-des-Levées, a parish in Anjou which illustrates the
demographic revolution of the eighteenth century

The call of profit was also strong elsewhere, even if the routes to it were different and the 'multiple shock' (*ébranlement multiple*) had less decisive consequences.[4] Here, in the sharecropping regions, the *nouveau riche* was the parasitic *fermier général*; in Provence it was the 'bourgeois' living in an agro-town from the proceeds of his rents. In the countryside, the process of social change resembled that of agricultural innovation – the abolition of fallow, the introduction of continuous crop rotation – which has been described by more than one writer as radiating out from extremely modest beginnings, a small enclosure or a curé's garden. Everywhere (though to an unequal extent), claims were staked, and here, too, the bourgeoisie installed themselves.

This happened all the more easily because the eighteenth century, if not yet a period of true economic 'revolution', was certainly one of important changes.

Population growth

The assumption that the eighteenth century was 'glorious' is not unchallenged, and one historian who works on Provence, René Baehrel, thinks that the so-called 'tragic' seventeenth century has more claim to glory than its successor.[5] Some qualifications can be made. All the same, thanks to the work of Labrousse and his school, a few points may be taken as proved.

We know that the eighteenth century saw a noticeable increase in the population. Of course it is difficult to give exact figures since there was no census in this pre-statistical period. However, the calculations of Vauban at the end of the seventeenth century and the estimates of Abbé Terray twenty years before the Revolution allow us at least to compare relative magnitudes. In 1700, and even in 1750, the French population remained close to 20 million; in 1789 it would not be rash to calculate it at about 26 million. Six million in under a century is considerable progress, even if the increase was less than elsewhere. There has been a discussion about the real reasons for this demographic 'take-off' in eighteenth-century France: it seems that the mechanisms, if not all the causes of this increase, are now known.

The rash term 'demographic revolution' seems misleading. There was no true revolution in this world where there were no new weapons in the fight against death. The birth-rate remained constant or even declined so that the basic reason for the increase in population was a

4 Labrousse (47).
5 R. Baehrel, *Une Croissance: la basse Provence rurale* (Paris, 1961).

decline in the death-rate. However, all that happened was that the great mortality crises, which, almost every ten years, used to wipe out the surplus accumulated since the last visitation, now came less often and in a less severe form.[6]

This schema is subject to a few qualifications. Population growth was greatest in the plains of northern France with their large-scale farming; elsewhere in the countryside and in the towns (where the death-rate was higher than the birth-rate) progress was much less visible. It is also possible to suggest a chronology for population growth. The trough of the wave came around 1700 and there was little progress until around 1720. This progress accelerated between 1750 and 1770, and still further in the last 20 years of the *ancien régime*.

It can be seen from this schema that the idea of continuous and 'revolutionary' progress is unacceptable without qualifications. The beginnings of a true demographic revolution are to be found elsewhere, in the decline of the birth-rate and the widening of birth intervals in certain country areas (Quercy), an indicator of the diffusion of birth control among the peasants, and so of a new attitude to human life. This shift was itself a response to the most important demographic fact of eighteenth-century French history, the first continuous and important population increase for centuries.

Price movements

An increase in population does not necessarily mean an increase in prosperity or a rise in the standard of living. Far from it. For Goubert, the middle part of the eighteenth century, until the 1770s, was characterised by economic growth as well as population growth, with each trend supporting the other. After that time economic growth slowed down or was blocked while population growth continued, producing unemployment and vagabondage.[7]

This leads us to look at the least controversial indices of economic trends: prices, profit, and production. So far as prices are concerned it is the agricultural sector, by far the most important in the French economy, which reflects the trend most faithfully. Since the magisterial study by Labrousse, we know the general movement of eighteenth-century prices. A long-term rise in prices began between 1725 and 1730 and continued in several stages. From 1726 to 1760 (or 1763) the rise

---

[6] These facts have been made familiar by the work of Pierre Goubert, especially his *Beauvais et le Beauvaisis, de 1600 à 1730* (Paris, 1961). [7] Goubert (43).

was a gentle one, a 'slow take-off'. Then came a decade of more rapid increase until a new level was reached in the years 1770–5, though the long-term rising trend had not come to an end.[8] If we take the years 1771–89 as our base of 100, then we may describe the long-term rise as going from 57 in 1726 to 119 on the eve of the Revolution. This long-term trend had various causes, from a decline in the value of money to changes in the climate. There were also regional variations: the sudden end to growth in the north and the Paris region contrasts with the pattern in the Midi, where growth hardly slowed down at all. The trends were also influenced by events: subsistence crises, falls in production, famines and sudden price rises. We will discuss these events when we reach the immediate causes of the Revolution (see Chapter 3, p. 83). At the moment it is the general trend which is important, with all its consequences. A rise in prices meant a rise in rents, particularly in the rent from land which the *fermier* collected. Between 1730 and 1789 these rents doubled or even (according to recent research) tripled, essentially following the direction of the price curve, perhaps a little behind it but proceeding more smoothly.

To discuss the relationship between price rises and rent from land we have to consider another variable, the volume of production.

The problem of French economic 'take-off'

It is difficult to be sure about this, because of regional variation, the vagueness or even the absence of the sources and the fact that research on this subject has not been going on for very long. In spite of land clearance, the area under cultivation did not increase by more than a small fraction; but could more have been hoped for? The slow decline of fallow was responsible for another limited gain. With the area more or less the same and the crops identical, there could be no revolution in productivity. Since agricultural techniques were more or less the same yields hardly varied. Despite all these minor variations, or adding them all together, we arrive all the same at an increase in agricultural production of something like 20%, if one can risk a precise figure. If we ask the Malthusian question about the relation between increasing production and increasing population, we discover an important fact. Production 'did not lose the race' but kept up with population.[9]

---

[8] E. Labrousse, *Esquisse du mouvement des prix et des revenus au XVIIIe siècle* (2 vols., Paris, 1933).   [9] Labrousse's phrase.

We must now compare agricultural productivity with that of trade and industry. In this case we do not have to rely on prices but can measure productivity and trade directly by looking at statistics of ships and cargoes. The conclusion is clear: between the 1720s and the eve of the Revolution the volume of trade increased by 400–450%, which shows the extent of progress. There are qualifications. European trade quadrupled. Colonial trade (Antilles, then India and the Far East) did best of all, because it increased tenfold. There were also variations by period. It was between 1716 and 1748 that the increase was most rapid, followed by a period of consolidation between 1750 and 1780 and after that a slight rise. However, the long-term trend remains an exceptionally favourable one, confirmed by the steady rise of internal trade which was translated into spectacular national prosperity in a kingdom where the volume of coin in circulation increased from about 700 million *livres* at the beginning of the century to more or less 2,000 million at the end.

Industry showed a similar spectacular increase, for which the statistics are more detailed. Although the increase was a general one, different sectors were affected unequally. The woollen cloth sector grew by only 61%, while the more dynamic linen sector grew by more than 80%, and this growth was easily surpassed by the performance of silk, cotton and printed cloths.

Then there was the beginning of the 'industrial relay race' which is revealed by the exceptional growth of certain sectors; the supremacy of textiles began to be challenged. Coal production increased by 700–800%, smelting by 200% and iron by 300%. Some historians believe that French industry was growing faster than that of Britain, while others think the rate was at least comparable (Crouzet).

Prices confirm this picture of variation. They increased sharply for raw materials and more slowly for finished products, apart from the dynamic linen and cotton sectors. However, the result of these two factors, production and profit, especially the rise of profit, was spectacular almost everywhere, even in the sectors of most sluggish industrial growth: in the Sedan woollen cloth industry, turnover increased fivefold between 1732 and 1788. By comparison with the considerable and constantly increasing profits of big business, the rise of nominal wages for the industrial proletariat (perhaps 10–25%) was very small: it represented in fact a fall in real wages.

Not all Frenchmen did well out of the 'glorious' eighteenth century.

On the eve of the Revolution we may return to the question, which is not a rhetorical one: was this Revolution prompted by prosperity or poverty?

'*Prosperity Revolution*' or '*poverty Revolution*'?

In the catalogue of clichés it is no doubt Michelet's image of the poverty of the French peasant at the end of the *ancien régime* that is most vivid. 'Look at him lying on his dung-heap...poor Job.' Others express a different point of view with equally striking metaphors. Thus Taine compares the precarious existence of the French peasant to that of a man fording a river: as soon as the water gets deeper, he loses his footing. Jaurès, reacting against the earlier stress on poverty, described the Revolution as the victorious movement of a self-confident bourgeoisie, the culmination of a century of expansion. Today, thanks to Labrousse and his school, we can see that they were all right in their own ways.

However, it is necessary to distinguish the winners from the losers. Among the latter were the 'natural' losers, as vulnerable at the end of the century as they had been at the beginning. This group includes the most important sectors of the rural population: farm-hands, owners of tiny patches of land, and, more generally, those peasants who had to buy their own food. For this group, the Revolution was, at least in part, a poverty Revolution aimed at securing subsistence. It might be asked whether they had gained nothing from a century of economic expansion. To this it could be replied that they 'gained their life'[10] at least, because the great famines which had regularly wiped out the demographic surplus of the previous period had become less frequent in the eighteenth century. However, this gain was not an unqualified one. The other side of the coin was overpopulation, especially in the countryside, and its concrete results: migration, vagabondage and the vast increase of a floating population which had no place in the village community.

The economic trend of the eighteenth century also claimed many urban victims. As far as can be seen the sluggish increase in nominal wages in the course of the period was not enough to compensate for the rising trend in prices. Real wages, despite their short-term oscillations, declined in the course of the century: at best, the wage-earners got no more than the crumbs from the rich man's table.

[10] Labrousse's phrase.

It may seem odd to associate these men who experienced the 'poverty Revolution' in all its brutal reality, with another group of losers, the nobles; for the nobles were an important part of the land-owning class which had profited from the eighteenth-century rise in rent. In their case the term 'pauperisation' has a very precise meaning. Their income had certainly increased, in an uneven way, but the landed nobility paid a price for their idleness by their decline relative to the productive bourgeoisie, just as the rise in prices hit the life-style of these extravagant consumers particularly hard. The mainspring of their revolt was not poverty, but their resentment at their downward social mobility.

On the other side, among that productive bourgeoisie who were the essential beneficiaries of the trends of the time we see the opposite phenomenon: the aggressive frustration of a class to which society did not give the position it deserved. This is the class which took the initiative in revolt. It deserves a more extended discussion. The first question to ask is whether it existed.

THE BOURGEOISIE: MYTH OR REALITY?

The controversy over the 'bourgeois' Revolution

The term 'bourgeois Revolution' is neither a commonplace nor a recent rash invention for which Jaurès and his successors take the responsibility. This analysis of the class component of the French Revolution was made with astonishing prescience by a contemporary, Barnave. The historians of the last century, from Louis Blanc to Tocqueville or Taine, came to accept this view to a greater or lesser degree, though in a very different spirit and by very different routes. Then came the 'Jacobin tradition' of French historians from Jaurès to Mathiez, Lefebvre and Soboul, all more or less influenced by Marxism. Through their work the social interpretation of the bourgeois Revolution seemed to impose itself almost unanimously.

However, a whole series of criticisms of this view were now put forward, initially by English and American historians such as Cobban, Taylor and Palmer, followed by certain of the French.[11] A bourgeois Revolution, they argued, requires a bourgeoisie, pointing out in one of their most pertinent criticisms of the orthodoxy how important

[11] For a useful survey, see Palmer (58).

'non-capitalist wealth' (real estate, rent from land, royal offices) remained for this emerging bourgeoisie.[12] They also argued conversely that the aristocracy held a sometimes preponderant place in the rise of industrial capitalism: for more than half the forges and the mines were in their hands.

They also insisted on the fact that the term 'bourgeois' as it was used at the end of the eighteenth century could refer to a member of the middle class 'living nobly' on income from *rente*. It was not so much a 'bourgeois' Revolution as a Revolution of landowners, they argued, or simply a movement which could not be defined in class terms, or even sociological terms, because it was essentially political in inspiration.[13]

Certain positive aspects of this severe critique deserve emphasis. It was no doubt influenced by mid-twentieth-century political attitudes, but it may also be said that this revisionism was inevitable. It became inevitable from the moment that quantitative social history expanded to take in those urban societies where the multiplicity of social positions made classification necessary. It became clear that the bourgeoisie, discussed by historians since the beginning of this century, was nowhere near being satisfactorily defined. Georges Lefebvre had posed the problem in his last studies without being able to resolve it.[14] What about using the *ancien régime*'s own concept of 'orders'? He had too sharp a sense of social reality not to be aware of the sterility of an approach which (as Goubert says, and Abbé Sieyès had said before him) put 5 % of the population, the nobles and the clergy, on one side, and the remaining 95 %, the third estate, on the other. But when he tried to break this group down, every empirical method turned out to be disappointing. For Lefebvre, the bourgeoisie of 1789, in very broad terms, included, within its hierarchy of upper, middle and petty bourgeoisie, some extremely diverse groups: from the banker to the merchant, the entrepreneur, the lawyer, the *rentier*, the shopkeeper and the craftsman. This definition was no doubt too wide since it only excluded the wage-earners of the towns, but at the same time it was perhaps too narrow for the rural world because it did not even hint at the birth of a new rural bourgeoisie or even a 'peasant bourgeoisie'.

Following certain recent approaches, of which Régine Robin's is certainly the most suggestive, we may return to the problem of defining and assessing the importance of the French bourgeoisie at the end of

[12] R. Taylor, *Non-capitalist Wealth at the Origins of the French Revolution*.
[13] Mazauric (18), pp. 75–9.   [14] Lefebvre (38).

the *ancien régime*.[15] Let us follow her uncompromising definition of
the bourgeoisie as

the class which was legally of commoner status, and which groups together
all those in town and country who were in an economically and socially
dominant position in the sphere of capitalist social relations...opposed to
privileged groups who were not involved in the same social relationships in
so far as it postulated, consciously or unconsciously, an alternative state
apparatus and in the long term (allowing for cultural lag) an alternative
economic and social framework.

This working hypothesis has the advantage of taking into account the
objections formulated by the Anglo-American school by presenting the
ancien régime in terms of a complex of overlapping social relationships.

We must not expect to find this bourgeoisie numerically preponderant or triumphant. Its power was limited by all the classes (still
of central importance) who lived not from profit but on income from
rente, and whose social relationships were conditioned not by the 'free
contract' of economic liberalism but by a diversity of links between
patrons and clients, and by the formal hierarchical structures of a society
of orders which was not yet an empty show or an anachronism.
According to this definition the term 'bourgeoisie' undeniably excludes
the aristocracy, the still dependent peasantry, and in the towns, the
important group of master craftsmen, who belonged to the guild
system. While the bourgeoisie in the strict sense may run the risk of
emerging 'bled white' (as Robin puts it) from this definition by
elimination, the 'mixed' classes have had their importance in this
transitional stage assessed anew: the classes, that is, who were on the
frontier between the two worlds in their social status, their income,
their aspirations and their attitudes.

Financiers, businessmen, bosses

The true bourgeoisie and the mixed, marginal bourgeoisie of the *ancien
régime* coexisted and intermingled to such an extent that they were
inextricable. Consider the financier, apparently the most mobile of all
these groups. The old pre-capitalist world had produced its own type
of financier, a specialist in loans and public moneys, the financial expert
for a State whose weak point was fiscal. Once this figure was installed
'in the regime', as Herbert Lüthy puts it, he certainly seemed
indispensable.[16] To define him as a man of the past is not to

[15] Robin (59).   [16] H. Lüthy, *La Banque protestante en France* (Paris, 1961).

underestimate either his power or his development over the century
which led from the equivocal figure of the *traitant* (resented by Samuel
Bernard) to the more solid and less volatile role of the financier,
symbolised by the *fermier général*. However, alongside this new financier
there sprang up a new figure, especially in the last twenty years of
the *ancien régime*, that of the modern 'banker' who was beginning to
turn towards the *rentier* public and look after their capital, just as he
was elaborating an investment policy, adding industrial enterprises to
his portfolio along with the more traditional items of shipbuilding and
international trade. Mallet, Perrégaux, Hottinguer, Delessert and Périer
were the great names in this new style of finance.

We will come to similar conclusions if we move from this world
of finance, which was, after all, marginal, to the group which was at
the centre of bourgeois society: the merchants and industrialists. In the
first instance we have to deal with them together. The merchants were
far more important. It is true that the boundaries of the group were
less solid, and that it rose from a crowd of small traders in town and
country, through the intermediary group of 'merchants' (*marchands*)
in the strict sense (a vague term to cover a multitude of activities), to
its peak in the person of the businessman (*négociant*) as portrayed in
Savary's handbook *Le Parfait Négociant*. To this social hierarchy there
corresponded a geographical one, from the market town to the more
important cities, and from these cities to the great ports where the
business élite met one another, a highly structured world where the
cohesion of the group was reinforced by commercial, family, and, in
some cases, religious ties (Protestants in Marseilles, Jews in Bordeaux).
Their life-style, like their wealth, was sufficient in any case to distinguish
this group from those around them. It is relatively easy to identify the
threshold between the merchant and the businessman (a capital of
100,000 *livres*), but there was no upper limit. In Nantes, Bouteiller left
8 million *livres*; in Marseilles, Joseph Hugues was worth more than 4
million, and legend has it that Georges Roux 'of Corsica' had 30
million. However, it is difficult to judge whether this group was still
triumphant, with the future in their bones, or whether what we have
just seen is no more than the apogee of merchant capital, of a
commercial capitalism adapted to the *ancien régime* by its internal
structure as well as the nature of its operations. It would be good to
know – and the problem is by no means a theoretical one – to what
extent and as a result of what processes commercial capital was
transformed into the industrial capital of the following century. A link

in the chain is provided by the cloth merchant or the owner of a small
furnace, who gave work to men in town and countryside, operating
within the framework of the commercial capitalism whose importance
we have stressed already. By his side, however, we begin to see the
modern industrialist or manufacturer. This large-scale entrepreneur
might have a distinguished social origin. Some nobles took a close
interest in manufacturing: the Ségurs or the Montmorencys at
Saint-Gobain, the Prince de Croy and the Marquis de Cernay at Anzin.
Others became captains of industry: de Wendel in metal-working in
Lorraine, the Chevalier de Solages in the mines of Carmaux. However,
it may be seen that, even in metal-working, the bourgeoisie overtook
the privileged in a number of regions, and in the cloth industry, this
bourgeois preponderance turned into a monopoly. Industrial capital
was moving towards autonomy although it had not yet reached the
goal, whether it derived from commerce (the Périer family, linen
merchants of Grenoble) or was accumulated within industry by the men
who have been called the 'technocrats' (*patrons techniciens*). What are
the limits of this 'true' bourgeoisie? To take what has become a classic
case since Jaurès, Duplay the cabinetmaker, who had Robespierre as
a lodger, was a craftsman, but he employed some 20 journeymen and
did not eat at the same table. He was certainly a bourgeois, but at the
same time he was a *rentier*, owning houses which brought him in an
income. Where is the break? The ambiguity does not reside in the
definition but at the heart of the historical process itself.

Mixed types: 'rentiers' and professional men

From this it follows that the bourgeoisie at the end of the *ancien régime*
needs to be extended – carefully, of course – to include these 'hybrid
groups, mixed types, deriving income from different sources', classes
at the turning-point, 'the product of the type of transition resulting
from the penetration of capital into the feudal mode of production'
(Robin). Besides those already involved in capitalist social relations,
there was a whole network of groups of more ambiguous status. Their
position as *rentiers* or owners of offices made them part of the structure
of the *ancien régime*, but at the same time fitted them for the battle for
the destruction of traditional class relations. This goes for the group
which was known in the eighteenth century as 'bourgeois' in the strict
sense; for a term which used to be employed more widely now came
to refer only to those who lived nobly on the income from their

property. This narrower group was not insignificant in size: it included
3·5% to 6% of the population of an average town. Their status and
even their income varied from one place to another. In Paris they were
investors in the national debt or in that of the municipality, and owners
of real estate. In small towns, on the other hand, they derived their
wealth essentially from local farms and other land. This *rentier*
bourgeoisie was often urban, but not exclusively so. In the urbanised
villages of the Midi they took a central and active place in rural society,
even though, here as elsewhere, they were turning into a true
bourgeoisie, engaging in rural trade, laying acre to acre, and nibbling
away from the inside at the power of the seigneurs whose estates they
administered.

The same dialectic between complicity and hostility can be found
in the relationship of the *ancien régime* with the liberal professions and
civil servants, in other words, the *officiers*. If we try to assess their
numbers in the towns of this period, we shall find them to be both
large and small. In other words, an *intendant* administered a province
with half a dozen secretaries and three dozen mounted constables. On
the other hand, municipal officers and magistrates proliferated, and so
did notaries, advocates and solicitors, of whom there were dozens, even
in a small town. This large group lacks all unity at first sight since it
goes from a legal proletariat of half-starved solicitors to the *président
à mortier* of a *parlement*. The pivot of this group is the *conseiller secrétaire*
to the king, ennobled by his office and to be found in even the smallest
town. He marks the transition from commoner to noble. However,
no matter how diverse and hierarchical, the group did have a common
way of life and common attitudes. It was the ease of its access to land
that facilitated its links with the *rentier* bourgeoisie, and indeed its
incorporation within it. This was true even at the bottom but still more
at the top of the social ladder. It is very easy to understand how Pierre
Vilar could exclude the liberal professions from his strictly defined
bourgeoisie 'because in every society they provide services paid for by
the upper classes'.[17] Neither these groups nor the 'land-owning
bourgeoisie' really belong to the troops who led the assault against the
ancien régime.

All the same, one often finds lawyers and office-holders in the front
ranks of the Revolution, while at village level it was often led by the
local 'bourgeoisie'. To be surprised at this, to describe the French

[17] Quoted by Robin (59).

Revolution as a 'landowners' Revolution' or (questioning the traditional interpretation still more fundamentally) as a political Revolution free from social determinants, is, to my mind, simply to produce a more sophisticated version of the sad conclusion of the nineteenth-century scholars who discovered ingratitude as a historical phenomenon. If a scholar from Chartres were to study the problems of one of the largest cathedral chapters at the end of the *ancien régime*, he would surely discover that the lawyers, such as Jérôme Pétion, who instigated the Revolution either locally or in Paris, had grown up and prospered in the shadow of this body whose privileges they were now undermining. Because a whole network of groups were part of the system they were not necessarily dependent on it. They entered by the back door, by ennoblement or investment in land, but only a fraction of them, notably the caste of magistrates in the *parlements*, became fully part of the system. For the majority of the others, the bourgeois demand for the destruction of the old political and social regime could be all the more seductive because they had nothing to lose by it, and a great deal to gain. This point leads us to look at the ideological element in the assault on the *ancien régime*. But before doing this, we must discuss other groups of attackers, who were not bourgeois at all, but no less energetic for that.

The other revolt

Having left behind the urban and rural bourgeoisie, we return to the middle and lesser peasantry, the greater part of the rural world which contained the majority of the population. They too had something to say in the coming crisis.

This group included smallholders on the poverty line, such as wine-growers or the share-cropper of the south-west, who could not subsist without working on other men's land. Their revolt was set off by what was still one of the most powerful triggers: hunger and high prices. A subsistence crisis was always likely to be followed by a peasant rising. However, we must not reduce the rising of the middle peasants to a mere reaction of 'primitive rebels' unaware of the consequences of their actions. This would make it impossible to grasp the significance, the obstinacy and also the continuity of these revolts, and it would mean viewing the French Revolution as nothing but a combination (possibly fortuitous) of movements which were in any case uncoordinated and unconnected. The small peasants had to fight on several fronts in order to survive. There was the rearguard action against the bourgeoisie (and often the nobles as well) in defence of customs in common as opposed to the agrarian individualism which would lead to future agricultural revolutions. There were different names for this struggle. In Provence, it was the defence of the mountain pastures or of the rights to *terres gastes* (known elsewhere as 'wasteland') and the enemy had several different faces. It might be the urban bourgeois, exempt from taxes, laying acre to acre and tactlessly determined on agricultural innovation. It might be the 'cock of the village', a rich peasant bent on the division of the common lands (which was bound to be to his advantage) and on the enclosure of his own property. In many cases it was the seigneur, ruthless in insisting on his rights to the best of the harvest, the forest and the fishing (*triage* and *cantonnement*), reviving ancient servitudes and exclusions as part of the 'seigneurial reaction'. In that case, it became the defence of customary rights, the poor man's cow and the inadequate survival kit of the most deprived elements of the rural community. This apparently 'reactionary' defence, swimming against the stream of history, in fact formed part of the attack on the seigneurial regime by a common front of bourgeoisie and peasantry. The peasants' struggle against the seigneurial levy in all its direct and indirect forms – from the *champart* to the tithe – meant the destruction of traditional society, the emancipation of the land, the same *tabula rasa* which was the goal of the urban bourgeoisie. There were cracks in the common front, as the fact of bourgeois participation in the seigneurial levy makes evident. As a result, the 'village Revolution' took very different forms in different regions.

The multiplicity of urban society

Let us move on to the town. It is difficult to calculate the proportion of townsmen who belonged neither to the privileged or 'bourgeois' groups nor to the wage-earners of the modern type. We find ourselves faced with a great variety of statuses and roles including the majority of the urban population. Master craftsmen and retailers represented about 30% of the population of the average small town, and the wage-earners accounted for at least the same proportion. Let us start at the bottom of this crowd which was going to become revolutionary. The industrial proletariat of the modern type had only a very limited place here, apart from particular towns, or, more exactly, particular quarters. In Marseilles, where I have been able to trace them to their furnished lodgings, the workmen formed no more than a tenth of the floating proletariat.[18] No doubt the percentage was higher in Paris and the great textile towns, but the order of magnitude is significant. The most important group is that of servants, especially maid-servants, who accounted for around 10% of the total urban population. Next came the wage-earning journeymen, employed in the building, furniture and clothing trades and in the sale of food: men, young for the most part, and usually living in the house of their employer and sharing his preoccupations. One of the main features of this old-style system was the almost equal importance of an unskilled proletariat of *journaliers*, *gagne-deniers* and *manoeuvres*, whose numbers were constantly being swelled by rural immigrants driven to the towns by subsistence crises. This group included the lumpenproletariat of the large towns, and the professional beggars the age of Louis had been unable to banish altogether. The relative importance of this non-specialised wage-earning group was no doubt increased by the proximity of the rural world. There was hardly a town which did not have a fifth of its population made up of country folk: market gardeners, or wine-growers.

At the other end of the wage-earning scale, close to the masters of the guilds, we find the important transitional group of 'sworn crafts' (*métiers jurés*), of considerable local importance. A typical example is that of the stevedores and porters of the ports and markets: a closed, hereditary aristocracy of muscle with a stake in the traditional system which gave it what were possibly the most conservative attitudes of all. Although the wage-earning group was on the fringe of the 'society of orders' it was to some extent structured by it. As for the lower part of the world of the guilds, this included a whole hierarchy of positions which faded into those of the wage-earners. Outside the guilds there was a mass of free crafts (*métiers libres*), generally low in status; then there were the *chambrelans*, who eroded the closed shop operated by the guilds by working at home; and finally there were those who made up materials provided by the customer. Craftsmen and shopkeepers, with their stalls and workshops, defined by eliminating the groups we have just mentioned, nevertheless retained an essential place in this society. This was the world of independent producers, whose framework had been the guild, which offered them insurance and stability until its decline, especially after 1775: a world which defended itself in its own way by cutting itself off from new inventions, competition and the rise of free enterprise.

[18] M. Vovelle, 'Le Prolétariat flottant à Marseille sous la Révolution française', *Annales de Démographie Historique* (1969).

The 'workshop' and the 'stall'

The world of the guild was, if not yet in decline, a world on the defensive against direct competition and more insidious conquest. Does this mean that it should be placed on the side of those who defended traditional society? On the contrary, it is well known that it was in this milieu that a fair proportion of the *sans-culottes* originated. This raises the problem of collective attitudes and social change within the urban groups on the fringe of the triumphant bourgeoisie. How were class attitudes and class conflicts formulated? The least ambiguous answer is probably to be found among the wage-earners, but we have already seen the semi-archaic complexity of its organisation, and the cohabitation of some of its members with the independent craftsmen. Above all, Labrousse has pointed out how, in a world where the stability of wages was almost universal (while the prices paid by the wage-earners were still rising with savage speed), grievances were naturally concentrated on prices. The food riot and the attack on the baker's shop played the part in the behaviour of the urban populace that would be taken by strikes in the nineteenth century. As a result, it was not always clear that the true enemy was the bourgeoisie. Strikes had of course begun, but we should not be surprised to find a master craftsman participating in a food riot together with his journeymen. The essential social conflict was that which united master and man against the aristocracy and the *ancien régime*.

It is easy to see the ambiguity in the position of craftsmen who suffered in the same way as wage-earners from subsistence crises, unemployment and economic depression. We shall see the *sans-culottes* forging in the fire of experience their ideal of the independent producer, their safeguard. However, we must not expect these craftsmen to break with the programme of the bourgeoisie. Before the splits which appeared in the course of the Revolution, they tended to accept the revolutionary ideology of the triumphant bourgeoisie, and to share the slogans which had been popularised by the spread of the Enlightenment.

AN ENLIGHTENED REVOLUTION?

The diffusion of the Enlightenment

'Je suis tombé par terre,
      C'est la faute à Voltaire,
Le nez dans le ruisseau,
      C'est la faute à Rousseau.'

('I fell on the ground, / It was Voltaire's fault, / My nose in the water, / It was Rousseau's fault')

Gavroche's song in *Les Misérables* parodies the nineteenth-century bourgeois assessment of the importance of ideology in the French Revolution, for good or ill according to taste. The Voltairean bourgeoisie was proud of this heritage; later, a repentant bourgeoisie followed Taine in denouncing the *philosophes* for having undermined society. Better still, in the days of the Revolution itself, Abbé Barruel and others saw it as the result of a Masonic plot.

They were followed by historians, or historians of literature, from Paul Hazard to Daniel Mornet, who reacted against the animosity towards the Revolution in much late-nineteenth-century literary criticism by beginning to disentangle the problem.[19] It cannot be doubted that the French Revolution drew support from the philosophical or more generally the intellectual movement of the century, just as it drew on changing structures of feeling. Its leaders knew this, and said as much. Even if they had not done so, the vocabulary, themes and doctrines of the Revolution would all have proclaimed this. Within the history of ideas, which is currently, as part of a more general movement, dissolving itself into the history of mentalities, the problem is now often seen in terms of the diffusion of the Enlightenment. How, and how far, did the key ideas penetrate society? To solve this problem we have had to turn to new sources, to study book production in eighteenth-century France, or, on the side of the consumer, to analyse the contents of libraries – following more and more sophisticated methods – to discover changes in emphasis on different areas of interest, studied as signs of changing tastes and ideas.[20] It is much more difficult to discover the thoughts of those people who owned no books, let alone libraries, but lived for the most part outside literate culture.

[19] See especially Mornet (62).
[20] R. Estivals, *La Statistique bibliographique de la France sous la monarchie au 18e siècle* (Paris and The Hague, 1965), and the suggestive examples in *Livre et société* (60).

The attempt has therefore been made to study the most humble forms of popular literature, or mass culture.[21] Here, however, attitudes and behaviour are experienced rather than read or expressed in writing, and they have to be approached obliquely, by every possible means. In the privacy of their homes, their attitudes to life and death have been investigated; while in public the festival, a privileged moment, has been a particular focus of study.[22] In a world in which religion had an essential place, students of religious practice have begun to concern themselves with the *ancien régime*. This is an enormous break-through for a historiography which was long blocked by the contradictory clichés of Enlightenment 'dechristianisation' on the one side, and on the other the formula that 'France was completely Christian in 1789'. Collective attitudes may also be expressed in action. The study of the rejection of the established order or of revolts against it reveals the attitudes of the silent majority, and the tensions in society. From thefts and tavern brawls to organised popular risings, the criminal records provide a whole gamut of essential pieces of information. To draw up a balance we must be careful to make distinctions, and to follow the lines of cultural and social cleavage.

The culture of the popular classes

At first sight the immense world of the 'illiterate', as Goubert defines them, was on the margin of the Enlightenment.[23] It is possible to make a rough calculation of their number (Figs. 13, 14, 15). Old studies, such as Maggiolo's, rediscovered and brought up to date, tell us how many people were unable to sign the marriage register.[24] The proportion was a high one: 65% on the eve of the Revolution. However, we need to break it down by sex, region and social group. Women were much more ignorant than men, some 50% of whom were illiterate. This figure reveals an undeniable progress over the long term: in 1685, 79% of Frenchmen were unable to sign. However, this progress varied according to the region. From this point of view there was a sharp contrast between the two Frances. Suppose we draw a diagonal

---

[21] Mandrou (61).
[22] M. Agulhon, *Pénitents et Francs-maçons dans l'ancienne Provence* (Paris, 1968).
[23] Goubert (43).
[24] The information collected by this nineteenth-century scholar has been analysed by M. Fleury and P. Valmary, in 'Les Progrès de l'instruction élémentaire', *Population* (1957); and by F. Furet and J. Ozouf, in *Lire et écrire* (Paris, 1977), trans. R. Swyer, as *Reading and Writing* (Cambridge, 1982).

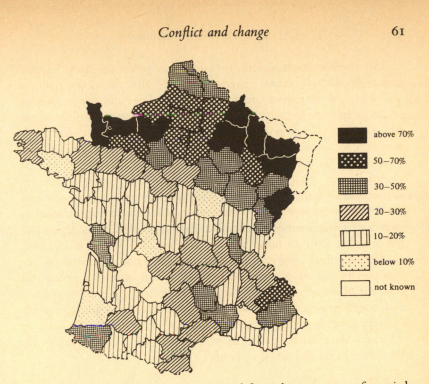

Fig. 13. Literacy in France in 1789 derived from the percentage of married couples able to sign their names. The superior performance of the north will be obvious

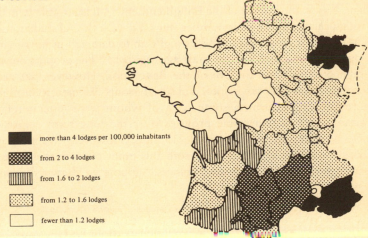

Fig. 14. Distribution of Masonic lodges in different *généralités* in 1789. The dominance of the Midi will be obvious

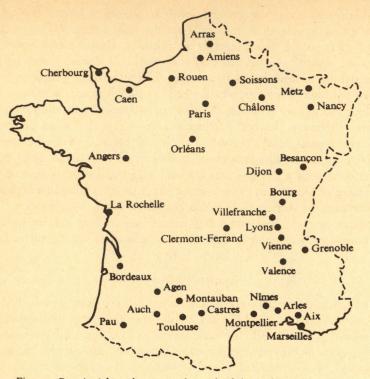

Fig. 15. Provincial academies at the end of the eighteenth century

line from the Cotentin to Franche-Comté, via the Loire region and
Burgundy. North-east of the line was an area of above-average literacy.
South-west of the line, people were ignorant, sometimes extremely
ignorant, as is shown by the example of lower Provence, where less
than 20% of the men and less than 10% of the women could sign their
names. The literate north was also the France of the more important
towns, and more elaborate studies than those of Maggiolo allow us to
show the relationship between literacy and social position. The vast
majority of the peasants were ignorant. Illiterate France overlapped
with rural France, especially in the Midi.

   Illiteracy does not mean lack of culture. In certain forms, the written
word reached the least educated groups, as in the case of the chapbooks,
which were read in public at the *veillée*. A recent study has drawn up
an inventory of the attitudes expressed in these chapbooks.[25] In this

   [25] Mandrou (61).

world religion, in the form of devotional booklets, lives of the saints, and hymns, was still dominant. The other major themes were escapist or supernatural. From legends to folk-tales, almanacs and books of white magic, we see an irrational world of miracles and fairies, searching in legends and news items for the hero the people needed, the redresser of wrongs, whether he was called Roland, Gargantua, Till Eulenspiegel or Fortunatus. There were two crucial areas omitted from this literature: history and science (even in the most concrete, technological sense). The world of popular literature seemed closed to all progress or Enlightenment, unconcerned with social grievances, imbued with a fatalism which found its grimmest expression in the Dance of Death, and its hero in the character of Bonhomme Misère:* literature of alienation, so it has been said, or of compensation.[26] It is not in these chapbooks that conflict and change can be studied. Long-term shifts hint at these tensions, and actions reveal them.

Popular religious practice

Religion, the importance of which has already been shown, had an essential place in social life. It gave the year its rhythm of festivals and offered a framework for associations such as the confraternities of penitents in Provence or Aquitaine. However, these forms of 'sociability', recently studied, reveal a change in the course of the century which has been described as 'secularisation'.[27] The weekly festival gave the young people an opportunity to dance. The declining confraternities of the Midi became no more than the formal framework for a social life which needed a focus and often found it in the tavern, a place of ill repute, but much frequented all the same. Was a process of dechristianisation taking place?

Another important problem was the following. In a State where the outward forms of religious practice were compulsory and the parish registers of Christian baptisms gave a misleading impression of unanimity, it was long possible to claim that popular religious practice did not change. The Revolution appeared to be a brutal, traumatic break with the past, and its rapid success required explanation. Certain writers, studying the records of diocesan visitations, had already noted exceptions to the rule of unanimity: foresters, quarrymen, tavern

* Character in a French folk-tale: a poor peasant who manages to cheat Death. [Trans.]
[26] Mandrou's phrase.
[27] Agulhon (see note 22 above).

keepers and soldiers were all unorthodox.[28] Whole regions of lukewarm religious practice were discovered next, even in the countryside, let alone the towns. The question has been raised whether the explanation should be given in geographical and social terms (the religion of the plains, contrasting with the devout *bocages* of the west), or in terms of traumatic historical events from the period before the Revolution; areas where Protestantism had never been successfully uprooted, turning into regions of religious indifference; zones of rural Jansenism where orthodox practice fell off. It has even been asked whether certain regions had ever been Christian in a deep sense. The point is not difficult to argue: the magical vision of the world, to which the chapbooks bear witness, corresponded to the experience of villages where the witch and the wise woman had an established position. To speak 'enlightened' language, we may point out that no more witches were burned after the intellectual revolution of the seventeenth century, that the law no longer recognised this category of person, just as the decline of the 'panic' pilgrimages of earlier centuries was an established fact everywhere.

We must not exaggerate, however. Some sources, such as wills, allow us to make the picture less crude. It seems clear that in more than one part of the countryside the highest and most regular level of religious practice was reached in the eighteenth century, up to about 1730, or even 1750. It was only after this time that we see a falling trend in the indicators of religious practice such as the demand for masses, the membership of confraternities or the legacies left to them or to charity. Were social attitudes changing? The currently debated question of the origins of contraception in the countryside, with all its indirect consequences – the men lapsing, while their wives remained faithful to the Church – is still too obscure to permit a definite answer.[29] In Languedoc, for example, the change did not take place until the shake-up of the wars of revolutionary and Napoleonic times. Can we then speak of a world on the fringe of history, its movement fettered, its mentality dominated by tradition? Yes and no. There were traditional means by which the world of the illiterate, the world of the subordinate, could make its voice heard.

The challenge to the established order could begin with apparently meaningless everyday violence. The criminal records tell us about delinquency in this still uncivilised world. As it organised itself, this

---

[28] G. Lebras, *Etudes de sociologie religieuse* (2 vols, Paris, 1955–6).
[29] A useful survey is in J.-L. Flandrin, *L'Eglise et le contrôle des naissances* (Paris, 1970).

movement of resistance could be lost in local brawls and fights between villages. However, it often took the form of collective action, such as salt and tobacco smuggling or anti-tax riots. People turned against the seigneur over the common lands or illegal feudal rights, or against the hoarder, the baker or the grain merchant when corn was dear. The riot remained the ultimate and virtually the only expression of popular opinion. In contrast to the long series of popular revolts in the seventeenth century, the age of Enlightenment may appear well-behaved, especially in the second half of the period, apart from exceptions such as the 'Flour War'. These spontaneous movements which spread throughout a whole province seem to have become rare occurrences, replaced by small-scale flare-ups which quickly died away. Had the provinces quietened down? The explosions of the pre-Revolution prove, if proof be needed, that attitudes had not changed.

Between illiterates and élites

Between the world of the people and that of the élites, there was an important third force. This was the intermediate level, to put it crudely, of those who could generally sign their name but were unable to read or did so only with difficulty. We find this group mainly in the towns, although they did exist in the countryside, especially in the urbanised villages of the Midi. They centred on the group of independent master craftsmen and shopkeepers who would soon provide the leadership for the revolutionary *sans-culottes*. We may add to this group the wage-earners immediately below them in the social hierarchy, journeymen for the most part. It is harder to define the upper limits of this intermediate world. If the criterion is the ownership of a few dozen books, this is likely, according to some sample surveys, to take us quite high in the social scale, to professional men, to churchmen and finally to the notables.[30]

This is not to say that this intermediate group lacked its own culture. It read books, although it owned few or none at all. Foreign observers, exaggerating somewhat, described Paris as a place where shopkeepers, dockers and coachmen all had the habit of reading. We are beginning to discover the cheap literature they read, still largely traditional (50% of the works were devotional), but with a place for innovation exemplified by the fashion of the novel. It is even possible to draw a map of reading habits, contrasting the north, where people read a good

[30] A point made by Daniel Roche on the basis of a study of Châlons-sur-Marne.

deal, with the area south of the Loire, where they did not, and the readers of devotional books in the east and west, with the readers of more secular literature, again in the Midi.[31] There were other forms of reading matter as well: news-sheets, pamphlets, flysheets, better adapted to a semi-popular clientele, like the popular songs of later times. The diffusion of the written word and the forms it took suggest that the sensibility of townspeople was different from that of the rural world, less hostile to change and more easily influenced.

This point is confirmed by what is known about religious attitudes. Not that we believe it legitimate to take the later schema of the towns as centres of damnation spreading dechristianisation throughout the neighbouring countryside, and apply it anachronistically to this period. The towns were privileged centres of the Catholic reconquest, rich in religious houses, parishes and confraternities. They were not yet under-equipped for the task: quite the reverse. As far as we can judge by making local studies of the demand for masses, pious bequests and the membership of confraternities, the urban middle classes, broadly defined, showed a remarkably high level of religious practice – higher than that of the countryside – and this often persisted until the middle of the century. Then came a turning-point – often a dramatic one – affecting craftsmen and shopkeepers as well as other sectors of the lower middle classes.[32] It may not be misleading to suggest a relationship between the changes in religious behaviour and what we know from other sources about changes in attitudes and values. The ideas of Rousseau, for example, apparently spread far down the social scale, and affected the structure of the family and the way in which children were treated.

As sensibility changed, so sociability took different forms. As we have remarked already, the festival long remained a dominant form of social life. Religious and secular festivals remained important, but their character changed. As a certain type of 'baroque' sensibility declined, even rejoicing changed its tone.

The inverse and, as it were, the complement of the festival was the riot. The urban riot had its own tonality. Here too the food riot, outside the bakers' shops or in the market-place, was the dominant form, but there was more diversity. The rioters often attacked town oligarchies or the tax policies of the government. Riots became more political. In

---

[31] See the suggestive study by Bouissy and Brancolini in the second volume of *Livre et société* (60).

[32] M. Vovelle, *Piété baroque et déchristianisation* (Paris, 1973).

towns of some importance, and above all in Paris, Jansenism was an issue which was taken very seriously and which allowed the crystallisation of a strong popular opposition which was quick to be provoked. The magistrates of the *parlements*, in the different phases of their ambiguous opposition to the monarchy, had long benefited from this popular support. These conflicts were often equivocal, of course, but their importance in creating an urban popular (or semi-popular) political consciousness deserves recognition. One should not be astonished, then, by their openness to the key ideas of the Enlightenment. There was an undeniable movement of ideas from the enlightened élite to those who had only what was at times an extremely indirect access to the Enlightenment.

A debate over the élite

Thus the élites appear to have been the repositories of the programme of the Enlightenment, and invested, as it were, with the task of diffusing it. This means that we need to reflect for a moment about what these élites represented, all the more because this problem has recently been raised once again.[33]

The oversimplified schema of a bourgeois Revolution opposed by the aristocracy has been replaced by a view of a culturally united élite including not only the nobility but also the upper fraction of the third estate, the educated *haute bourgeoisie*. These groups had in common not only a certain cultural level but also a set of options, and even a programme, all of which can be summed up as the 'culture of the Enlightenment', in which all the élites were equally involved, whatever their origins. This reinterpretation has important consequences. It might be extended so far as to reduce the Revolution to an accident, or a misunderstanding between two factions of the élite from which a new ruling class could and should naturally arise. Thus the problem of élite culture leads us to the question of the role of the Enlightenment in the Revolution and so to the Revolution in general. We can look at the question of this unity of the élite in terms of culture, tastes, sensibility, options, and programmes and the answer need not be the same in every case. It is possible to map the contours of this élite at different levels. Let us begin in a simple fashion, by distinguishing the producer and the 'consumer', in other words someone who can read and has access (however limited) to high culture.

[33] Richet (63).

The culture and the structures of the élite

Literacy, measured by signatures, is no longer a useful criterion for deciding who belonged to élite culture: in this milieu at the end of the eighteenth century everyone could sign their name. The other possible criterion is secondary education. We know that the number of secondary schools was relatively high, though their distribution varied cruelly from one region to another. These schools were run by the religious orders and dominated by the long-standing rivalry between the Jesuits and Oratorians. They remained the places where these young men (recruited less exclusively from the aristocracy than people used to think) were trained in the humanities. At the time of the Revolution they were still brought up on a diet of Petrarch and the Latin classics. There were perhaps modest signs of incipient modernisation in the introduction of new disciplines, but a certain neo-classical revolutionary heroism would have been inconceivable without this traditional humanist background. These 'consumers' of the Enlightenment can also be identified, now grown to manhood, in the meeting-places which multiplied during the eighteenth century: discussion groups and Masonic lodges.

Nowadays we no longer subscribe to the legend, put about at the time by Abbé Barruel and a few others, that the French Revolution was the result of a Masonic plot. This does not mean that the Masonic lodges did not play a very important part in the propagation of the Enlightenment. Let us look at them on the eve of the Revolution, at a time when the establishment of the 'Grand Orient' in 1773 and the absorption or federation of some lodges with other rites enable us to gauge their success. There were lodges in every town of any importance: at least 363 French towns contained lodges, and many had more than one.[34] The distribution of the lodges is uneven, and revealing. They were most densely concentrated in the Midi, in Provence, in Languedoc and in part of Aquitaine. On the other hand, they did not 'take' so well in the west, in Brittany and the Loire valley or, despite the military lodges, in the north-east. This distribution reveals local attitudes, and also deep socio-geographic structures: recent work has shown how, in the urbanised Midi, the notables shifted their allegiance from the old confraternities to the Masonic lodges which were better adapted to new forms of sociability as well as to new

[34] H. Le Bihan, *Loges et chapitres de la Grande Loge et du Grand Orient de France* (Paris, 1967).

attitudes.[35] A study of the sociology of the lodges would perhaps reveal the cultural élite in its widest and most diffuse form. The work has only just begun but it suggests that the social 'landscape' varied from town to town and from lodge to lodge. On the whole, the lodges were composed of nobles and ecclesiastics, the upper ranks of the legal and liberal professions, members of the bourgeoisie, merchants and businessmen, together with a few clerks, artisans and shopkeepers: a cluster that we have learnt to recognise. We have approached these cultural élites via their meeting-places; we would like to get to know them from inside to catch the Enlightenment in the act of spreading. We may well be disappointed. We should not expect to find that they were great readers: libraries are not often mentioned in inventories *post mortem* and when they are mentioned they are not well-stocked: books are to be counted in tens and only rarely exceed the hundred mark, in the case of nobles or priests. Could the cultural élite have been, paradoxically, aristocratic?

One would be inclined to believe this if one moves from a consideration of what we have rather irreverently called the 'consumers' to look at the 'general staff' of the Enlightenment. The provincial academies, known for the subjects they proposed for essay prizes, were one type of institution from which this conquering culture originated: there were 9 of them in 1710, 24 in 1750 and 35 in 1789. But if we look at their members we find, in general, that a fifth of them, on average, were ecclesiastics, and often more than half were nobles, frequently those who had bought their way into the nobility through offices. The third estate was reduced to a bare minimum, and included in particular members of the liberal professions and a middle class of 'talents': trade was scarcely represented at all.[36] All the same, it would be very naïve to be surprised at this imbalance. In the first place these academies, though a faithful reflection of provincial hierarchies (in Voltaire's words, 'good girls who never harmed anyone'), did not represent the whole of the movement: it is significant that the group of Encyclopédistes was distinctly more open to the bourgeoisie and to the élite at least of the crafts. In any case, a message does not have to be carried in person. This is shown by the example of the businessman, who was almost totally absent from the academies (although found in other groups with a less rigid structure). Did this absence reflect a lack

[35] Agulhon (see note 22 above).
[36] D. Roche in the first volume of *Livre et société* (60).

of interest in culture? Apparently not: as far as we can tell, these men went well beyond the narrow ideal of Savary's 'complete merchant'.*
In any case, the literature and drama of the end of the eighteenth century, as Ehrard has pointed out, very often presented the businessman as a hero, in contrast with the aristocrat. There was a significant shift from Molière's *Le Bourgeois Gentilhomme* (1670) to the gentleman merchant of Lesage's *Turcaret* (1709).[37]

A turning-point in sensibility

Whoever was responsible, a new style had imposed itself and a profound change had taken place. It affected behaviour, practice and taste, which became increasingly 'enlightened'.

We can follow this change by looking at the titles of books in libraries at the end of the century. A breakdown by subject bears witness to the continued importance of law and history, but also to some astonishing switches. At the beginning of the century, religious literature had been easily the most important subject, thanks to the Jansenist controversy, but it now went into an irreparable decline. The rising subjects, which included the sciences, the arts, 'curiosities' and belles-lettres (within which there was a shift from the epic and the tragedy to the romance), showed that there had been a fundamental change in the tastes of the public. This new public, more politically conscious, required a new kind of literature, from large treatises to the incisive essays in which Voltaire excelled.

A whole spectrum of collective attitudes, sometimes half conscious or implicit, may be discerned. Attitudes to life and death suggest that the traditional ideal of the 'honnête homme' was taking a new form. Large families were no longer fashionable: the ideal of a small family began to spread downwards from the aristocracy. This ideal owed more to the rediscovery of childhood by Rousseau and his followers than to Christian trust in Providence or the indifference of libertines. This rediscovery of childhood was part of a wider movement of the period, the rehabilitation of feelings. Now they were secularised, emotions had changed their nature.

It is among these élites that the process of dechristianisation can be discerned most clearly. This has been known for a long time, even if

---

* Jacques Savary's guide to business, *Le Parfait Négociant*, was published in 1675. [Trans.]
[37] In his contribution to *Niveaux de culture et groupes sociaux*, ed. L. Bergeron (Paris and The Hague, 1967).

it was described in the convenient clichés 'Voltairean bourgeoisie' and 'frivolous aristocracy'. Recent quantitative studies of religious practice allow us to be more precise. The world of the notables, extremely devout at the beginning of the century (to judge from its masses and its bequests), changed little, or if anything became even more pious until the years 1730–50 (according to region) thanks to the increasing importance of Jansenism.[38] However, whether it came early or late, the turning-point was a sudden one and the indicators of religious practice generally fell by 50% (at least in Provence). The change affected different social groups unequally: in the religious domain, the élite reveals a diversity which calls its cohesiveness into question. Among the nobility, religious practice remained at a very high level, while it declined sharply among the bourgeoisie, professional men and businessmen setting the example.

This rapid secularisation of the life-style of the upper classes was a major element in the formation of a new sensibility, even if it appeared to some contemporaries as a new form of religious experience. Changes in art, however, make the direction clear, revealing the desire for solidity and majesty and even heroic aspirations in the buildings or projects for buildings of Ledoux or Boullée, and the simplicity aspiring to austerity of Louis XVI furniture. Painting, on the other hand, moved in two apparently diverse directions: heroism in the ancient Roman style, as in David's profession of neo-classical faith, *The Oath of the Horatii* (1785), and the affected sentimentality of the moralising genre scenes of Greuze.

Was the élite revolutionary?

This leads us to the unavoidable problem of the social and revolutionary content of all these innovations. It would be too simple or mechanical to make the neo-classicism of David (to say nothing of Greuze) the expression of a rising bourgeois culture opposed to the decadent frivolity of Boucher and Fragonard. However, despite the apparent consensus of élite culture, there were cracks in the edifice. They will seem even wider if we pass from the 'collective semi-unconscious' of tastes, acts and practices to the domain of clear ideas and joint decisions.

There is no doubt that the philosophy (or programme) of the Enlightenment, despite internal contradictions, included a body of common ideas. Despite Rousseau, this philosophy may be defined in terms of optimism and a faith in progress and in reason. It was a

[38] Vovelle (see note 32 above).

conquering rationalism which wanted to change the world by attacking everything which attached it to the past: despotism (if it was not enlightened), abuses and superstition. A system of new values, with liberty as the key word, seemed to impose itself on almost everyone. In his *Esquisse d'une histoire des progrès de l'esprit humain* (*Sketch of a History of the Progress of the Human Mind*), Condorcet summed up the trend and carried it forward. However, we must be careful if we are not to be misled. In this body of Enlightenment writings, one word is lacking almost everywhere (except in Marat's *Les Chaînes de l'esclavage* of 1774): the word 'Revolution'. Once the Revolution itself began, its ambiguities became apparent. Aristocratic liberalism, typified by Montesquieu, a liberalism which was the child of nostalgia rather than hope, now revealed its true face. Whether or not it was the creation of an élite which could appear – from the social point of view – extremely traditional, the message of the Enlightenment was to become the weapon of the bourgeoisie. There could be no homogeneous élite where there was no true community of interests.

3

Birth of a Revolution (1787 to May 1789)[1]

ARISTOCRATIC REVOLT OR PRE-REVOLUTION (SUMMER 1786
TO SUMMER 1788)

Various titles have been suggested: an 'aristocratic Revolution'
(Lefebvre), a 'revolt of the nobles' (Mathiez) or 'of the aristocracy'
(Soboul), or even a 'pre-Revolution' (Egret), not to mention a
'Revolution of the notables'.[2] These modifications and revisions in
terminology are very revealing, since they raise the whole problem of
the interpretation of the period from 1787 to 1789. It is tempting to
list the 'immediate' causes of the Revolution here, in contrast to the
'deep' causes we have already tried to describe in the previous structural
chapters. But the point is that it is not just a question of the initial
upheavals; whether one opts for 'revolt' or 'revolution', 'nobles' or
'notables' to some extent colours one's view of all the rest. These years
can be seen as no more than an unfortunate incident, or as a major
episode which could have brought about a revolution without the
Revolution if the notables had had a common programme; we should
moreover make due allowance for the effects of an economic crisis
which mobilised the masses.

A mediocre monarch

We would deserve criticism if we failed to give the representative of
the French monarchy in 1789 his rightful place. Louis XVI had been
on the throne for fifteen years, having succeeded his grandfather Louis
XV in 1774. 'We are too young to reign', he might have said at the
time, with his new queen, Marie-Antoinette, daughter of the Empress
Maria Theresa. This anxiety was justified by an awareness of his
personal limitations in a serious situation. Much has been said about
the integrity and the undoubtedly good intentions of this big man of

---

[1] The title echoes a famous phrase of E. Labrousse.   [2] Egret (68).

73

limited intelligence. He came alive when hunting or making locks in his workshop, but slept through council meetings and, as his diary shows, he was to live through the decisive days of the Revolution in a state of semi-consciousness. In any case, he had little personal distinction. He was obese; it was said that he drank, that he made a poor showing as a lover, and that he needed an operation to enable him to perpetuate the royal line: the hopes of the monarchy were pinned first on a girl (1778) who was to become Madame Royale, then on the first dauphin (1781–9), and then on the Duc de Normandie (1785). This caused a dynastic problem: the king's brothers kept a watchful eye on this fragile line of succession. The Comte de Provence and the Comte d'Artois had very different personalities but they were both ambitious, and therefore intransigent in their defence of privilege. At a greater distance there was the king's cousin, Philippe d'Orléans, a danger even in disgrace, the richest man in the kingdom and skilled at manipulating the forces of change to his own advantage. The queen, Marie-Antoinette, had a political role in this family circle. This seems paradoxical when one thinks of this young woman with a taste for escapism who rapidly became the symbol of the spendthrift frivolity of court life. But her dresses, her overflowing self-interested entourage (Madame de Polignac) and the scandalous reputation she acquired (she was suspected of a love affair with Fersen, Colonel of the Royal Swedish Regiment) turned her, in spite of herself, into a symbol of the old regime. There was another factor: the queen's influence on the king was gradually increasing; public opinion accused her of not thinking French at all. She quickly became known as 'the Austrian'.

None of this need have mattered much. The monarchy had survived many other palace dramas, and Louis XVI's inhibitions cannot explain the decline of the reforming zeal of the regime. The real problem was political: Louis's policies were extraordinarily erratic, in a period which could not tolerate wavering. Louis XVI wanted to 'barricade' himself with men of integrity, but he nevertheless ousted the 'triumvirate' (Terray, Maupeou, d'Aiguillon) who had offered a French road towards a form of enlightened despotism. He did not support his minister Turgot (1774–6), who brought new ideas inspired by the physiocrats into the corridors of power, and he replaced him, without much benefit, by Necker, an enlightened banker from Geneva who was competent rather than brilliant. Although the publication of Necker's *Compte rendu au roi* concerning the income and expenditure of the kingdom was essentially a propaganda exercise, it revealed to the public the disproportionate expenses of the court, and the hostility of this pressure group provoked Necker's dismissal in 1781.

Political crisis: the deficit

In this last decade France entered a political crisis. Participation in the War of American Independence had been a success in terms of international prestige but a financial disaster, costing two thousand million *livres*, which had to be borrowed. Calonne, Necker's successor and minister of Finance from 1783 on, pursued a policy of systematic borrowing to cover the needs of the Treasury. The heavy weight of debt (which had increased threefold in 15 years) at last forced him to raise the question of structural reform by presenting a *Plan d'amélioration des finances* (*Plan for Improving the Finances*) in August 1786.

This deficit was a major factor in triggering the Revolution, so much so that it was, according to Mirabeau in 1789, 'the nation's treasure'. We can have no more than an approximate idea of the gravity of the situation. The Treasury did not draw up budgets for the years to come, in the modern manner, since the practice of *acquits au comptant* allowed the king to find whatever money he needed. However, certain documents from the end of the *ancien régime* allow us to form at least a relative idea of the situation: the 'Treasury accounts' for 1788 show an income of 503 million *livres* compared with an expenditure of 629 million. The problem is not difficult to see. Taxation no longer provided a solution, since taxes had already increased by 140 million in ten years. Money had to be picked up wherever it could be found, where the physiocrats had noticed it accumulating, among those who drew their income from land. However, this meant doing away with the whole fiscal system, which was based on the exemption of the privileged. The budget seems out of proportion on the expense side too. Military expenses accounted for more than a quarter of the total (165 million, or 26%). On the civilian side (145 million, or 24%), we must not be too surprised by the tiny proportion (2%) devoted to welfare or education; it would doubtless be anachronistic to use these categories to describe a system in which they were unknown. The court and pensions, on the other hand, accounted for 6% of income: not the bottomless pit that public opinion imagined, but an enormous sum all the same, and it is natural to be shocked by such limited examples of royal generosity as the 23 million to pay the debts of the Comte d'Artois and the 14 million for the Comte de Provence: it was too much, of course. Yet the most important item in the account was the interest on the debt, which absorbed 51% of annual income in 1788. It was a vicious circle in a situation where expenditure exceeded income by some 20%, where anticipated revenue and advances allowed the government to live from hand to mouth. This was the system Calonne tried to break by presenting his reform plans to an Assembly of Notables.

Calonne and the notables

This too complaisant minister had been an effective provincial *intendant*, and hence he left a poor reputation behind him. In any case his plan of reform went beyond a set of fiscal expedients, as he explained to the notables himself: 'In this vast kingdom it is impossible to take a step without finding different laws, contrary customs, privileges, exemptions...and this general disharmony complicates administration, interrupts it, clogs its wheels and multiplies expense and disorder everywhere.'

Such a diagnosis involved a fundamental reform. On the fiscal side, it implied not the abolition but the limitation of the old inegalitarian, irrational system. The *taille* was reduced, and so was the *gabelle*, and its application was made more uniform. Above all, much was expected from a new tax, the *subvention territoriale*, which rose and fell in proportion to income from land, and, most important of all, was levied on all landed property. The old *vingtième* was limited to movable goods: a levy of 5% on profits and offices. By this attack on the fundamental fiscal problem Calonne proposed to resolve the urgent question of the moment, the deficit, by the alienation, spread over 25 years, of royal lands in order to pay off the debt. He also planned the conversion of the Caisse d'escompte into a State bank.

Outside the strictly financial domain, Calonne planned to increase economic activity, and so revenue, by freeing the grain trade and suppressing internal customs and certain impositions, such as the branding of leather, which caused irritation without bringing in great profit. Above all, in order that 'the distribution of public office might cease to be unfair and arbitrary' he envisaged radical administrative reform involving a hierarchy of assemblies in towns, districts and provinces whose members were nominated by the well-to-do. Although they remained consultative in function, this was an attempt to extend the system of provincial assemblies which Necker had introduced as an experiment in Guyenne and Berry.

What did Calonne's plan amount to? It was a helping hand, held out – not for the last time – to the traditional aristocracy. They would save the financially sick monarchy, but they might have to agree to give up a fair number of their tax exemptions and implicitly accept plutocracy in the provinces. At this price, the basic structure of the old regime would be saved, including most of the aristocracy's privileges.

This compromise failed. The Assembly of Notables met on 22 February 1787, along the lines of the traditional model: 144 people attended, including princes of the blood, dukes, 40-odd peers and marshals, 33 magistrates from the *parlements*, a dozen prelates, 25 mayors and aldermen; it is hard to imagine a group more thoroughly conditioned to endorse the royal propositions than these dignitaries, who were caricatured as chickens ready to be plucked. However, remembering their own privileges, these notables reacted against the minister. Shocked from the start by Calonne's speech revealing the size of the deficit, they demanded to see the accounts: had Necker not, six years before, counted on a surplus? This clever move forced Calonne, in order to justify himself, to show how Necker had cooked the accounts, even though, in so doing, he annoyed those for whom the banker of Geneva remained the man of progress and of the Enlightenment. Calonne was then attacked where he was weakest. Mirabeau took him to task in a 'denunciation of speculation'. The minister attempted in vain to revive the debate by denouncing the egotism of the aristocracy. Whether from lack of confidence in Calonne or from lack of information, public opinion did not support him against the prelates and *parlementaires* who obtained his dismissal and forced him to flee.

The Brienne ministry

In May 1787, the Archbishop of Toulouse was called to office by the king. Loménie de Brienne, known for his opposition to Calonne, was a man of the Enlightenment, ambitious as well as intelligent, and ready to implement the politics of the man he had supplanted. However, the opposition had not given up: far from it.

In order to conciliate the notables, Brienne agreed to show them the accounts and announced spending cuts. At the same time, attempting with a certain skill to split the aristocratic–bourgeois coalition, he put forward a series of reform measures. This prelate was prepared to take

on himself the hostility of the clergy by giving the Protestants civil
liberties. As a gesture of conciliation to the leaders of the third estate,
he set up assemblies in all the provinces. Their members were appointed
and their functions were purely consultative but – an innovation which
would not be forgotten – the third estate was represented on the same
scale as the other two orders combined. He also offered the peasants
the opportunity to commute their *corvée* for the king into a tax.
However, he came to grief over the financial question. Having been
forced to revive Calonne's *subvention territoriale* and indeed to increase
it with a stamp duty he found himself facing renewed opposition from
the notables. There was a new theme in this opposition: by declaring
itself incapable of granting a tax, the assembly made implicit reference
to a summoning of the Estates General and La Fayette demanded an
American-style assembly complete with a 'Great Charter', in other
words, a constitution.

There has been much discussion of the importance and the reality
of the options still open to the monarchy at this stage. Would the king
have saved the regime if he had taken the notables at their word and
backed the bourgeoisie against the privileged? The problem is a false
one, because it assumes that it was possible for the king to act as arbiter;
he was in fact part of the old system.

Unable to liberate himself from those 'intermediary bodies', the
parlements, Brienne was forced to submit his edicts to them for
approval. He had the insight to give way, at least so far as the 'liberal'
edicts (*corvée*, provincial assemblies) were concerned, but the Parlement
of Paris did not miss the opportunity to exploit the ambiguity which
allowed it to defend its privileges by mystifying public opinion (which
shouted 'down with taxes', 'long live the fathers of the people'). It
remonstrated against the stamp duty and rejected the *subvention
territoriale*, appealing to the Estates General. The old eighteenth-century
game started up again: forcible registration of the edict at a *lit de justice*
(6 August 1787), followed by its repudiation by the Parlement,
followed in turn by the usual exile of the Parlement to Troyes, the
support of the provincial *parlements* and other courts, the active support
of the lower classes of Paris, talks and recall from exile, the monarchy
having given way and withdrawn its fiscal edicts.

However, the game had gone too far. Brienne proposed to borrow
420 million *livres* spread over five years, and agreed in return to
summon the Estates General in 1792. A *séance royale*, held on 19
November 1787, was transformed into a *lit de justice* by the king and

his Keeper of the Seals, Lamoignon, who decided on strongarm tactics: a move which might in other circumstances have been a genuine act of royal authority. There was a classic exchange between the king and his cousin the Duc d'Orléans: 'It's illegal'...'I want it, so it is legal.' This expression of the doctrine of absolutism revealed the discredit into which it had in fact fallen, thanks to a changing way of thinking. After this confrontation both sides were entrenched in their positions and the game could go no further. The Parlement responded to the exile of the Duke and a number of its magistrates by reiterated and increasingly bold protests, for example on 4 January 1788, and on 3 May: the denunciation of *lettres de cachet* in the name of natural law, and the proclamation of the 'fundamental laws of the kingdom', of which they declared themselves the guardians. These laws recognised the hereditary monarchy but proclaimed the liberty of the individual, the independence of the judiciary and the right of the Estates General to be summoned regularly to grant taxes: an ambiguous mixture of the very old and the very new.

The revolt of the *parlements* culminated in the tragi-comic, or at least grandiloquent, session of 5 May 1788, when the magistrates refused to deliver two of the leaders of the opposition, d'Eprémesnil and Montsabert, to the authorities. At this point, late in the day, the monarchy decided to revive the policy which had been that of Chancellor Maupeou at the end of the previous reign, and to break the *parlements* by taking away their powers. Six edicts prepared by the Keeper of the Seals (Lamoignon) made profound changes in the legal system. Torture was abolished, to the benefit of humanity; litigants also gained, because a number of lower courts were abolished. The whole system was rationalised with the *tribunaux présidiaux* as the courts of first instance and with appeals to 45 *grands bailliages*. This change had the effect of reducing the power of the *parlements*, whose right of registration passed to a 'plenary court' of royal officials. A central part of the old system survived, since the sale of offices was not abolished, but in any case this important reform was never put to the test, for the revolt of the magistrates was followed by another stage of confrontation.

The 'Revolution of the notables'

This is the title which has been given to that remarkable phase which essentially covered the summer of 1788, from the edicts of Lamoignon, in May, to the fall of Brienne and the recall of Necker at the end of August.[3] This change of terminology characterises a change in the pace, nature and scope of the movement. Although Paris did not altogether lose the initiative, for a while it was upstaged by the provinces, still rooted in the past, where the old provincial estates, refuges of the nobility, and the local *parlements* had a centrifugal effect. Nevertheless, it was here, rather than in the Paris of May 1788, that a new, independent collective force began to emerge: that of the bourgeoisie. This resulted in the elaboration of a genuinely revolutionary programme, which went beyond the reactionary aims of the aristocratic revolt.

However, this programme varied from place to place, and from moment to moment. Initially, the movement took the form of a backlash from those who had suffered as a result of Lamoignon's edicts: we refer, of course, to the *parlements*; geographically, the disturbances extended from Dijon to Toulouse, and from Rennes to Pau or Grenoble. This had a ricochet effect on those urban groups whose livelihood depended, directly or indirectly, on their *parlements*; where would Grenoble have been without 'these Gentlemen'? By itself, this would simply be an example of traditional solidarity. But there was more than this. First of all there was the fact that in the *pays d'états*, or areas which had formerly been *pays d'états*, there was strong local patriotism amongst the different nobilities, partly distinct from one another but ready to converge. Where these assemblies survived, they gave support to the militant fervour of the local aristocracy (Rennes). Elsewhere, however, we can see that the new assemblies could themselves provide the framework for demands which were sometimes aggressive (as in Auvergne, at the instigation of La Fayette). As the *parlements* had their network of sympathisers, the demands of the local nobilities could arouse popular support. It is not difficult to find local examples of this in May and June. In Pau, on 19 June, the country people, incited to revolt by the *parlement* and the nobility, besieged the *intendant* and brought him to terms. In Rennes the nobility, united with the students, met only feeble resistance, thanks to the collusion of the *intendant*.

[3] Egret (68).

The example of Dauphiné

In these areas, the initiative for revolt remained with a coalition
between the parlementary caste (*caste parlementaire*) and the other
branches of the nobility. However, the real turning-point occurred in
Dauphiné. There were no doubt good reasons for this: there was a
parlement in Grenoble, and Dauphiné contained both a large nobility,
which resented the abolition of the provincial assembly, and an active
and varied bourgeoisie. This ranged from the great capitalist
entrepreneur of the modern type, such as Claude Périer, 'Lord Périer'
('Périer Milord'), to that apparently very different group whose
members, it seems, were close to the *parlement* from which they derived
their living: the lawyers of Grenoble, of whom Mounier and Barnave
were two eminent representatives. But we should not confuse these two
groups; these men themselves did not. Barnave was very well aware
of the criteria for defining the bourgeoisie with which he identified,
and in the name of which he was to negotiate with the privileged groups
of society, toning down their initial demands and finally suggesting a
kind of compromise. In Grenoble, as elsewhere, it was the *parlement*
which took the initiative: it refused to register the edicts, and was
ordered into exile (end of May). Encouraged by the local legal
fraternity, popular reaction took the form, on 7 June 1788, of the
famous 'day of Tiles' (*journée des Tuiles*) when the crowd stoned the
troops and brought back to the Palais de Justice the magistrates who
had been ousted. But this time the consequences were much more
significant. This popular movement led to an assembly being held in
Grenoble on 14 June 1788: it was a spontaneous coalition of the
notables, consisting of 9 clergy, 33 nobles and 59 representatives of the
third estate, most of whom were lawyers. Led by Mounier and
Barnave, this bourgeois faction put forward a programme which
already went far beyond mere support of the *parlementaires*; they
certainly called for the reinstatement of these men, but they also
demanded the convening of the provincial estates in which the
representatives of the third estate would be 'equal in numbers to those
of the clergy and of the nobility combined, and chosen by means of
free elections'; this assembly was itself to be a prelude to the convening
of the Estates General.

This plan took shape and was more or less worked out during the
general assembly of the municipalities of Dauphiné which was held on
21 July 1788 at the Château de Vizille, lent for the occasion by 'Périer

Milord'. There had been a real electoral campaign, which had been both active and selective, since just under 200 of the 1,200 parishes were represented. As it was, the assembly of Vizille consisted of 50 clergy, 165 nobles and 276 representatives of the third estate, a carefully selected third estate, but one which still managed to be dominant, thanks to the initiative of its leaders (Mounier). The resolutions adopted demanded the reinstatement of the *parlements*, but stripped of their powers of registration and of their political influence. They also called for the re-establishment of the provincial estates on the basis of parity between the third estate and the other two estates combined: this was felt to be a particularly important step in a political reorganisation culminating in the revival of the Estates General, which alone were able to 'struggle against the despotism of ministers and put an end to the corrupt administration of finance'. As it triumphed, this strong provincial feeling prepared the way for its own elimination: the people of Dauphiné declared that they would never isolate their cause from that of the other provinces and that 'by supporting their own particular rights, they would not abandon those of the Nation'.

Was a compromise possible?

What had happened in Dauphiné marked a change in pace in the events leading up to the Revolution. It went beyond the aims of aristocratic revolt. Equally important, the notables had offered a compromise. The national and libertarian aspirations of the bourgeoisie remained and there was a new assessment of merit, though limited enough to be satisfied by the doubling of the third estate. The privileged groups did not stand to lose anything really essential, even if the *parlements* were to be restored and provincial identity to suffer a setback after being exalted. This can be seen the following month in the drawing up of a constitution for the projected new estates of Dauphiné. By deciding to rely on the system of orders, the notables produced some very significant results; the nobility did not include those recently ennobled; the clergy excluded the poor priests, despite the fact that there were many of them in Dauphiné; and the third estate imposed a property qualification and was closed to the country *fermiers*, in other words, to a whole sector of the peasantry. These decisions ensured the cohesion of a hand-picked 'élite', and the notables even went as far as giving a specific guarantee of the category of so-called 'noble lands'. One of Mounier's friends explained the basis of this decision: 'it would be better to run the risk of not seeing the restoration of perfect equality in our lifetime than to slow down our march towards liberty. Should our citizens be concerned today only with being less poor? Should they not begin by wanting to be free?'

Was there not a measure of self-deception, not to say contradiction in this programme of the notables which, to obtain freedom and political equality, agreed to make very serious concessions to the old social structures? This overestimates the realism of the nobility, the acquiescence of the bourgeoisie as a whole, and also the passivity of the people, duped by the compromise of the notables. Mounier had hoped that after the initial fillip of the 'day of Tiles', the people would restrict themselves to a silent role: 'The lowest classes of the people calmly awaited the results of our work. The multitude never influenced our assemblies.'

This hope was seriously misguided: the fragile equilibrium necessary for this programme of revolution without the Revolution no longer existed; the machinery of government was breaking down as a result of lack of authority and especially for lack of money since Brienne, short of funds, had to suspend Treasury payments. He was forced to promise (5 July 1788) to convoke the Estates General on 1 May 1789, and to suspend the plenary court set up by Lamoignon to replace the political powers of the *parlements*. It was on the basis of an almost complete surrender that the king accepted the resignation of Brienne on 24 August, and humbled himself sufficiently to reinstate Necker.

On the other hand, the 'submissiveness' of the urban and rural masses would not long withstand the assault of a violent economic crisis.

CRISIS AND REVOLUTION

Taken as a whole, the eighteenth century has been described as 'glorious' because its economy was carried forward by a long-term increase in prices and production. However, since the work of Labrousse, we know that the 'poverty Revolution' was not a myth: it was within the context of a violent economic crisis that the Revolution broke out, and poverty was one of the most important of its immediate causes.[4] This is not to suggest that there was not long-term prosperity; but during the period leading up to the Revolution, as far as the economy is concerned, there was a short-term 'intercycle of recession' (1778–87), followed by the 'revolutionary cycle' (1787–91).

[4] Labrousse (66).

The crisis in the French economy at the end of the *ancien régime*

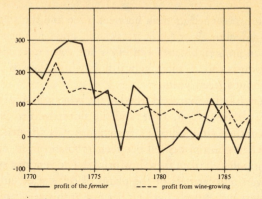

Fig. 16. An 'intercycle of recession' according to two indices of agricultural prosperity: the profit of the *fermier* and the profit from wine-growing

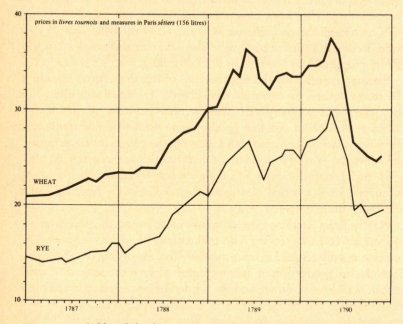

Fig. 17. An 'old-style' subsistence crisis: monthly variations in the price of wheat and rye between 1787 and 1790

An '*intercycle of recession*'

Economic progress reached its peak between 1760 and the 1770s: after this there was a decline. It was not irreversible and did not mark the end of the 'economic eighteenth century', but was rather a phase of the kind economists call an intercyclical fluctuation; in this case, one which lasted about fifteen years.

There was a marked downward trend in the wine industry: the price of wine fell by about 50% in 1781, and the slump was to persist for seven years. Another vital sector of agriculture was affected, though less severely, when grain prices fell between 1770 and 1780, and again until 1787. Who suffered from these low prices? The vendors, of course, the wine-growers and farmers of the plains of large-scale cultivation. The peasants were particularly hard hit because at this very time of low prices the landowners increased their rents. This apparently inopportune action was an attempt by the landowners to raise revenue by cutting the profits of their *fermiers*. It was certain to increase the problems of the peasantry who were now more numerous and therefore in no position to argue about higher rents, at the very time when their profits were declining. Other sectors were also affected: there was a crisis in fodder crops, and, as a result, in stock-breeding, after 1785.

Industry experienced the repercussions of this depression: no doubt the rising sectors, for example coal-mining, remained dynamic: but they were still so marginal! The essential branches of the textile industry – cotton or woollen goods – were weakened and stagnated: there was a lack of raw materials following the cotton shortage during the American War of Independence and the crisis in sheep-rearing after 1785. As for long-distance trade, the great boom had already been over for several years; a period of stagnation set in before the American War and lasted until 1785–6.

Nearly every sector of the economy experienced this recession, or at least an end to growth. The population, however, continued to increase and this resulted in acute social *malaise*. According to Labrousse's formula, the production of men increased while at the same time their output was slowing down, and the burden of rent became heavier just as the farmer was obliged to sell at a lower price. This situation had persisted for more than ten years when the 'revolutionary cycle', dominated by the crisis of 1789, broke out in 1787. It was to last roughly from 1787 to 1791.

The economic crisis

The crisis comes into the category of those 'old-style' accidents which preceded the industrial revolution. They followed a familiar pattern: the initial, decisive, impetus came from the countryside, but the whole economy was to be affected.

The cereal harvest of 1788 was very bad, and that of 1789 mediocre. We must give 'the history of events' in the economy its due when its consequences were so severe; the storms and hail of July 1788 which ravaged the crops of Normandy and Champagne contributed to the revolutionary climate. They were followed by the harsh winter of 1788–9: the average *annual* prices of cereals rose by 50% in this bad year. This is at once a large and a small increase. If we compare the *monthly* prices from one year to another we sometimes find an increase of over 100%, and there were also areas which suffered particularly badly (the north-east) in relation to others which escaped more lightly (the Midi). On the other hand, this upward tendency was still distinctly less sharp than that of 1770, which was the most comparable year in the recent past. So why was there an explosion? This crisis, which was in itself limited, occurred within an economy, and hence a society, which had hardly recovered from the slump of the last few years.

The crisis in cereals was reproduced in other areas of production: the wine-growers did not know whether to laugh or cry over the mediocre harvests which kept prices steady. In the end they lost out, after three poor harvests. Thus, the crisis of under-production in agriculture had a contagious effect, and provoked a crisis of falling industrial demand.

Industry, mainly textiles, took the blow head-on. It had its own specific problems: French manufacturers complained bitterly of the consequences of the Anglo-French treaty of 1786 which reduced import duties on British goods. More generally, it has been pointed out that even in normal times the people spent half of their daily budget on bread. The surge in basic food prices therefore resulted in effect in the loss of the urban market as far as textile goods and other consumer products were concerned. In 1789 textile production had fallen to half the level of 1782, and the building industry, that barometer of collective prosperity in the old regime, was in decline. Thus, from 1787 to 1789 the crisis affected various sectors of an economy which had already been weakened: this helps to explain its major social implications.

The social crisis

It is quite easy to describe what happened. Some groups may have profited from the agrarian crisis: landowners whose rents were paid in kind, beneficiaries of tithes or *champarts* and wealthy *fermiers* with produce to sell. In various ways, these groups may have profited from the high prices from which the consumer suffered. But there were not many of them; the majority of the peasants, obliged as they were to get their supplies on the open market, reacted in the same way as other consumers. The lowest, most numerous categories of peasant were also affected by unemployment: a poor harvest meant little work for the day-labourer or the thresher. There was unemployment in the countryside, and also in the towns: the level of employment was seriously affected by the problems in the textile and other industries. Moreover, there was a constant process of osmosis between the two worlds: the crisis provoked an influx of country people seeking work in the towns, and seasonal work above all was affected by the crisis in certain sectors such as building. Here and there, it is true, we find the setting-up of charity workshops, the old remedy of the urban bourgeoisie intended to keep 'their' poor occupied. They were not much of a palliative: this was the period of roaming bands, such as those described by Lefebvre, wandering across the plains, sometimes in large numbers. In the eyes of many people, still susceptible to collective panics, it was only one step from being part of these bands to being a brigand. This threshold was easily crossed in the summer of 1789.[5]

Of course, the unrest took different forms in different places. In the towns – those at least which had a modern-style wage-earning class – there were demands for higher wages: there were strikes in Marseilles, and it was in Paris, in the Faubourg Saint-Antoine, that attitudes were most clearly defined. The premises of a wealthy wallpaper manufacturer, Réveillon, were sacked because he had maintained that the workers could live perfectly well on their meagre wages; the troops intervened brutally and the riot ended in bloodshed. Although these clashes were spectacular, they were less common than those provoked by the high cost of living: the food riots experienced in more or less all the towns at this period, disturbances over buying and selling, the high-handed fixing of the price of grain and bread by the authorities, pillaging. As they had been fifteen years before, the government and its agents were

[5] Lefebvre (71), and cf. (70).

once again accused of being involved in a 'famine pact' to keep the
people starving. The measures taken by Brienne in 1787 concerning
free trade in grain and the licence to export it fuelled the idea that the
government had cornered the market, even though these measures had
been revoked by Necker. To this common basis of dissatisfaction each
group added its own specific demands, which went beyond the price
of bread. The towns became incensed against city tolls. Hostility was
often turned against the municipal or consular oligarchies who were
held responsible for the situation.

Risings in the town and in the countryside

In the countryside the agitation centred on demands which had been
intensified by the crisis: the recovery of common land, the destruction
of the seigneurial ovens (*fours banaux*), and, in particular, the struggle
against the seigneurial dues which the poor harvest had made even more
odious: in some areas they took back grain which had been paid as
rent, in others they refused to part with any grain for the following
year. These signs of unrest became apparent in certain areas after the
winter of 1789: from February to April conflicts broke out over the
collection of rents and *champarts* in Dauphiné. Other provinces, from
the Lyonnais to Languedoc and Brittany, experienced similar movements. The most spectacular example, without doubt, is to be found
in Provence, where the 'pre-Revolution' in March–April 1789 illustrates the similarities and the differences between the urban and the rural
movements. The action started in the towns: in Marseilles, Aix, Toulon
and Arles there were uprisings in protest against the high price of grain;
granaries were pillaged and there were revolts against the consuls and
against the municipal taxes, of which the most unpopular was one on
flour, the *piquet de la farine*. Very soon, however, the countryside was
infected; wandering bands spread the movement from village to village
through a large part of the countryside of lower Provence. Its
programme changed, of course: the fight against dear bread was not
forgotten but most of the hostilities were now directed against the
châteaux which were pillaged and sometimes burned by the rioters.
This movement owed part of its national celebrity to Mirabeau, the
prodigal son of Provence, who intervened to cool it down, but it should
also be seen as an episode in the campaign leading up to the meeting
of the Estates General.

   The economic and social crisis was a kind of backcloth, serving to reveal, or to catalyse, collective attitudes. The political crisis which was developing at this time was to become much more embittered and was itself to contribute to the renewal of social unrest in the widespread outbreaks of July 1789: the sequel to the events of the spring.

Let us not anticipate but instead draw up a provisional balance. The economic crisis focused the discontents of the Revolution but was not 'the cause' of the Revolution: it has been observed that crises occur every ten years, but revolutions do not (Labrousse).[6] All the same, this crisis was extremely important as a precipitant.

FROM COMPLAINTS TO DEMANDS

The interval from August 1788 to May 1789, in other words, from the convocation of the Estates General to its meeting, was much more than a period of waiting, or even an election campaign. While the complaints (*doléances*), which were to have been the 'last will and testament of the old-style monarchy', were being formulated, an irreversible process was set in motion.

New problems, old-fashioned spokesmen

Necker returned to power in August 1788. He was not really a new man, though he gave that impression to the people around him. This banker from Geneva was without doubt a self-made man. He had risen from the ranks to become Director General of Finances from 1777 to 1781 and enjoyed some renown at that time for his famous and ambiguous *Compte rendu au roi*. He deceived people both as to facts and as to his character. Necker was not the financial wizard the holders of government stock believed him to be: stockholders maintained their confidence in him until 1789, a confidence which he abused. At most, he was a competent financier, when what was needed was someone who would reform the system. We can take his measure from his first actions. By giving a good impression he obtained a loan of 85 million *livres*, a sum too small to do more than tide things over; nothing was resolved, at a time when structural reform had become necessary. Necker, who gambled on public confidence and so had to remain flexible, squeezed out Lamoignon, renounced his judicial reforms, reinstated the *parlements*, and, so as not to compromise himself too

---

[6] E. Labrousse, 'Comment naissent les Révolutions', in *Actes du Congrès Historique du Centenaire de la Révolution de 1848* (Paris, 1948).

deeply, recalled in November 1788 those notables who had proved a
stumbling-block to Calonne.

However, the major problem concerned the future and was
impossible to formulate in traditional categories. Public opinion was
waiting for the Estates General to meet. No one yet knew what form
this assembly would take. Would the three estates be summoned
separately, according to the procedure which had been followed in
1614? This would put the third estate in an obvious minority, with
two against one. Should the number of the third estate's representatives
be doubled? The measure would have no more than a symbolic value,
unless it was accompanied by a change from voting 'by orders' to
voting individually, the only way of making the third estate equal to
the other two.

On 21 September 1788 the Parlement of Paris decided that the
Estates General would be 'summoned according to rule and composed
as they had been in 1614', in other words, of three equal estates. The
popularity of the Parlement instantly slumped. In the eyes of public
opinion it was unmasked and seen in its true light as one of the pillars
of intransigent conservatism.

Necker tried another tactic, and in November 1788 he summoned
a second Assembly of Notables, a carbon copy of Calonne's. It was
no more flexible than the previous one and declared itself in favour
of the traditional system. They were supported by the princes of the
blood who issued what was virtually an ultimatum disguised as a
petition: 'Could Your Majesty possibly decide to sacrifice and
humiliate Your brave, ancient and honourable nobility?' By this act,
any illusion there might have been of the notables as a revolutionary
force was dissipated. However, one might also say that the illusion of
the king as arbiter revealed itself to be as wavering as its spokesman,
Necker.

Necker was shrewd enough to see what was coming. It would have
been difficult to do anything else as soon as the Parlement itself, on
5 December 1788, reversed its decision and declared for parity between
the third estate and the rest. The decisions of the *conseil du roi* (Council
of State) on 27 December 1788 were presented in a reassuring manner,
as the result of a skilful piece of 'market research'. Necker proposed
that they should fix the number of deputies to the Estates General in
proportion to the population of the various *bailliages*. It was necessary,
according to him, to take account of the increased importance of the
third estate, whose growing wealth and education gave it a larger stake

in the country, and so to double its share of seats. This official programme lacked precision in one crucial respect: would the voting be individual, or estate by estate? The ruling issued in January 1789 as a result of this meeting of the Council was deliberately ambiguous. But public opinion was quite clear on this point.

'Patriotic party' or 'national party'

Besides, the royal government itself, for the first time, made a direct appeal to this collective force. The message was read from the pulpit that 'His Majesty desires that everyone should be assured that from the ends of his kingdom and its most obscure corners, their grievances and their wishes would reach him.' These were not empty words. In the majority of cases, the *intendants* displayed an attitude of neutrality to reform, or even sympathy (Amelot in Dijon). This self-effacement on the part of the government made the new political forces mature more quickly. People have spoken of the formation of the 'patriotic party' or 'national party' at this time. The phrase does not refer to an organisation of the modern type but rather to a cluster of more or less structured groups. One finds them above all in Paris. The clubs which had been closed down about ten years earlier now multiplied: the Club de Valois at the Palais-Royal under the aegis of the Duc d'Orléans, the Club des Colons (of Santo Domingo), the Société des amis des Noirs, and the Société des Trente, the rendezvous of the liberal nobility founded by Adrien Duport, a magistrate of the Parlement of Paris. These clubs included new men who would soon be famous or were already famous: political writers like Brissot, scholars and philosophers like Condorcet, and liberal nobles such as La Fayette, La Rochefoucauld, Montmorency, Talleyrand and Mirabeau. The man of the moment was Sieyès, a canon rejected by the estate of clergy who returned to his origins in his famous pamphlet, *Qu'est-ce que le tiers état?*, in which, in January 1789, he proclaimed: 'What is the third estate? Everything. What has it been until now? Nothing. What does it demand? To become something.'

Far from being isolated, this work belongs to a large group of publications in Paris (Target's *Lettres aux états généraux*), and the provinces (in Aix, Mirabeau's *Appel à la nation provençale*; in Arras, Robespierre's *Appel à la nation artésienne*, in Rouen, Thouret's *Avis aux bons Normands*).

In this proliferation there was no confusion, but on the contrary an attempt at co-ordination and common tactics. Paris was linked to the provinces in many ways and models were drawn up for the *cahiers de doléances* which were the order of the day. How far did this co-ordination go? It is important not to evade the issue, because some people have spoken of a plot in a period when plotting was common enough. The 'Committee of Thirty' doubtless played a co-ordinating role by circulating models for *cahiers de doléances*. More precisely, there has been talk of an Orléanist plot. The character of Philippe d'Orléans is clearly vulnerable to this accusation. Ambitious and enlightened, he surrounded himself by a 'brains trust' where men of talent, like Choderlos de Laclos, the army officer who was the author of *Les Liaisons dangereuses*, drafted petitions and models for the *cahiers* which can be found in the Loire region. In Paris, the gardens of the Palais-Royal, which were owned by the Duke and let out by him for commercial purposes of extremely diverse kinds, were a centre of political life as well as the centre of fashion. The Duke was also Grand Master of the Lodge of the French Grand Orient, which was enough to make many people more suspicious: could he not have used all this influence to further his own ends? In fact there is no need to invoke a Masonic or Orléanist plot to explain what happened in France between 1788 and 1789: the 'patriotic party' was not the same as the Orléans faction.

Although Paris played a leading role, the provinces were not far behind. They had already been politicised in more than one area by events which had occurred before the pre-revolutionary period: this was the case in Dauphiné, in Provence and also in Brittany, where things turned out badly. Illusions faded here even more quickly than elsewhere; the nobility, supported by the Parlement, made use of the estates to demand the restoration of the status quo in the *élections*. The nobility clashed openly with the students from Rennes, who supported the third estate: in January 1789 the Breton nobles were forced, literally, to leave Rennes for their country seats, swearing resentfully that they would not send delegates to the Estates General. There were similar incidents in Franche-Comté, at Besançon. The various forms of unrest which were to be found from Alsace to Languedoc (Agde) were not confined to the provincial capitals (Arras) or to the towns which had a *parlement* and could therefore be expected to be politically conscious. This spread of unrest can be explained by the pressure of the economic crisis which mobilised first the popular masses, and then the bourgeoisie. It has also been noted that, at the most humble level of the village community, the new rural municipalities were able to

exert an important influence.[7] They had been established two years
earlier by Brienne and were elected by those inhabitants who paid the
highest taxes. These municipalities were an obvious sign of increased
political maturity. If we follow the diffusion of key ideas from Paris
to the level of the village, we find ourselves in the thick of an electoral
campaign.

The 'cahiers de doléances'

The royal assurance that all 'grievances and wishes' would reach the
king was taken very seriously. The electoral assemblies were charged
with drawing up the lists of grievances (*cahiers de doléances*). It was the
first time such large numbers of French people had had the opportunity
to express themselves. We still have nearly 60,000 *cahiers*, compiled by
the rural communities, or, in the towns, by the guilds. They were
synthesised in the *cahiers généraux* at the level of the *bailliage* or
sénéchaussée.

These *cahiers* are an impressive source, but what can we expect them
to tell us? Since Michelet, who wanted to see them as evidence of a
consensus, and Taine, who did not regard them as an authentic
expression of popular feelings, there have been changes in the methods
of studying them and also in the value ascribed to them.

At the instigation of Jaurès, in the early twentieth century, research
on these documents began and some of them were published.[8] Two
things became obvious: that the task was enormous, and that the need
to interpret this mass of documents was an urgent one. Once the
method of editing the *cahiers* had been determined, and once the topics
with which they dealt had been listed and analysed, this extraordinarily
rich source could still be exploited in a number of other ways. For
example, it is possible to read the *cahiers* between the lines by analysing
their vocabulary according to the methods of modern linguistics. A
group of historians are currently working on this.[9]

How were the *cahiers* drawn up? A study of the corpus of original
cahiers enables us to distinguish 'families' of these documents and this
helps to clarify what we can expect from them. It was known that
models of *cahiers* were distributed and we can assess the influence of
these models in various regions: in Normandy, for example, we know

---

[7] Mathiez (6).
[8] 'The publication was organised by the 'Commission de recherche et de publication de
textes et de documents relatifs à l'histoire de la Révolution française'.
[9] Following A. Dupront.

that one-fifteenth of the *cahiers* in the Rouen area were derived from the model drawn up by the lawyer Thouret; this enables us to assess the limitations of propaganda at the national level. There were also humbler, less far-reaching models, transmitted from village to village or at random through the movement of a clerk. This does not mean that we should conclude that the *cahiers* are a stereotyped source. In most cases local demands were able to make themselves heard; however, the influence of the lawyers and the local bourgeoisie, who very often did the actual writing, did determine the tone of the *cahier*. Did they make a faithful record of local opinion? The *cahier*, which was drawn up with care and often in considerable detail, article by article, generally gave considerable space to the state of the nation. In modest villages, on the other hand, where the lesser peasantry were able to make themselves heard, the *cahier* describes, with an often touching naïvety, the burdens and miseries of the community. Between these two possible schemata, there are many mixed *cahiers* which pass from a general preamble to a list of concrete local demands. The abundance of the spontaneous *cahiers* makes them a richer source, but the structure or the vocabulary of the ones drawn up by educated men (the *cahiers savants*) enables us to estimate the influence of the Enlightenment. This is also true for the *cahiers* of the *bailliages*, where the contents of the *cahiers* of the local communities were remodelled in a highly selective manner.

Content of the 'cahiers'

As far as the content is concerned, the *cahiers* are both descriptive and prescriptive: they reveal a society as it saw itself, and as it dreamt of being. Let us start with the most spontaneous category: the simple *cahier* of an ordinary village. The seigneur appears as the main adversary in the list of grievances which include complaints about the tithe, the *corvée* (forced labour), the militia, and royal taxation, in particular the *taille* and the *gabelle*. Another form of hostility also emerges, sometimes obliquely: the village's resentment of the town and 'foreign' landowners reveals the bitter anti-bourgeois feeling of certain parts of the country-side. At this level, the political demands often seem superimposed, and it is here, too, that we find the clearest expression of total loyalty to the king as father-provider. It is easy to contrast this type of *cahier* with those influenced by the towns where the emphasis is quite different, but we should bear in mind that there were distinct regional variations: in one province (the *bailliage* of Semur-en-Auxois)[10] the imitation of the model of the country town spread unevenly through the surrounding country; whereas elsewhere (in the Mediterranean Midi) almost the whole province was under the influence of the towns.

The campaign against the feudal system became less severe and merged with the desire to protect the property rights of the *rentier* class. Political demands were of prime importance; in this respect the content of the more advanced village *cahier* and the town *cahier* overlapped. However, the urban communities responsible for drawing up the *cahiers* did have their own specific concerns, one of the most common of which was the defence of a corporate system, which was often narrowly conceived.

What about the demands for political reform? It has often been emphasised that this movement was both well advanced and timid or hesitant. Loyalty to the monarchy had been energetically reaffirmed, but there was a widespread condemnation of absolutism, though it was not formulated in this way. In most of the *cahiers* the concept of France as a united country seems to have been assimilated, but this process was not complete, as we can see from the number of demands with a strongly regional bias: 'The king of France will not be recognised in Provence except under the title of Comte de Provence', claimed the inhabitants of Vitrolles; while the nobility of Roussillon announced that 'His Majesty will only appoint Catalans to livings.' The persistence of these regional demands would seem to be backward-looking. There were, however, a certain number of common themes: the attack on absolutism took the form of a denunciation of the *intendant* and the condemnation of the judicial system, in particular the arbitrary use of *lettres de cachet*. There was also criticism of the tax system, on the grounds that it was inegalitarian and, what is worse, irrational. On the positive side, the *cahiers* assumed that there would be personal freedom and freedom of opinion, and that these liberties would be guaranteed by a constitution which would limit royal absolutism, and set up a nationally representative body whose consent to taxation was necessary. This much was common; however, there were some clearly marked, and predictable, differences. The *cahiers* of the nobility and of the clergy reveal their own specific concerns and reservations. The nobility were doubtless in favour of the various forms of liberty, and were more or less resigned to accepting a fairer system of taxation, but they clung

[10] Following the pioneering study of Robin (59), part 2.

to the inegalitarian social structure, of which the vote by 'order' was at once the expression and the guarantee. The *cahiers* of the clergy express a greater variety of attitudes, and sometimes align themselves more clearly with the third estate, when they reflect the views of the lower clergy. They also sometimes vehemently condemn the spread of new ideas and speak out against any notion of tolerance or freedom of thought.

Such a catalogue of themes is now standard. The vocabulary of the *cahiers* has recently been studied in new ways. The frequency, meaning and relationships between significant words or groups of words ('king', 'nation', 'seigneur', 'constitution') have been examined. This has revealed that certain ideas fundamental to the philosophy of the Enlightenment are not to be found. The word 'nature' hardly features at all, except in the expression *droits en nature* (dues paid in kind). Is this surprising? Most of the *cahiers* are expressed in language which reflects the mental world of the jurists who drew them up: to be aware of the limitations of the *cahiers* is by no means to diminish their importance: they are an outstanding source for the history of attitudes.

The elections to the Estates General

It still had to be decided who would be eligible to vote. It has sometimes been observed that the electoral regulations of January 1789 were in the end extremely liberal. This is true in some respects, but not in others. All taxpaying men over 25 were eligible to vote, but in different and fundamentally unequal ways, because of the structure of the orders and of the estates. In each *bailliage* or *sénéchaussée* the privileged groups elected their representatives by a direct ballot; all those of confirmed noble status were entitled to vote, a fact which did not fail to annoy a certain wealthy sector of the nobility, especially in the *pays d'états*. Amongst the clergy, paradoxically, the system appears to have favoured the lower parish clergy, since all the priests attended the assembly and voted in person, whereas the convents or chapters were only represented by delegates.

As for the third estate, the electoral system was more complex and operated on two or three levels. In the rural communities, the parish assembly nominated two representatives for every 200 households to the electoral assembly of the *bailliage*. The representatives from the towns, who also attended this assembly, were nominated in two stages. Each corporation chose one representative for every 100 voting members in the trade guilds, and two in the most prestigious guilds (merchants and liberal arts). These representatives then formed the electoral assembly of the third estate of the town, which distilled the separate *cahiers* into one and selected the representatives it would send to the electoral assembly of the third estate of the *bailliage*. The rural and urban representatives then proceeded to elect the deputies for their constituency. This was a hierarchical pyramid, apparently biased in favour of wealth and also talent. The results of the ballots bear this out.

The electoral processes themselves leave a mixed impression. They were conducted with great solemnity, but the atmosphere was often very tense. The privileged groups were far from presenting a united front. The most severe internal conflict was to be found in the assemblies of the clergy. Here, the interests of the upper clergy were threatened because the parish priests were in the majority and they elected only about 40 prelates. The nobility also turned out to be divided, in complex and often ambiguous ways: there were protests from those unenfeoffed nobles who were not allowed to vote; while on the other hand, the upper nobility from the *pays d'états* were so hostile to the idea of sharing power with the lower nobility that they abstained from voting.

As for the third estate, we should not ignore the efforts of the bourgeoisie to gain power and the deflection of the original aims, revealed by the comparison of a rural *cahier* with one from a *bailliage*. At every level the notables became the spokesmen: in the village, the *laboureurs* opposed the *manouvriers*; the urban bourgeoisie did not take rural grievances seriously, and the lawyers in the big towns as well as in the country towns took over the often exclusive right to act as spokesmen for the rest. All this was bound to create tensions: as we can see from the two sets of *cahiers* which were produced after a split in the electoral assembly. However, this makes the cohesion of the third estate, which still appeared almost unanimous, all the more striking.

The deputies

There were 1,165 deputies, divided almost equally between the third estate and the privileged orders: 578 commoners, 291 clergy, 270 members of the nobility and 26 not classified. We should examine these groups as collective entities as well as discussing individuals who had already emerged as important.

The sociology of the third estate confirms what has been said about the structures of the bourgeoisie of the *ancien régime*: it had a certain homogeneity since none of its members were either artisans or peasants. On the other hand, the producers, the up and coming bourgeoisie – the shopkeepers, financiers and industrialists – accounted for only about 100 members. This figure was low compared with the compact group of *gens de robe*, which included about 200 advocates. The most significant sector of the bourgeoisie, both quantitatively and qualitatively, were the professional men: from Arras, Rennes, Rouen, Chartres and Grenoble came the thinkers of the group, Robespierre, Le Chapelier, Thouret, Pétion, Mounier and Barnave. There were also about 50 'bourgeois' landowners who lived on their income from *rentes*. The rest of this group was made up of men of talent: writers and theorists like Volney and Dupont de Nemours, and the astronomer Bailly. The third estate had also recruited two brilliant men from the clergy and the nobility: Sieyès and Mirabeau.

The privileged orders were not homogeneous groups: amongst the clergy there were only 46 bishops, and even they were sometimes liberal, like Mgr de Boisgelin, the Archbishop of Aix, or Talleyrand, Bishop of Autun. Amongst the members of the lower clergy, it was the parish priests who held the majority. They were mostly in favour of change; the separation of Abbé Grégoire and Abbé Maury into different camps had not yet taken place. The schisms within the nobility were different: the majority were opposed to change, and with good reason, and it was often the lesser nobles, like Cazalès, an office-holder from Languedoc, who were most enthusiastic for tradition. On the other hand, there were some great names amongst the 90 aristocrats who could be described as more or less liberal: d'Aiguillon, Noailles, La Rochefoucauld and, of course, the Marquis de La Fayette, the 'hero of the Old World and the New'.

The opening of the Estates General was fixed for 27 April 1789; it was postponed till 5 May, no doubt as a result of dissension in the circles around the king over the plots to get rid of Necker. It was on 2 May at Versailles – where the Estates were to meet – that the famous procession took place, the parade of the society of orders of the *ancien régime*, frozen in their age-old hierarchies.

4

The constitutional Revolution

A single or multiple Revolution?

The five months from 5 May to 6 October 1789 were to give the French Revolution its specific character. The commonplace images of our childhood textbooks include the oath at the Jeu de Paume – the symbol of the bourgeois, the lawyers' Revolution – then the storming of the Bastille, which marked the explosion of the Revolution of the people, and finally the night of 4 August which was an echo of the peasant Revolution which led to the collapse of the social structures of the *ancien régime*. No doubt this does not account for the whole of the Revolution: but it is already beginning to look like a radical and complex upheaval.

So complex that it has become commonplace to talk about the 'Revolutions' of the summer of 1789 in the plural. This is no doubt a salutary reaction against the artificial unanimity of a certain old-fashioned style of interpretation which, whether it was hostile or favourable, was simplistic and did not go into detail. According to Mathiez, there was first a Paris Revolution, then a Revolution in the provinces, which gained urban support, and then finally a Revolution in the countryside. According to Lefebvre, the phases were not geographical but social: the process began with an aristocratic Revolution (which would be our pre-Revolution) and moved on through a bourgeois Revolution, to a Revolution of the people, and finally to a Revolution of the peasants. This was also, more or less, the schema adopted by Soboul.[1] These schemata are certainly useful pedagogically but, more important, they take into account the genuinely diverse

[1] Soboul (14).

99

strands of a Revolution which was not monolithic. The reactions of
the bourgeoisie to the Grande Peur indicate that the revolt of the
peasants was an autonomous movement; on the other hand, the
bourgeois militia offer us the spectacle of an armed bourgeoisie,
opposed both to absolutism and to the dangers of a popular explosion.
Having said this, is it legitimate – other than for the sake of clarity – to
isolate three autonomous Revolutions in the summer of 1789?[2] This
would be to distort reality. Although the unity of the revolutionary
movement was distinctly shaky in many respects, it involved more than
a simple, or even fortuitous, coexistence of two elements: the
progressive bourgeois Revolution and a traditional revolt provoked by
the mixture of economic interests and nostalgic millenarianism which
characterised popular attitudes in both town and country. By very
different means, there emerged a common aim, and a common result:
the destruction of the old social and political regime. Without the
popular revolt in the towns, the bourgeois Revolution would not have
succeeded, and the peasant riots of the Grande Peur again served the
interests of a bourgeoisie who – although it was thoroughly alarmed –
gained as much from the night of the 4 August as the peasantry did,
if not more. Beyond the misunderstandings, the mistrust and the
hostility, this Revolution of 1789 retains its unity, a fact which does
not absolve us from the obligation to pick out its individual strands.

The Revolution at the top (May to July 1789)

There was an interval of two and a half months between the opening
of the Estates General and the spectacular entrance on stage of the
popular masses on 14 July. During this time the monarchy and the
privileged groups – in other words, the representatives of the old social
order – came into contact with the Estates General, the mouthpiece of
the bourgeoisie. Relations were at first uncertain, then openly hostile.

It is worth considering these events at an almost day-to-day level.
At the inaugural session of the Estates General in Versailles on 5 May
1789, the speeches of the king and then of Barentin, the Keeper of the
Seals, warning against the spirit of innovation, caused disappointment.
Similarly, Necker, who was the next to speak, disillusioned those who
counted on him by restricting himself to a statement about the financial
situation: had they come there merely to discuss deficits? The
opposition seems to have crystallised as a result of a procedural problem.

---

[2] As is done by Furet and Richet (9).

The numbers of the third estate had been doubled, but this concession was useless if voting was carried out by order and not by head: this latter was the only way the third estate could win. These two interpretations emerged during the initial talks; the royal government, wavering, allowed the third estate the opportunity to state its claims from the beginning. On 5 May, in the evening, deputies from the same province met and initiated a plan of concerted action for the third estate. Commoners from Dauphiné led by Mounier, from Artois led by Robespierre, and from Brittany led by the lawyers Le Chapelier and Lanjuinais were all in agreement. They called themselves, in the English style, 'members of the Commons', and they invited the other orders to convene for the purpose of establishing the relative voting powers of the three estates. This was rather more than a skirmish, as the privileged groups realised. Some of them became more entrenched in their attitudes: the nobility, where those who insisted on voting by order outnumbered the liberals by 141 to 47. Others were divided: the clergy, where there were 133 conservatives to 114 in favour of joining up with the third estate. The following month only appeared to be unfruitful; the most important thing was that the third estate remained unshakeable and believed, as Mirabeau remarked, that it 'only had to remain immobile to make itself formidable to its enemies'. Then the third estate took the offensive. It invited the other orders to join forces with it, and on 12 June began the verification of the powers of the deputies, one by one. Three priests from Poitou, followed by sixteen others, deserted their order to join the third estate (13–16 June). But was this still the third estate? At the instigation of Abbé Sieyès, the participants decided to call themselves the 'National Assembly'. They affirmed their right to consent to taxes, and denied the king the right to go against this decision. This symbolic act split the privileged orders; on 19 June, on a majority vote, the clergy decided to join forces with the third estate, whereas the nobility, on the contrary, appealed to the king, declaring that 'it is not only our interests that we are defending, Sire, but yours, those of the State and ultimately those of the French people'. The monarch was not indifferent to this appeal from his nobility and decided to hold a plenary session along the lines of the *lits de justice* to overturn the decisions of the third estate.

On 20 June the third estate, finding that it was locked out, moved into the hall of the Jeu de Paume. Here, presided over by Bailly, the deputies accepted the formulation suggested by the Dauphinois Mounier and undertook 'never to separate and to meet anywhere that circumstances dictate until the Constitution has been established and placed on solid foundations'. A virtually unanimous vote agreed to what has become known to us as the 'oath of the Jeu de Paume'. In the face of this dynamism the clergy and even two nobles from Dauphiné joined the National Assembly on 22 June; the *séance royale* of 23 June was unable to break the momentum of this movement. It was a session designed to intimidate: the king commanded that the orders should deliberate separately. He overturned the decisions of the third estate with regard to taxation, though he accepted that taxation should be shared out equally and he agreed that the Estates General should be consulted (in a vaguely defined way) on this subject. However, he vigorously defended property rights, by which he meant 'the tithes, *cens*, *rentes* and feudal and seigneurial dues, and, in general, all the rights and prerogatives both substantial and honorific which pertain to the possession of land and fiefs'. He concluded: 'If by some dreadful chance, far from my thoughts, you were to abandon me in this fine enterprise, then I should do what is right for my people alone, and I should consider myself alone to be their representative.' The deputies were ordered to disperse. This marked a turning-point in the rebellion. Their reply to the master of ceremonies, the Marquis de Dreux-Brézé, was that 'the assembled Nation does not have to take orders' (Bailly) and Mirabeau hurled his famous apostrophe: 'we are here by the will of the people, [and] only bayonets will force us from our seats'. His exact words are in dispute and the phrase may have been improved later, but this is irrelevant. Despite his own inclinations, the king did not dare resort to force against the assembled third estate; the next day the majority of the clergy rallied to the National Assembly and they were followed by a minority of the nobility, 47 members, including the Duc d'Orléans.

The king appeared to give in. On 27 June, not without reservations, he invited the privileged orders to come together at the Assembly. However, the deputies exploited their strong position; on 9 July they styled themselves the 'National *Constituent* Assembly'. Two days earlier they had set up a committee for the Constitution; the whole political regime was being called into question. But would this delegation of the bourgeoisie be able to impose its demands on the established powers without enlisting the support of the masses?

Disturbances in the towns

Up to this point the Revolution had been a matter of laws: now it came down to street level. The most important incident was the storming of the Bastille, on 14 July 1789. Did this mean it was a Parisian Revolution? No doubt: but it was both followed and, in some cases, preceded by a whole series of revolts in towns throughout France. Was it a popular Revolution? Certainly: the emergence of the urban masses was the most significant aspect of these events. However, it was also a bourgeois Revolution, the revolt of a bourgeoisie which was still very far from having achieved its aims, and which was therefore not yet reluctant to become involved.

Historians have emphasised the importance of the economic crisis, which was then reaching its peak, in mobilising the urban masses. Food shortages, expensive bread and a further increase in prices in the summer of 1789, combined with unemployment in a number of urban trades, accounted for popular feeling; the people paid a fixed price for bread, they pillaged granaries and storehouses and they were also hostile to the indirect taxes (both municipal and State) which were collected at the town gates. In Paris, as elsewhere, the town dues (*octroi*) had come under attack before the Bastille. It was a vicious circle: as always, the crisis provoked a massive influx of homeless and jobless men into the towns, where they swelled the numbers of the urban proletariat in a similar situation. All the same, to describe the causes of the popular urban revolts purely in terms of socio-economic trends is to be too reductionist: these movements had been recurrent for a long time, since the Fronde, if not the Catholic League.* There was among these groups a genuine political consciousness and an acute sensitivity to events. The myth of an 'aristocratic plot' (which had an element of truth in it), supported by the movement of troops, tended to unify the demands, both social and political, of the people and the bourgeoisie.

The bourgeoisie had its own reasons – more complicated, no doubt, but pressing – for taking up arms. The bourgeoisie in Paris kept a close watch on events at Versailles, but the bourgeoisie in the provinces was not unaware of what was going on, thanks to the communications network set up by the deputies to the Estates General. This meant that the provincial bourgeoisie was also sensitised to the possibility of an aristocratic plot, and that it was aware of what was at stake. Although this group was less directly affected by the crisis, it had its own specific

* Mid-seventeenth century and late sixteenth century respectively. [Trans.]

anxieties: the Paris *rentier* feared for Necker, whom he saw as his
defence against bankruptcy. Besides these general concerns, these
bourgeoisies also had their local war aims and their local adversaries:
the municipal oligarchies, with their exclusiveness and family monopolies in which the bourgeoisie no longer recognised itself. Finally the
bourgeoisie also took up arms because it feared disorder. The civic
militia took up arms spontaneously against the 'dangerous classes'. This
was the case in Paris on 12 and 13 July, as can be seen from the fact
that a declaration was issued that 'the establishment of the civic militia
and the other measures which have been taken have allowed the city
to pass a quiet night. The fact is that a number of individuals who were
carrying arms have been disarmed, and order has been restored.'
However, for the moment the people and the bourgeoisie faced the
same adversary.

It was in fact the monarchy which took the offensive. Unsure of
the loyalty of the French guards who had their barracks in Paris and
shared the people's aspirations, the King decided to bring in some 20,000
men belonging to foreign regiments. This threat had a strong impact
on Paris and also on the National Assembly, which on 8 July demanded
their removal. The king had no intention of giving way, and on 11
July he dismissed Necker and formed a militant administration led by
the Baron de Breteuil with Marshal de Broglie at the ministry of war.

Paris, the centre of the Revolution

The threat of this action provoked the people. Paris became the centre
of the Revolution. Political activity was concentrated in certain areas
such as the Palais-Royal, the haunt of popular orators like Camille
Desmoulins. However, agitation spread. On 12 July there was a riot
in the gardens of the Tuileries and the Royal German dragoons of the
Prince de Lambesc charged a procession of demonstrators who were
supported by the French guards. Then the toll gates were set on fire,
as economic and political demands met. The Bourse (Stock Exchange)
closed and some bankers (Delessert and Boscary) enrolled themselves
with their employees in the civic militia. A new political system was
coming into existence: parallel to the Hôtel de Ville, the 407 electors
of the Estates General formed an alternative municipal government
under the direction of a permanent committee. On 12 and 13 July they
completed the establishment of the civic militia. This was an attempt
to divert popular feeling, but it turned out to be uncontrollable. On

13 July revolt became general, and the people looked for arms everywhere.

On 14 July, at the Invalides, the crowd managed to capture 32,000 muskets and then went off to the Bastille in the hope of similar results. The taking of the Bastille, the high point of the French Revolution and the symbol of the fall of the *ancien régime*, is a historical fact which has to be analysed on different levels. The facts themselves have been regarded in very different ways by the revolutionaries themselves and by the historians of former times and of today. Conservative historians have ridiculed the siege of this fortress of the *ancien régime* in which only eight prisoners could be found, and these either madmen or rakes placed there at the request of their families. However, this is to misunderstand the meaning of the act. It was in order to look for arms that a large crowd appeared before this fortress, which was redoubtable, although guarded by a mere hundred or so invalids and Swiss guards. The governor, de Launay, negotiated with the crowd but after a series of misunderstandings fired upon them. This was followed by an assault, and then the surrender of the fortress. About a hundred of the attackers were killed; de Launay and some of his men were massacred after the victory. But who were the 'vainqueurs de la Bastille' (victors of the Bastille)? Very few of the upper middle class, but certainly not the 'wretched', as has often been said: most of the crowd were artisans or shopkeepers, two-thirds of them from the Faubourg Saint-Antoine.[3] Even at the time, however, the taking of the Bastille was much more than an ordinary episode of the Revolution. The event was very quickly given a symbolic interpretation and made the expression of the collective emancipation of a whole people. In any case, the incident had immediate practical consequences. On 15 July, Louis XVI went to the Assembly to announce the withdrawal of the troops; the next day he recalled Necker; the day after that he went to Paris and received from the hands of the mayor, Bailly, the new emblem of the triumphant Revolution, the tricoloured cockade. This meant a recognition of the legitimacy of the Paris Commune, which had replaced the permanent revolutionary committee. However, in a wider sense, this also meant a recognition and an acceptance of the dramatic changes which were taking place. A court faction led by the Comte d'Artois understood this very well, and left France in the first phase of emigration. Enlightened opinion and the rest of France had no illusions either. 'Thus', wrote Jefferson, 'came to an end an *amende honorable*

[3] Rudé (24).

of a kind which no king, had ever made before, and no people ever accepted.'

In fact, Paris was very far from being appeased. On 22 July the *intendant* of Paris, Bertier de Sauvigny, and his father-in-law Foulon de Doué were hanged in the Place de Grève and their heads were carried round the city on the ends of pikes. They were accused of hoarding grain. These victims of the poor, crazed by food shortages and by the idea of a 'plot', drew a stronger reaction from Babeuf than from a responsible member of the bourgeoisie like Barnave. Babeuf wrote: 'The masters, instead of controlling us, have turned us into barbarians because they are barbarians themselves. They are reaping and they will reap what they have sown.' Barnave, on the other hand, asked: 'Was the blood which was shed all that pure?'

The 'municipal Revolution'

The Revolution which took place in the streets of Paris found an echo in every provincial town in a process which has been called the 'municipal Revolution'.[4] In fact it is not fair to see this provincial movement as a consequence of the upheavals in the capital; as far as we can tell in the confusion, events in the provinces often took place at the same time as events in Paris, and sometimes even before. Without going back to the risings in Provence in the spring of 1789, we may note the troubles in Rouen from the beginning of July. This was followed, in July and early August, by a massive reaction to the dismissal of Necker, and finally by an explosion at the news of the taking of the Bastille. The point is that different local factors provoked or revived unrest in the towns. In Rouen, as in the area around Paris (Saint-Denis, Saint-Germain-en-Laye), it was food riots which brought the people out on the streets. Elsewhere, customs dues and municipal taxes were what provoked the people. In yet other places, bourgeois grievances were dominant and were encouraged by national slogans, while being directed against municipal oligarchies. In the majority of cases, we find a mixture of these motives. On some occasions, different causes produced similar effects. In one place, a food riot was repressed by the notables; elsewhere, they turned it to their advantage.

The geography and chronology of these municipal revolts are extremely revealing. They were particularly violent in the areas most

---

[4] See D. Ligou, 'A propos de la Révolution municipale', *Revue d'Histoire Economique et Sociale* (1960).

affected by food shortages: around Paris (Chartres or Orléans), in Normandy (from Vernon to Evreux, Rouen or Caen), in the middle-west (from Rennes to Angers, Tours or Le Mans). In the east also there were violent clashes, in Sedan, Troyes, Nancy and Metz, while the pillage of the town hall at Strasburg on 21 July made a more than purely local impact. Lefebvre and others have noted that the movement was not as violent in regions which had an old municipal tradition, especially in the Midi or the extreme north of France.[5] For example, Toulouse, Albi and Aix all escaped without violent confrontation. However, qualifications are necessary. In some parts of the south there were serious conflicts, as in the case of Lyons, where the 'consulate' did not give in without resistance; and in other places, such as Nîmes or Montauban, there were clashes between Catholics and Protestants.

However, it is possible to discern a number of common features in these movements. Traditional authorities gave way. Virtually every-where we find that the *intendants* withdrew without resisting, and the almost total defection of the army (Strasburg, Rennes) should be noted. The local bastilles usually fell without a shot being fired, as in the case of Bordeaux (Château Trompette), Lyons (Pierre Ancise), or Caen (Tour Levi). The new *de facto* administrations were as various as those they replaced. In some places they reinstated or enlarged the old town council (Toulouse) while in others they destroyed it (Strasburg). In many cases we find the coexistence of two parallel hierarchies, with the new administration, the 'permanent committee', gradually pushing out the old. The top priority of these permanent committees was to organise a local military force, at first a 'civic militia' and then a 'national guard'. The fear of the people was clearly an important motive underlying this reaction, and in practice it was the notables who provided the officers, just as it was they who took over the new municipal administrations.

Was this the triumph of the 'Revolution of the notables', the compromise rejected by the aristocracy and now imposed by force, and, more especially, with the support of the people? The equilibrium was much too unstable and its results too uncertain for us to affirm this with confidence, all the more so because there were other figures coming on stage: on 20 July the Grande Peur began.

[5] Lefebvre (71).

Rural risings

For those historians who insist on seeing the Revolution as just one of
several revolutions at the end of the eighteenth century, this appearance
of the peasant masses in the forefront of the revolutionary struggle
constitutes the most original feature of the French Revolution.[6]
Everyone is agreed on this point, but not on its interpretation. Did not
the peasants, motivated by nostalgia for the past and liable to panic,
merely get in the way of a bourgeois Revolution which could very
well have done without them? At the very least, did these various levels
of revolutionary activity have anything in common other than the fact
they were taking place at the same time? Or, on the other hand, was
this formidable initiative on the part of the peasants not the decisive
element in enabling the bourgeois Revolution to triumph, to a much
greater degree than elsewhere, over the social order of the *ancien régime*?
The accounts of contemporaries are not necessarily our best means of
reaching a balanced view. The fear with which the bourgeoisie
responded to the Grande Peur confirms that they had not wanted the
peasants to come on stage in this way. But let us pause to consider the
evidence.

The Grande Peur erupted in a rural world which was already in
revolt over more than one issue, from Provence to Cambrésis. Social
and economic grievances were closely linked in these revolts, which
reached a peak in the second fortnight in July. In the plains around
Paris there was a cluster of isolated outbreaks, while in certain regions
there were uprisings on a massive scale. From 17 July the revolt in the
bocage spread across the western edges of the plain from Caen to
Alençon. At the same period the abbeys throughout the region of the
Sambre were devastated, and an incident near Vesoul in Franche-Comté
sparked off a series of risings against the nobility from Pontarlier to
Langres. This movement died out just outside Belfort, but was revived
in upper Alsace at the end of July, from the area around Colmar to
Montbéliard. At the same time, châteaux throughout the Mâcon area
were burnt down; the peasant revolt was stopped by outright force
at the gates of Cluny, and the new bourgeoisie who had assumed power
condemned and executed about thirty of the participants.

[6] Notably Godechot (10).

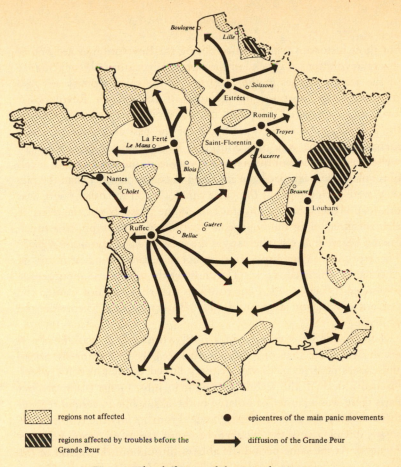

regions not affected

regions affected by troubles before the Grande Peur

● epicentres of the main panic movements

→ diffusion of the Grande Peur

Fig. 18. The diffusion of the Grande Peur

The Grande Peur

These revolts lead up to and explain the Grande Peur proper, but this movement remains distinctly different from them. Lefebvre, the authority on this subject, remarked that the zones of open revolt did not usually experience the Peur, which leads one to suspect that there was a contrast between the regions which were already mobilised and armed, and those which were less active, where panic could gain a hold and suddenly flare up.[7] It is Lefebvre, again, who describes the motives

[7] Lefebvre (71).

behind this panic, as well as the stages of its development. The typical pattern of what seems to have been the most spectacular of the old-style panics is to be found repeatedly throughout the records of parish meetings. There was a rumour — and this began around 20 July — that a band of armed brigands was on its way, looting and destroying. These were not any old brigands, but very often enemies: Piedmontese in the Alps; in Brittany, the English who had landed, they said, at Brest; and in Limousin, the Comte d'Artois who was supposed to be coming from Bordeaux at the head of an army. The age-old fear of brigands took on a mythical form and became associated with a rural version of the aristocratic plot. Imaginary massacres and fights were talked about — an echo, it has been said, of the taking of the Bastille which reverberated in a distorted form throughout the provinces. This provoked a rush to arms. The market towns and villages went on to the defensive, which encouraged their neighbours to see armed bands everywhere. Later, contacts were made and information was gathered, and it became apparent that there was no cause for panic. But this is not the end of the matter; at this point in the analysis we should, like Lefebvre, remind ourselves of the objective facts underlying the panic: were these brigands imaginary? Yes and no. Famine had resulted in an increase in the numbers of homeless beggars: the activity ('gang' begging, as it has been called) of these able-bodied rootless men who roamed the plains was constantly mentioned, and feared. It is only too true that there was a natural progression from begging to banditry. We are dealing here not so much with a distorted echo of the taking of the Bastille, as with a dramatic amplification of the disquiet in the countryside.

The initial panic gave way to a second phase. When the fear had passed, the villagers did not lay down their arms: the national guards of the country towns developed as a result, and the municipal Revolution at village level was born of the Grande Peur. Before this stage, however, there was another phase during which the fear turned to Revolution. Troops of armed villagers descended on the local châteaux, demanded the records, land registers, and ancient documents entitling the seigneur to his feudal dues, and made a bonfire of them. However, these gestures against the nobility often ended up more seriously in arson or plundering. Anyone who resisted was roughly treated and sometimes there were deaths, though on the whole there was little bloodshed. The duration of the Grande Peur was short — it lasted barely a fortnight from 20 July to the beginning of

August – but this makes its diffusion over such a wide area all the more spectacular.

Six original centres of panic have been identified. From these epicentres the movement spread by contagion, becoming reanimated in certain places while elsewhere the original stimulus was replaced by a 'panic of anticipation'. One of the original epicentres was at Estrées, in the Beauvaisis. This spread as far as Flanders, across the plains of large-scale cultivation to the north-west of Paris. Another covered the whole of Champagne, the plains to the south of Paris and Burgundy, and stretched, via the Bourbonnais, to the heart of the central plateau. In the west, a movement spread from the forests of Perche (Montmirail), throughout the plain bordering Brittany, from Caen as far as Tours. Vendée and Poitou were affected by a wave of panic from Nantes, and that originating in Ruffec, in Poitou, spread across the whole of the western Massif Central and affected most of Aquitaine. Finally, in the south-east, the wave which originated near Louhans spread through the Rhône valley, but it also penetrated deep into the Alps and stopped only at the edge of lower Provence. Altogether most of France experienced these waves of panic, with the exception of Brittany, Lorraine and Alsace in the north-east, the Landes area, Languedoc and lower Provence. It is easy to understand that this provoked an outcry both among the urban bourgeoisies and in the National Assembly. At Versailles, the Grande Peur became involved (in a way which was incongruous, but also perfectly relevant) in the discussion of the 'Declaration of Rights' which was to open the Constitution: the problem underlying all discussion was that of the destruction of the old social structures and hierarchy of orders, together with the network of dependence which constituted the feudal system.

Reaction to the Grande Peur

The bourgeoisie found themselves in a dilemma, which can be interpreted at different levels. The immediate reaction (which was not the least important) resulted in a wave of anti-popular feeling. In many cases, the bourgeois élite received feudal dues; and more generally, the whole notion of property rights, so dear to the bourgeoisie, was now being called into question. It was up to the bourgeoisie at any rate to try to reformulate these rights, by differentiating between those rights which affected themselves, which were based on a free contract, and the archaic, oppressive forms; this, in turn, presupposed careful consideration on the part of the jurists, whose frame of mind was naturally legalistic.

Another factor was political. The patriotic majority were not unaware of the fact that they had derived their power from the 'fires of sedition'; to embark on repressive measures would be to give way to the king who still held the power of coercion: if he attempted to regain control, the results could be serious. Political considerations here tempered the first impulses of an alarmed bourgeoisie, and no doubt made them aware of the advantage of a new start, free from the old feudal dues. On condition, of course, that the situation was carefully controlled, it was in their interests to renew the attack on the privileged classes and to turn the immense power of the peasant revolt to the advantage of the new bourgeois regime. For this to succeed, the operation no doubt had to be well led, and, as one deputy declared, this could not happen without a little 'magic'. This was provided by the night of 4 August.

The night of 4 August

The romantic historians have left us with the impression of a collective upheaval, or an almost unforeseeable wave of enthusiasm, a kind of miracle, in which the generous outpourings of the well-endowed élites matched the great panic of the poor. The miracle had been well prepared. On 3 August the relevant committee (*comité des rapports*) could only recommend the restoration of order by force. During the night of 3 August the leaders of the 'patriotic' party assembled in the 'Breton club' and drew up a plan which skilfully made members of the liberal nobility responsible for proposing a settlement. During the night sitting of 4 August 1789, the Vicomte de Noailles spoke first, then the Duc d'Aiguillon. They agreed on an offer which was generous but restrained. There was to be equality (above all, equality with regard to taxation) and, in addition to this, the privileges of the 'feudal' regime were to be destroyed. Some, which were concerned with personal liberty, were to be abolished without compensation: this included the *corvée* and *mainmorte*. Others, the *droits réels* which were concerned with land, were held to constitute a form of property: they were deemed to represent the counterpart of concessions based initially on a contract; on these grounds, the nobility offered to declare them redeemable. This decision covered the *champarts* and, more generally, all the dues which affected the peasant most severely. This was a clever distinction and it assured the success of a plan which inspired a wave of enthusiasm. This was not the end of the matter: in an atmosphere of increasing effusiveness, nobles and prelates proposed that everyone should be liable to the same legal penalties, that the sale of offices should be abolished, that admission to all forms of employment should be on equal terms, and also that seigneurial courts should be abolished, together with the rights of hunting, fishing and keeping dovecots. This spirit of renunciation was contagious: it spread to all the privileged areas of what was to become, from this moment, the *ancien régime*. Everyone, so the gossips reported, was eager to sacrifice the privileges of his neighbour. The clergy lost the tithe and its fees, and the provinces and the towns lost their exemptions, their local assemblies of estates, and their franchises.

This apparent clean sweep was made in the enthusiasm of a sleepless night. In the morning, they took stock, and from 5 to 11 August the definitive decrees were drawn up in an atmosphere of harsh bargaining. They did not go back on the main principle, since they declared from the beginning that 'the National Assembly is destroying the feudal regime entirely'. However, in determining the practical details, the aristocrats found apparently unexpected support amongst certain leaders of the 'patriot' party (Sieyès and Mirabeau). The clauses governing the redemption of the *droits réels* were not designed to facilitate this process: the seigneur did not have to show proof of his rights, and there had to be a unanimous decision by all members of the peasant community before the redemption could take place. In addition, the clergy fought hard to retain the tithe, though without success; and finally the abolition of the guilds, which had been proposed prematurely, was dropped from the final draft.

The peasants were the most disappointed group: they thought they had been cheated by the so-called 'abolition' of dues which could only be redeemed at an impossibly heavy price. The new law did not go far enough, but common practice began to correct this: from this time onwards communities began to refuse to pay the ancient dues.

In spite of its limitations, the night of 4 August remains a milestone in the development of the Revolution, and more generally, in the history of modern France. All the complicated, institutionalised divisions which made France less than a nation were swept away at a stroke. The old regime of a society of orders was replaced by a system based on civil equality, in keeping with the philosophy of the Enlightenment. The legal liberation of the individual was one of the conditions essential to the rise of capitalism in the nineteenth century; on these grounds, there is a case for saying that it was the bourgeoisie which triumphed on 4 August, though they could not have been aware of this at the time. The peasantry, the original plaintiff in the case, also benefited. France now took on the appearance of a country of small landowners, emancipated from feudalism, and this was to last for more than a century. Without looking so far ahead, this beginning was itself to change the course of the Revolution; there would no doubt be major disagreements, even radical misunderstandings, between the bourgeois Revolution and that of the peasants, but for most of the peasantry the night of 4 August sealed an irreversible commitment to the new regime.

The difficulties of the Revolution of the 'parlements'

Had it been possible to do so, this would have been the moment to reach an amicable settlement, without reservations or regrets.

During August the bourgeoisie in power formulated its 'Declaration of Rights'. Mounier had suggested the need for this even before the taking of the Bastille, when he declared: 'A good constitution must be based on the rights of man and it must protect those rights.' As a principle, this was accepted on 4 August, but discussions about it continued until the 26th. Several obstacles were encountered, which were sometimes revealing. Mounier had requested that this message of the Enlightenment should be expressed in a 'short, simple and precise' form, but its formulation brought to the surface all the old problems. One of the most serious clashes centred on the definition of the freedom of conscience and of worship, which was, to say the least, timid. This infuriated Mirabeau; as Lefebvre has pointed out, the content of the Declaration of the Rights of Man (whose impact we shall assess later) still reflected a greater emphasis on the destruction of the past than on the anticipation of the future. Nevertheless, it is essential that we should see the Declaration – as Lefebvre has also pointed out – as the 'dying act of the *ancien régime*'.

In fact, nothing had yet been lost, and the *ancien régime* was reluctant to die. 'I will never allow *my* clergy and *my* nobility to be stripped of their assets', declared Louis XVI, and instead of sanctioning the decrees of 5–11 August, he reacted with what remained his outstanding characteristic, inertia. This was not the way to help those within the 'patriot' party who would have liked to arrest the course of a revolution they felt had already gone too far: Mounier, the lawyer from

Grenoble, plus others such as de Virieu, Malouet and Lally-Tollendal; they were to become known as 'monarchists'. They had worked out a social compromise, and they felt things had gone far enough. This conditioned their whole attitude. They were not aristocrats: their ranks contained a mixture of members of the bourgeoisie and a certain liberal sector of the nobility. They were partisans of liberty, of civil equality, and of national unity, but they were much more cautious with regard to the social changes brought about by the revolutionary upheaval, although the 'upper chamber' they dreamed of would have been composed of a 'gentry' rather than of the old privileged groups. These partisans of an English-style two-chamber system needed royal power to be strong; they did not hesitate to insist that the sovereign should have an absolute right of veto.

Such a compromise was deemed impossible and was even energetically denounced by the extreme wing of the 'patriot' party. In September the two related issues of the two chambers and the veto divided the deputies of the National Assembly. Sieyès and the group which became known as the 'triumvirate' – Barnave, Duport and the Lameth brothers – were strongly opposed to the monarchist party. As far as they were concerned, a single chamber remained the only way of ensuring that the aristocracy did not reconstruct its bastions; as for the veto, they were prepared to grant only the power of suspension, which would last for only two legislatures. This group won by a very wide margin in the two decisive ballots which settled these questions. The motion to establish two chambers was defeated by 849 votes to 89, and that to introduce a 'suspensive' veto was passed by 575 votes to 325. This success was slightly ambiguous: in the first vote the 'true' aristocrats, anticipating the worst, abstained.

For them, as for the king, the problem was different; they were not concerned with arriving at a compromise but with reconquering their position. Would they not be assisted in this by the difficulties facing the new regime? Necker, in power once more, was unable to make ends meet; he had securities to cover no more than a tenth of the 30 million *livres* he raised by borrowing. The crisis of government reflected a social and economic crisis which was as severe as ever. Food prices had reached a peak, and there was unemployment in Paris. In the Assembly, as in the municipal councils, all the new bourgeoisie in power could suggest was that there should be freedom of trade for grain, a suggestion which ran counter to the spontaneous demands of the people.

It is easy to see how, in such an uncertain struggle, the monarchy was strongly tempted to reassert its position by brute force: troops were concentrated at Versailles, though more discreetly than in July. But things had also changed on the other side. Precedents had been established, and they had some experience of revolution. Public opinion was more mature and was able to organise and express itself through the press. Its leaders were shrewd men: Desmoulins, Loustalot and Marat, writing in his *Ami du peuple*. They were theorists who were able to analyse the situation and go beyond the spontaneous demands – which still held a certain magic – of the craftsmen and shopkeepers of Paris: to remove the king from the influence of the court and install him in the midst of the people of Paris, as a symbol of rediscovered communal felicity. It was perfectly possible not to share this illusion and still reach the same conclusions. However, to take direct control of the monarchy, the 'fires of sedition' had once more to affirm the power of popular pressure.

The 'days' of October 1789

It is this historic encounter which makes the 'days' (*journées*) of October significant. The economic stimulus was important, and the events can also be seen as a rising of women, characteristic of food riots. But this is not the whole story, and behind the crowd of women there was a cohort of highly motivated men.

What triggered these events was not as trivial as has sometimes been said. During a banquet held at Versailles on 1 October to celebrate the arrival of the Flanders regiment, some soldiers and lifeguards took part in anti-revolutionary demonstrations: they trampled on the tricolour cockade and replaced it with the black cockade, that of the queen. Retaliation came almost immediately. At the Palais-Royal public opinion flared up; in the *faubourgs*, in particular, feelings ran very high.

The day of 5 October began with a demonstration in front of the Hôtel de Ville by women from the central markets and from the *faubourgs*. However, leading revolutionaries – such as the usher Maillard, one of the leaders of the 'vainqueurs de la Bastille' – had been warned, and now stepped in. The women, perhaps 5,000 to 10,000 of them, decided to march on Versailles, and this gave events a new twist. It led to a second demonstration, this time by men: the national guard, in arms, assembled at midday and marched in the same direction, led by its General, La Fayette.

The two processions arrived one after the other at Versailles, where the women invaded the Assembly and petitioned the king. They obtained a promise of bread. However, political considerations were already supplanting the original grievance: Louis XVI made it known that he agreed at last to sanction the decrees of 5 and 11 August. Even if this gesture was hardly likely, at this particular moment, to defuse the popular movement which was under way, it shows the link between mass movements and political conquests.

The armed people spent the night at Versailles. At dawn some of them got into the château and penetrated as far as the queen's apartments, killing a few of the lifeguards who had been defending the entrance. This was an abortive enterprise, but it had important consequences. After the Parisian national guard – which was in an ambiguous position – had restored order, the applauding crowd demanded that the royal family should return to Paris. The king, followed by the Assembly, which declared that it would not be separated from the person of the king, decided to comply. An extraordinary procession was formed to take back to Paris 'the baker, the baker's wife and the baker's boy' (*le boulanger, la boulangère et le petit mitron*). The royal family, guarded by La Fayette (a protector they had not wished for), were surrounded by the troops of the national guard, by a procession of women carrying branches, and by pikes on which were impaled a round loaf or the head of a lifeguard.

This episode marked a turning-point in the Revolution: an expression we do not use lightly. It was much more than an absurd side-show. The transfer to Paris of the royal family and the Assembly greatly reduced the chances of the monarchy reasserting itself by force. The physical proximity of the popular Revolution in Paris also reduced the likelihood of a compromise being reached by the 'notables'. The monarchists realised this: some, like Malouet, withdrew from the scene; Mounier himself emigrated. Does this mean that the whole of the bourgeoisie was at the mercy of a popular movement which had taken matters out of its hands, and that the course of the Revolution had thus been deflected? Certainly not, but the conditions of a new balance of power began to emerge. From this moment on, the bourgeoisie mistrusted the people as much as it mistrusted the monarchy (which the intervention of the masses had just enabled it to crush). As a result, the bourgeoisie urgently needed to consolidate the bases of its power.

THE FALSE RESPITE

Was there a 'fortunate year'?

After five months packed with decisive events, one can understand why more than one historian has been tempted to see the next phase as a lull in the course of the Revolution. For many writers this is a legitimate pedagogic device, which enables them to make a provisional assessment, but for others the lull has quite a different significance. They see this phase as a period of compromise which could have put an end to the Revolution; but they also know that the compromise was a failure, so they are drawn almost inevitably, in order to lead on to what came next, into further subdivisions. Two of the most recent historians of the period (Furet and Richet) have ingeniously distinguished between a 'fortunate year' which reached its apotheosis in July 1790 with the Festival of the Federation, and a period of renewed revolutionary activity – the divorce period – of which the most dangerous moments were the flight to Varennes (June 1791) and the massacre of the Champ-de-Mars (July 1791).[8] These events marked a turning-point in the Revolution; for better or for worse – for worse, according to those who feel this was the moment it went off course – the incongruous intrusion of the masses ruined any chance of a compromise.

We must not anticipate the events of 1791, but let us make clear that in our opinion the year 1790 only seemed to be a period of respite. It is easy to be misled if one restricts one's vision of the Revolution to events in Paris, since it is certainly true that there, at least for a time, the pace slowed down. If, on the other hand, one takes into account the different rhythm of the Revolutions in the towns and rural areas of the provinces one gets the impression that there was a constant renewal of activity. What is more, one gradually becomes aware that 1790 was one of the great years in the maturing process of the Revolution only because it was also one of the great years of counter-revolution. The aristocracy, which for a time had been disconcerted by events, recovered itself and ruined any hope of a lasting compromise. This made it very unlikely that there would be a further change in the course of the Revolution.

[8] Furet and Richet (9).

The organisation of political life

The surface indications of a period of stabilisation did exist, and so did
some of the preconditions. The most important of these was the
slackening of economic pressure. The harvest had been generally good,
the price of bread had fallen, and in Paris food shortages were less
common from November. However, the murder of the baker François,
hanged from a lamp-post for suspected grain hoarding, was still a
significant incident since the Assembly responded by introducing
martial law, aimed at repressing disturbances and banning unlawful
assemblies. Some realised the dangers of these measures, for example
the journalist Marat who asked anxiously: 'To what do we owe our
freedom, if not to the riots of the people?'

A new style of political life was emerging, with its own rhythm and
its own institutions. Let us stay, for the moment, at the centre – in other
words, in Paris. The king was installed in the Tuileries, with at least
the appearances of court life around him. But he was extremely
conscious of having lost respect, and of being very closely confined as
well. In spite of the wave of emigration, he was still surrounded by
a group which encouraged him to reject innovations out of hand. All
the same, it was necessary to come to terms with the new powers.

At the head of this group, we should put the king's ministers. As
far as politics were concerned they were fairly insignificant figures in
the face of a Constituent Assembly which was becoming increasingly
powerful. The politicians working with Necker after 14 July included
some nobles who were liberals, at least by reputation: Champion de
Cicé, La Luzerne, Montmorin, La Tour du Pin, Saint-Priest. These
men, liberals of 1788 or 1789, very quickly found themselves out of
sympathy with the opinions, and even the spirit, of an Assembly which
had begun, rightly, to treat them with suspicion. In the autumn of 1790,
their successors, Delessart, Duport and Duportail, were to be the spokesmen of the group which was then dominant in the Assembly, that led
by La Fayette. In fact, the new regime was finding it very difficult to
manage the actual relationship between the executive and the legislature,
let alone change it by constitutional reform. Mirabeau proposed that
the Constituent Assembly should admit ministers (24 October). This
would have been a step in the direction of the English parliamentary
system. Mirabeau was also offering himself as a candidate; at least, this
was what the Assembly understood. They rejected his proposal (7
November) and decreed that no minister could be admitted to the

Assembly. Relations between the two powers tended to take the form either of a hostile rivalry, or of clandestine contacts.

The Assembly was installed in the Archbishopric, and then in the Salle du Manège, near the Tuileries. The sittings were held in public; the audience was at first composed of the higher social groups but, as the months went by, access was less restricted. It was here that the great orators made their impact: first, Barnave and Mirabeau, then, gradually, Robespierre. The essential work took place in the *comités*, or committees. There were thirty-one of these, and they were responsible for the reshaping of institutions.

The Constituent Assembly: factions and individuals

The men whose task it was to achieve this reorganisation gradually split into groups rather than into 'parties' in the modern sense. The 'patriots' were opposed to the aristocrats: but this initial division became more complicated. The aristocrats themselves were divided into the true aristocrats, known as the *noirs*, and the monarchists. The first group would not accept the Revolution and fought a bitter, rearguard action in defence of the royal prerogatives and privileges. They included old-style nobles like Mirabeau's brother, who was nicknamed 'Barrel' (Tonneau); lesser nobles, such as Cazalès, their most impressive orator; and commoners, sometimes of very humble origins, who supported the old regime: Abbé Maury, for example, who was their most violent spokesman.

The monarchists represented another level and, one might say, a further stage in the rejection of the Revolution. These were the men who, as we have seen, inspired the Revolution of the notables. Their leaders were originally commoners, like Mounier, but it is not surprising that they included among their ranks a fraction of the nobility who had initially been liberal (Clermont-Tonnerre, Lally-Tollendal, de Virieu). No doubt the October 'days' had irremediably dashed their hopes of an orderly Revolution; but they remained a pressure group with a noticeable effect on the Assembly, on public opinion (they founded the club called Amis de la constitution monarchique) and on the ministers.

The old 'patriot' party had a majority, but rifts were already apparent here. The so-called *constitutionnels* were the most numerous group. These included the most enlightened members of the old privileged groups (from the clergy: Abbé Sieyès and the prelates Boisgelin, Champion de Cicé and Talleyrand; from the nobility:

Montmorency, La Rouchefoucauld, La Fayette and the Lameths). However, the bourgeoisie of the old third estate included the serried ranks of the élite of talent, wealth and ability such as Bailly, or lawyers like Le Chapelier, Lanjuinais, Thouret, Target, Merlin de Douai and Tronchet. The group was held together by slogans (a limited monarchy) and also by the influence of certain leaders (La Fayette). It benefited from the growing strength of the clubs. The most important of these was formed following the meeting of the Breton deputies: the 'Society of the friends of the Constitution', commonly known as the Jacobin club. This was an essential organ of political life, which we shall have to give the place it deserves. In Paris it was open to a wide, though still well-to-do, public, and it was also influential in the provinces. It stimulated political life by offering a platform to speakers of the 'patriot' party. The moderate 'patriots', grouped around La Fayette, could not control the Jacobins as they would have liked. They did not break off relations with them, but they preferred to meet in a more exclusive environment; this was the purpose of the '1789 society' which was open only to moderate politicians.

It is clear from these divisions that the 'patriot' party was unified only in name: on the 'left' of the supporters of La Fayette, more radical groups were emerging; these included the 'triumvirate' of Barnave, Duport and Lameth, an incisive coalition, at least at this period, which led the attack on the compromises of La Fayette and Mirabeau. There were also a few deputies – though they still stood alone in the Assembly – who could already be described as democrats: Robespierre, whose moral authority was becoming established, Pétion, Buzot and Abbé Grégoire.

The very uncertainty involved in this distribution of roles reflected a stage in the class struggle during the French Revolution, though the political microcosm must not be seen as a true image of this struggle. There were at least two elements missing: on the one hand, the people, the *petit peuple* as they were called by Marat, who became their official spokesman in his newspaper the *Ami du peuple*; and on the other, the majority of the aristocracy which had already withdrawn from the parliamentary game (or had refused to enter into it) and had moved on to open counter-revolution. It was men from those groups which made up the new political class who were prepared to accept the compromise by which they hoped the Revolution would be stabilised: men from the upper fringes of the bourgeoisie of notables and also from the liberal nobility whose political influence remained essential.

La Fayette: a new Caesar?

The difficulties this coalition encountered in trying to follow the aim
it had set itself, consciously or not, are reflected in the major feature
of political life at this period: the influence of certain individuals and
what might be called the temptation of 'Caesarism'. This stemmed no
doubt from the decline in significance of a monarchy which had been
reduced to resisting in a way which, though certainly not passive, was
clandestine and obstinate, while in the provinces it was the result of
the dissolution of the old authorities. There was a temporary power
vacuum, and the bourgeoisie were fully aware of its dangers. It left
a space for strong men, and so the bourgeoisie, at the same time as
it drew up its literal Constitution, set about finding some heroes to
defend a new order it felt to be fragile: there are plenty of examples
in the provinces (mayor Lieutaud in Marseilles); and at the national
level there was La Fayette, who enjoyed exceptional popularity in the
year 1790.

'La Fayette, the mayor of the Palace', Mathiez calls him, and this
is echoed by Lefebvre who speaks of 'the year of La Fayette'.[9] How
are we to explain the extraordinary popularity of the man, even if he
was by no means the pretentious nonentity some people have claimed
him to be? The 'patriot' party was not short of other candidates, and
Mirabeau could have canvassed considerable support. However, although Mirabeau was still very popular in certain circles, the political
class and the best informed journalists (Marat) had few illusions about
him by now. They knew perfectly well that Mirabeau had sold out to
the court, which he advised by correspondence, while the court had
settled his debts and paid him to defend the royal prerogatives as best
he could in the Assembly. La Fayette was not beyond reproach either,
though his treachery was less conspicuous. Since the October 'days' he
had come to see himself as taking on the role of the protector of the
royal family. He advised the king to commit himself to accepting the
Revolution, from which his power might well emerge strengthened.
The dice were loaded by both sides; the king joined in this game only
to go back on his word straight away, in secret; the hostility of the
queen towards the 'hero of the Old World and the New' was no
mystery. But at least they kept up appearances: the king accepted La
Fayette's offer of service, as he had accepted that of Mirabeau. He also
met the triumvirate, and on 4 February 1790 he gave an apparent proof

9 Mathiez (6); Lefebvre (11).

of his good faith by going to the Assembly to declare that both he and the queen accepted the new order without reservation. This session of the Assembly ended with the oath of fidelity to 'the Nation, the Law and the King'. From April 1790, the tribune from Provence and the 'hero of the Old World and the New' collaborated in the service of the king, and Mirabeau wrote to La Fayette: 'Your great qualities need my force, and my force needs your great qualities.'

This partnership was put to the test in one of the liveliest clashes of 1790, which arose in May: the question of the right to declare war. The incident which provoked this clash may seem trivial. As a result of a dispute between England and Spain over the possession of the Bay of Nootka, in what is now British Columbia, Spain appealed to France in the name of the family pact which linked the two Bourbon monarchies. The incident raised a fundamental problem: should the Revolution take over the legacy of the old alliances, and the foreign policy of the kings? Or should it not in future make its own decisions with regard to diplomatic policy, treaties and declarations of war and peace? This provoked a great debate. On one side there were the monarchists and La Fayette's group, who defended the royal prerogative; and on the other side there was the opposition of the left who were aware both of the fundamental problem and of the current situation. They were anxious not to allow the young French Revolution to be dragged into a hornets' nest.

Thanks to the audacity of Mirabeau, the defenders of the monarchy gained a partial success; putting his past services into the scale, he made one of his famous speeches which won the Assembly over; however, the impact of this session did not survive the vote on the final resolutions, which granted the king only the right to make proposals about peace and war, which would then need to be approved by the legislative body. One clause proclaimed for the whole world the new basis of international law, by asserting that 'the French nation renounces involvement in any war undertaken with the aim of making conquests' and that 'it will never use force against the liberty of any people'. The position of the monarchy – and also of Mirabeau, now discredited amongst the best informed of the 'patriot' party – remained uncertain. La Fayette, on the other hand, retained a great deal of authority, even though his sympathies tended towards the Jacobins and the extreme wing of the 'patriot' party. To assess La Fayette's power, we should no doubt take into account not only the bargainings at the highest levels that we have already mentioned, but also his real sources of influence. Certain contemporaries — Marat, for example — saw clearly what these were; they stressed the importance of gaining control of the national guard, a coercive force in the bourgeois Revolution. Since the crisis of the summer, the national guard had become widespread: the most insignificant country towns had one. But this very fact meant that the guard varied enormously from place to place: in some areas it was a spearhead of revolutionary activity, in others, the refuge of counter-revolution. By organising it from Paris with a hierarchical structure, and by bringing it up to strength with professional soldiers, La Fayette — followed, moreover, by the Assembly — certainly hoped to turn the national guard into an easily controlled instrument which would help bring about the new order he dreamt of.

The Festival of the Federation

The apotheosis of this system was the Festival of the Federation on 14 July 1790. The initiative for this did not come from Paris. It was on 29 September in Etoile, near Valence, that 12,000 national guards from Dauphiné and the Vivarais had taken an oath of federation. The following month the idea was taken up by the commune of Dijon, and then, between January and June, by Brittany, Anjou, Franche-Comté, Alsace and elsewhere. The Bretons were the first to propose sending delegations to the capital; after this the idea of forming a federation on a national scale was adopted by the Paris Commune. Pictures have made us familiar with the rituals of unity on the Champ-de-Mars, where the Festival of the Federation was celebrated on 14 July 1790. Bourgeois, aristocrats and the common people, both men and women, participated in this festival: they flocked to the ceremony itself, a religious service, after which La Fayette took the oath of federation.

We would certainly be wrong to underestimate the historic importance of the federal movement, a kind of converse of the Grande Peur, which spread (by example rather than by contagion) from the provinces to Paris. It was a symbolic expression of the sense of national unity born of the 1789 Revolution. History shows that this unity could not last, and also that it had its social limits, as was said at the time (although Marat dreamt of a 'popular' federation). This does not destroy the significance of an episode in which the Revolution affirmed its triumph — prematurely, doubtless, but spectacularly — over the forces of disunity.

The geography of the counter-revolution

In the year 1790 the counter-revolution was everywhere. To say this is not to share the misconceptions produced by the anxieties of contemporaries. Some historians, such as Furet and Richet, have spoken of the 'narrow road' taken by the bourgeois Revolution in the summer of 1790 between the constant outbursts of a popular Revolution on the one hand, and of an aristocratic counter-revolution on the other. Without wishing to clear the people of all responsibility for the breakdown of the bourgeois Revolution, we have to say that they were not the major cause. It is true that the deep-seated peasant Revolution was still in progress. In January 1789 anti-noble revolts erupted in Corrèze, Quercy, Périgord, and parts of upper Brittany; and again in May there was a rising in the Bourbonnais. In the towns, agitation was sporadic but it was often linked to the defensive reactions provoked by the fear of an aristocratic plot. This was the period when the tribulations of the journalist Marat, the 'friend of the people', who had to go into hiding and even flee for a time, showed that the 'people's Revolution' had been temporarily muzzled.

The real danger was the counter-revolution, and its ultimate failure should not lead us to underestimate it. There were no doubt some rearguard actions, such as the protests of the former privileged orders in the autumn and winter of 1789–90: that of the Bishop of Tréguier against the Declaration of the Rights of Man (14 October 1789), followed by the nobility of Toulouse, Béarn, Cambrésis and Brittany. The resistance of the *parlements* before their suppression was slightly more co-ordinated: protests came from Rouen, Cambrai, Metz and elsewhere which their true authors had to disown. The counter-revolution was distinct from these rearguard actions. It is true that it took over from them, but it was organised on different levels and so turned into something new.

In the first place there were the activities of the royal family and its entourage. At the very moment they were giving the impression of rallying to the new regime, they were really thinking of fleeing to one of the provinces, such as Rouen or Metz, from where they could work towards the reconquest of the kingdom. Attempt followed attempt: first that of the queen's secretary, Augeard, in October 1789; and then in February 1790 that of the Marquis de Favras who merely carried out a plan which had doubtless been organised by Monsieur, the Comte de Provence, but had the sense of style not to give away his accomplices even on his way to the scaffold ('jump, Marquis!').

The counter-revolution could scarcely derive its leadership from the royal family: the king, and also the queen, whose influence was growing, did not have enough elbow room or even a precise political strategy. However, initiatives came from elsewhere. As emigration increased it became more organised: the first wave, which left in July 1789, was swollen by another in the winter. In Turin, at the court of his father-in-law, the king of Sardinia, the Comte d'Artois organised a postal network to encourage plotting in all the provinces. Despite the difficulty of co-ordinating the action of families who hated one another, this counter-revolutionary committee had an effective or-ganiser in Calonne, the former minister, and found some resourceful informants such as the Comte d'Antraigues, who set up an information network. Unable, for the moment, to organise the king's flight, they planned a general rising. They were skilful enough to choose the weak points in the system. In Alsace they took advantage of the unrest pro-voked by the *princes possessionnés* on the other side of the Rhine who complained of being dispossessed, but the separatist attempts in Alsace misfired: Strasburg, it is true, did not move at all. In Franche-Comté, too, the projects failed.

Things were different in the Midi. Some resourceful notables (such as Froment, a lawyer from Nîmes) managed to exploit the hostility which existed between Catholics and Protestants: the Protestants were as a rule firmly committed to a Revolution of liberation, so the Catholics had chosen the other camp. In certain urban centres of activity (for example, Nîmes or Montauban) one can see how the various layers of disagreement – social, religious and political – were superimposed on one another. In Nîmes a silk town, the commercial and manufacturing bourgeoisie was Protestant, but the common people were Catholic and provided the clique of counter-revolutionary notables with an unexpected popular base. This explains the violence of the disturbances which took place in Montauban on 10 May 1790, and in Nîmes in June. Here, the Protestant national guard, together with the highlanders of the Cévennes, defeated their Catholic enemies, the Cébets, after a hard struggle. These were just two centres in what was a more or less widespread conflagration; in Toulouse there was serious counter-revolutionary unrest in April 1790, and this was followed by outbreaks throughout the region, from the Alps to Aquitaine: in Valence, Arles, Uzès and Aix. The conflict sometimes spread from the towns to the country. This was the case in the Vivarais, where the national guards' spontaneous formation of federations was manipulated by the counter-revolutionaries to their own advantage; in August 1790 at the camp of Jalès, in Ardèche, there was an assembly of 20,000 national guards which a committee of nobles induced to approve a counter-revolutionary manifesto impugning the National Assembly and its Constitution. The meeting was dispersed, only to reassemble in the same place on two further occasions, as we shall see.

Other urban centres of activity emerged. In June 1790, Avignon rose against the Pope and his vice-legate and demanded to be reincorporated into France: there was another scene of bloodshed. This was not a religious conflict, but it was certainly a social one; it involved a local struggle between Avignon, which was pro-French, and Carpentras, which had remained 'papist', or between the progressive lower Comtat and the conservative upper Comtat. The apparent confusion was worse confounded by the change of heart of the National Assembly which, in November, refused to reincorporate Avignon. This only heightened the tension: the Avignon army besieged Cavaillon, then Carpentras, and a genuine and bloody war broke out. At the same time, Lyons rose in revolt: the Lyons counter-revolutionary committee, led by a former consul, Imbert-Colomès, managed to provoke disturbances on 25 and 26 July 1790. The movement was quelled and did not spread into Beaujolais and Burgundy, as its instigators had hoped. However, the counter-revolutionary committee remained active. Was the danger of the counter-revolution illusory? Not at all: especially as in addition to these individual, if numerous, centres of counter-revolutionary activity, there was also an insidious but widespread attempt to regain control. It is with this in mind that we should look at what has been called the '*malaise* of the army' in the summer of 1790.

The attempt to regain control

We believe that it is a mistake to see this as a simple and ultimately technical problem of adapting to new structures.[10] It is true that the quality of officers had deteriorated as a result of emigration, and that the involvement of part of the army in the revolutionary movement made it necessary to adapt the old disciplinary system. But the problem was much more serious, as some people, including Marat, realised: for the aristocratic officers, regaining control of the army would ensure that

[10] Furet and Richet (9).

they had the means to make a reconquest on a grander scale. There was an increasing number of incidents: in Toulon as far back as December Admiral d'Albert came into open conflict with the 'patriot' sailors. In May and June the trouble increased and the minister La Tour du Pin had to agree that the army's situation was 'deplorable'. In August what was to become known as the 'Nancy affair' began. The soldiers of the Swiss regiment of Châteauvieux protested against the arrears in their pay and demanded to inspect their regimental chests. They were supported by local 'patriots', but the military and political authorities were determined to suppress them. La Fayette, cousin of the Marquis de Bouillé, who commanded the garrison at Metz, persuaded him to 'strike a great blow', although it was not until a pseudo-mediator, Malseigne, was sent from Paris that open conflict broke out. Bouillé reconquered the city on 31 August after a bloody conflict which left 300 dead. An extremely severe repression followed, and thirty-three men of the Swiss regiment were hanged or broken on the wheel, while others were sent to the galleys. Marat's headline was 'The Awful Reveille'.

It no doubt came as a surprise, but everything was leading up to it. The policy of compromise which was represented by La Fayette and symbolised by the Festival of the Federation turned out to be a trap. After the king had congratulated the Marquis de Bouillé for his bloody victory over the Swiss regiment, it was once again Marat who could write of La Fayette: 'Is it still possible to doubt that the great general, the hero of the Old World and the New, the immortal restorer of liberty, is the leader of the counter-revolutionaries, and the instigator of all the plots against the fatherland?'

In the summer of 1790 illusions were swept away and the two sides were in open confrontation: the religious crisis was to speed up the process still further.

The financial crisis and the birth of the 'assignat'

There was a state of open crisis after the Civil Constitution of the clergy was voted (12 July 1790), and especially after it was promulgated (24 August), but it would be true to say that the crisis had been latent for months.

To understand what was happening we have to go back to 2 November 1789, the day on which the Constituent Assembly decided to 'put the property of the clergy at the disposal of the nation'. The

reorganisation of the Church was the result of the financial crisis.
Following the October 'days' Necker had to admit that his policy had
failed. His loans were no longer covered, the Discount Bank (Caisse
d'escompte) went bankrupt and a patriotic fund produced virtually
nothing. The banker Lecoulteux invited the Assembly to do 'what
honest landowners do in a similar situation: sell up the estate'.

One of these estates was particularly sought after. It was the Church
lands that the Bishop of Autun, Talleyrand, suggested, in October,
should be used to pay off the public debt. The suggestion, as one may
well imagine, was not unanimously welcomed. From that time on,
there was a confrontation between two theories. For the lawyers of
the third estate, the Church was simply the trustee of goods which
belonged to the nation. The nation was therefore free to reclaim them,
on condition that it discharged the financial obligations of the Church
(pious foundations, worship and charity) and paid the stipends of the
clergy. The defenders of the clergy, on the other hand, such as Abbé
Maury or, with more qualifications, Mgr de Boisgelin, argued that
nationalisation meant spoliation, and Mgr de Boisgelin offered a loan
to the State in the name of the bishops. The third estate settled the
matter by deciding to assign the Church lands – claimed to be worth
3,000 million *livres* – as security for the public debt.

This plan came into operation by stages between the winter and
summer of 1790. In December Church land worth 400 million *livres*
was put up for sale payable in *assignats*, the issue of which was to
provide extraordinary revenue. In return for the land which was
alienated, these treasury bonds – in units of 1,000 *livres* – went into a
special fund, to be destroyed as they were redeemed. In this way, the
operation should have made it possible to liquidate the debts of the
ancien régime.

However, the results of the operation were modified by a succession
of unforeseen circumstances. The first *assignats* were not accepted
because there was no public confidence in them. In April, to clarify
the situation, the management of Church lands was taken away from
the clergy and the sale of 'national lands' was organised. However,
there were new financial difficulties and the Assembly decided to give
up the *assignats* or treasury bonds which the public had rejected, and
to issue paper money which they had no choice but to accept, since
it was decreed that it should be 'current like coin in public and private
transactions'. This modification was accompanied by a change of aim,
from liquidating the most urgent public debts to liquidating them all,

and providing for the needs of the State. This new plan was the subject
of prolonged debate in August and September 1790. After the
deliberations, the Assembly decided, in May 1791, to increase the issue
(to 1,200 million *livres* in denominations of which the lowest was 5
livres) of a true paper money, which did not bear interest. These notes
were supposed to circulate everywhere, and so to involve everyone in
the sale of Church lands. These advantages outweighed the major
disadvantage, the depreciation of the paper money, which became
inevitable since the coins were not taken out of circulation: thus the
competition between the two forms of currency verified the law that
'bad money drives out good'. Did not the State itself agree to change
its money at a loss? Henceforth there was a two-tier price system, for
coins and notes, and the value of the latter declined. In May 1791, 100
livres in paper money were worth no more than 73 *livres* on the London
market.

The members of the Constituent Assembly were not exactly
sorcerers' apprentices. They had calculated the risks in advance, even
if they were unable to predict how far the *assignat* business would go.
In the religious sphere – to go no further – this episode was a
turning-point in the history of the Revolution, which involved a
complete reconsideration of the place of the clergy in French society.

The religious problem

There were other reasons for this reconsideration as well. The abolition
of the tithe during the night of 4 August affected the financing of
masses; the abolition of the three estates naturally involved that of the
clergy as a corporate body; the liberation of the individual under the
new legal system prevented anyone from making perpetual vows
(February 1790); this meant that religious orders were suppressed, and
the end of religious enclosure was celebrated in numerous ways in a
flood of images. Other fundamental problems quickly replaced these.
In December and January the Assembly had extended official toleration
to non-Catholics, first to the Protestants and then to the Jews of the
Midi, despite strong protests (from the Catholics of Uzès, for example).
Within the framework of its general reorganisation, the Assembly saw
that a religious reform was particularly urgent: the Assembly worked
on this between April and May 1790 and at the end of May began to
discuss the plan for the 'Civil Constitution of the clergy'. These
discussions took six weeks and the measure was voted on 12 July.

The significance of this action, half way between the separation of

Church and State and the previous symbiosis between these two powers, will be discussed later, but it should be said that at the start this scheme did not seem to be unacceptable. In July the nuncio wrote to Pope Pius VI in the name of the liberal bishops to ask him not to condemn the Civil Constitution of the clergy. Mgr de Boisgelin, Archbishop of Aix, criticised the project, but not very severely, and it was on the advice of these prelates that Louis XVI gave his sanction to the Civil Constitution of the clergy on 22 July.

The mistake of the Constituent Assembly was to ask the Pope to 'baptise the Civil Constitution', as Boisgelin put it, in other words, to sanction it. Cardinal de Bernis, the ambassador to Rome, instructed to present the text of the law to the Pope, was personally hostile to it and was not a trustworthy messenger. In fact his lack of zeal made little difference: the Pope had already made up his mind. He had already condemned the Declaration of the Rights of Man. Extremely concerned as he was with his temporal power, the Pope was worried about Avignon,* despite the concessions of the National Assembly. He remained deaf to the pleas of the French bishops who begged him to prevent a schism from taking place in France. When, on 24 November 1790, the Constituent Assembly imposed the constitutional oath on the priests (who were now civil servants) – an oath which involved the acceptance of the Constitution – the break which followed came only a few days before the papal briefs of 11 March and 13 April 1791 condemning the Civil Constitution. A new element was thus introduced into the Revolution. The religious schism was not the crucial factor making the French Revolution take a 'wrong' turn but it introduced a new bitterness into the conflict.

THE HARDENING OF POLITICAL ATTITUDES (SUMMER 1790 TO SUMMER 1791)

Did the Revolution change course, or not? In the period from autumn 1790 to the breakup of the Constituent Assembly in September 1791, we encounter some familiar problems. The religious problems made the threat of counter-revolution more obvious, and the duplicity of the monarchy had become increasingly clear. The idea of a compromise seemed illusory. However, new factors now emerged, as a result of an upsurge in revolutionary activity.

---

* The city of Avignon belonged to Rome until 1791, when it became part of France. [Trans.]

Politics

The previous phases had ended, on 14 July 1790, with the artificial unanimity of a reconciliation under the aegis of La Fayette. On the surface, the general's triumph was certainly short-lived: it is true that the ministerial reshuffling imposed on the king by the Paris sections at the beginning of October meant that ministers who had become unacceptable after the Nancy affair were replaced by a 'Fayettist' team (Duport, Duportail and Delessart). But the popularity of the 'hero' was declining in Paris as well as in the eyes of the royal family. If La Fayette were to leave the stage, however, who could replace him?

In private, the attitude of the court, and above all, the royal family, became unambiguous. 'I would rather be king of Metz than remain king of France under these conditions, but it will soon be over', exclaimed the monarch in December 1790. He no longer had the slightest inclination to come to terms with a revolution he completely rejected, even if he sanctioned its acts officially. He was counting on foreign intervention to help him reconquer his throne, and he gave his emissaries (d'Agout and the Baron de Breteuil) full powers to enter into secret negotiations with foreign powers: foreign policy – both official and clandestine – thus took on a new significance. To make this foreign intervention easier, the king had come round to the idea of fleeing to the frontier where, under the protection of loyal troops, he would dissolve the Assembly and make a direct appeal to the nation. In the meantime he would have to wait patiently, accept what he could not avoid, exploit the situation whenever possible and, above all, turn to corruption in order to undermine the revolutionary front from within.

This was no doubt where Mirabeau came in; in the last few months of his life he was active in a number of areas. At the Assembly he sometimes took risks in support of the *émigrés* but, on the other hand, as far as religious questions were concerned, he pressed for a policy of intolerance (January 1791). In particular, he presided in a masterly fashion over the distribution of bribes, starting with himself and then corrupting other members of the Assembly as well as members of the most revolutionary popular societies (Danton at the Cordelier club). He died on 2 April 1791, the victim, it was said, of his own excesses. Public opinion was still confused, and he was given a splendid funeral, but he was already peripheral to a revolution which had managed to bypass the intrigues and corruption to which he was limited.

Was there a decline in leadership? The new team was already emerging. In the Assembly, the triumvirate (Barnave, Duport and the Lameths) sought to become the leaders of a government party. They were still regarded as leaders of the left, but in fact their revolutionary days were over, though they were not without principles. In his *Introduction à la Révolution française* Barnave shows that he was one of the most astute analysts of the period he had lived through. However, these reservations led them to lay down limits they felt should not be exceeded. Duport explained: 'The Revolution is over. We must preserve it, while resisting excesses. Equality must be restrained, liberty reduced and public opinion controlled. The government should be strong, solid and stable.' Was this, as has been claimed, the programme of an incipient 'great Tory party'?[11] For this to happen, no doubt the bourgeoisie would have had to be unequivocally triumphant from this point on. As it was, the new leaders could only resort to the methods of La Fayette and Mirabeau; without fearing contradiction, they relied on the support of the traditionalists and, in a straightforward way, sold out to the king and the court; this had been done by April 1791. The triumvirate, in turn, fell from power: the new split in the 'patriot' party became more serious in the spring of 1791 and in particular in May at the time of the debate on the colonies.

If we could go into more detail, this incident would no doubt deserve to be described for its own sake. The Revolution had spread to the colonies and had given rise, in the Antilles, to demands being made by the coloured free men – the half-castes – while at the same time the settlers had a powerful lobby in Paris with Barnave and the Lameths as their spokesmen. The debate on the colonies began on 7 May; it produced some remarkable exchanges when Barnave came into conflict with his adversaries, Grégoire or Robespierre. The final decree accorded political rights to half-castes born of a free mother and a free father, but it left on one side the problem of the black slaves, who were to revolt in August 1791. As far as the Assembly is concerned, however, it could be said that this clash confirmed the split in the old 'patriot' party. A new left was emerging and gaining public support: its protagonists were Pétion, Grégoire and above all Robespierre, whose integrity was beginning to earn him the reputation of an 'incorruptible legislator'.

There was a hardening of attitudes and a realignment of loyalties: these new conditions of political life in the Constituent Assembly

[11] Furet and Richet (9).

reflected a new mood throughout the country. In addition to the
Assembly, other organisations sprang up and multiplied: popular clubs
and societies which reflected an upsurge in grassroots activity.

Clashes at the base

Was there a social crisis? Yes and no. We cannot talk of food shortages
after the good harvest of 1790: this is clear from the moderate level
of prices. But other factors contributed to this renewal of activity. In
the towns, where the economy was still sluggish, the journeymen in
certain trades (carpenters, farriers and printers) were fighting for higher
wages and had formed an alliance in Paris. In the country, the agrarian
revolts, which had begun in 1789 and sometimes even earlier, continued
to spread from province to province. Some areas were more affected
than others: the Nivernais, the Bourbonnais, Quercy and Périgord were
places with an oppressive agrarian regime; here, where the remains of
the feudal system were being eradicated by violence, events had their
own dynamic.

The great innovation of the year 1791 was no doubt the increasing
politicisation of the masses: there was a shift from crowds to organisations. The process had begun earlier, but it now crossed a critical
threshold. At the end of April 1790 a new type of club had opened
under the title Société des amis des droits de l'homme et du citoyen
('society of the friends of the rights of man and of the citizen'),
commonly known as the Club des Cordeliers (Cordelier club) after the
place where it met. This club was distinctly different from the first
generation of societies: it had unrestricted admission, and its avowed
purpose was surveillance and denunciation, not to mention direct
action. During the winter of 1790–1 the example of the Cordelier club
led to the establishment of numerous popular or 'fraternal' societies:
these emerged spontaneously (like that of the hotelier Danjou) but were
quickly encouraged. They were soon to be found in every district of
Paris and in certain provincial towns. In May 1791 the Cordelier club
and the popular societies formed a federation and elected a central
committee.

Other structures now emerged which were to serve as institutional
supports for popular activity, in ways which were sometimes unexpected. The forty-eight Paris sections which replaced the sixty districts in the spring of 1790 were gradually opened up to leaders from
the people, who thus became involved in revolutionary activity. New

structures gave rise to new demands: by means of the journalists who were its appointed spokesmen (Marat, Loustalot, Bonneville) this popular movement drew up a programme of demands which were genuinely political. It is from this moment that one can date the birth of a truly democratic party, demanding political rights for all citizens and denouncing in advance the bourgeois Constitution. There has been particular mention of a real 'anti-clerical party' (Soboul); let us say that there was at least a strong current of anti-clericalism amongst the people, in the provinces as well as in Paris.[12]

The counter-revolution

The rise of the popular movement is inseparable from the success of counter-revolutionary action. Counter-revolution 'at the top' remained an ever-present danger. The court was known to be committed to it, and public opinion had become sensitive, reacting strongly to plots, both real and imaginary. This was evident in an incident in February, in a Paris angered by the emigration of 'Mesdames', the king's aunts. On 28 February a crowd went to the Château de Vincennes with the intention of destroying it, on the strength of rumours of a plot, rumours which had possibly been put about deliberately. While La Fayette rushed to the scene to re-establish order, several hundred nobles – 400 it was said – gathered at the Tuileries. The Parisians disarmed them and forced La Fayette to arrest these 'knights of the dagger'. Was this just an odd, isolated incident? It would be a mistake to reduce the counter-revolutionary peril to this scene, which verges on the tragi-comic. In the provinces, the counter-revolutionary gatherings at the Jalès camp, which had begun in summer of 1790, were not broken up until six months later, in February 1791. In the south-east there were constant disturbances: in Arles, the *chiffonistes*, who were temporarily triumphant, conducted a real counter-revolutionary terror campaign; in the Comtat the struggles between the French and the papal factions had never been so pronounced. From Dauphiné to Provence the princes' emissaries, such as Monnier de la Quarrée, established a network of conspirators. Even if we do not find clashes like these elsewhere, it is very difficult to see the aristocratic plot as 'one of those myths which make real history' (Furet and Richet); such myths have solid, objective foundations.[13]

---

[12] Soboul (14).   [13] Furet and Richet (9).

The religious schism

The religious schism opened up new possibilities for counter-revolutionary activity and these were very quickly exploited: in June 1791, the directory of Morbihan wrote to inform the minister of the Interior that 'the confessionals are schools where rebellion is taught and prescribed'. The obligation to take the constitutional oath and the papal briefs condemning the Civil Constitution of the clergy split the French clergy in two: there were the 'constitutional' priests (*jurants*) on the one hand, and the non-juring or 'refractory' priests on the other. The distinction was not always a sharp one: only the parish clergy were obliged to take the oath, but sometimes other clergy in addition to the parish priests and their curates took it; and there were also those who changed their minds and retracted, or who took the oath with reservations. However, two groups rapidly emerged: there was the episcopate, which was overwhelmingly non-juring – with the exception of only seven prelates – and there was the priesthood, which was more or less evenly divided between those who accepted the oath and those who did not. This split produced a tense situation and raised a whole set of new questions.

Should the non-jurors be allowed to hold services? The logic of the new regime would suggest this, but it would mean subjecting to unfair competition the priests who had taken the oath and who had committed themselves to the Revolution. Moreover, the defection of a part of the priesthood raised the problem of the responsibilities which were incumbent on them. The idea of secularising the registration of births, deaths and marriages came from the non-juring clergy themselves, as a way of getting round the monopoly of the constitutional clergy. What it amounted to was a situation in which there were rival, hostile clergies and churches in competition with one another: the non-jurors took refuge in the chapels of convents or almshouses, and the two groups ministered to different clienteles, with the pious following the 'good priests'. There was an increasing number of incidents: in Paris, and sometimes in the provinces, the market women attacked nuns who attended the services of the non-juring priests. On the other hand, in the spring of 1791 in a number of areas it was very difficult to install constitutional bishops and priests: there were technical difficulties in getting the new bishops elected and invested, since only Talleyrand would agree to consecrate them, and in more than one place – where public opinion was obstinate – it was difficult to get them accepted. A compromise had to be reached. At the instigation of the supporters of La Fayette the *département* of Paris agreed, in the spring of 1791, to tolerate the saying of Mass by non-juring priests in private buildings; the Constituent Assembly followed the Paris initiative in May 1791 with a decree on the freedom of worship. This half measure did not put an end to the conflict, and was very strongly opposed by the constitutional priests and by numerous local authorities, especially in regions where non-juring priests were in the majority (Brittany and Alsace). The non-jurors, for their part, were far from being satisfied with this measure of toleration. Positions hardened; this was one of the major issues which were to polarise public opinion in France.

At the very moment when, thanks to the religious schism, the counter-revolution was recruiting 'the infantrymen it lacked' at home, it seemed that it was also slowly but surely acquiring support abroad.[14]

The Revolution and Europe

It was during the year 1791 that the Revolution made itself felt as a European phenomenon. This statement needs qualifying in two ways: the most politically aware élite groups had felt the impact of the French Revolution from the beginning, but foreign powers only gradually became involved in what seemed to them to be a French problem.

Did the French Revolution inspire sympathy? It rapidly appeared that it did, throughout the Europe of the Enlightenment. We know of the enthusiastic reactions of the intellectual élite in the Empire: Kant, Fichte and Klopstock, who took it upon himself to extol the Revolution. A certain Forster from Mainz rushed to Paris to experience on the spot what many regarded as a supremely important upheaval. The response from England was similarly strong: there were reactions from poets (Blake, Coleridge, Wordsworth) and also from politicians, such as Fox (one of the leaders of the Whigs) and Wilberforce (who was campaigning for the emancipation of the Blacks). What had begun as an intellectual movement came everywhere to include a wider section of public opinion: in England the most radical Whigs formed clubs in support of the French Revolution (1790, the 'Constitutional Society' in Manchester). In the Empire, the Hamburg bourgeoisie ostentatiously celebrated the anniversary of the fall of the Bastille on 14 July 1790.

By 1791 this initial enthusiasm had already worn off: most of the

[14] Furet and Richet (9).

ruling classes had withdrawn their sympathy when they discovered the dangerous effect of revolutionary fever on social stability. This was the case in the Rhineland, where the peasants, following the model of the French, refused to pay their seigneurial dues. On the other hand, the intellectual élite became more deeply committed, and as they were often not looked on favourably at home, they gathered in Paris. The outlaws or exiled men from the Empire, the Netherlands, Savoy or the Swiss cantons constituted an active fraction of the political class in Paris. Personalities began to emerge, such as the American Thomas Paine, or the Prussian Anacharsis Cloots. The hardening of attitudes is reflected in the pamphlet war: one essential date was the November 1790 publication of Burke's *Reflections on the Revolution in France*, the fundamental expression of counter-revolutionary ideology.

The contest was continuing at the top, as well. What were the sovereigns doing? An ambiguous game was being played between the monarchs on the one hand and France on the other, a France which presented three very different aspects: that of the official government, that of the *émigrés*, and finally that of the court. The monarchs were not eager to intervene; they had other, more pressing problems elsewhere. For the Austria first of Joseph II and then of Leopold II, as for the Russia of Catherine the Great, the war against the Ottoman Empire was a major preoccupation from 1786 until the Treaty of Jassy at the beginning of 1792. During this time Leopold had abandoned the struggle (in July 1790) to concentrate on the Austrian Netherlands which had risen against him; in the winter of 1790 his troops crushed the rebels, entering Brussels on 2 December and Liège in January. Then these three sovereigns of central and eastern Europe turned uneasily towards Poland, where constitutional reforms of a liberal, forward-looking kind were introduced in May 1791. In these conditions it is easy to see how the sometimes very strong reactions against the French Revolution, notably in the case of Catherine II, did not at first have any effect. Only the king of Sweden, Gustavus III, who dreamt of a counter-revolutionary crusade, appeared to have made up his mind. Other sovereigns shared his opinion: Victor Amadeus, king of Sardinia, and Charles III of Spain, whose minister Florida-Blanca sent troops to the French border in March 1791 as a *cordon sanitaire* to protect Spain from the 'revolutionary plague'. However, these were not the leading figures. Joseph II, and Leopold II, who inherited the direction of these operations, saw the troubles in France as a desirable weakening of

French power and did not want to get involved; English policy was characterised by a similar attitude of calculated delay.

In the end, the sovereigns did intervene. Was this the fault of France? The new regime remained faithful to the declaration of world peace that it had formulated at the time of the Bay of Nootka affair: an attitude which was consistent both with its principles and with its sense of realism. But the French Revolution had only to exist to be seen by the sovereigns as a provocation. This can be seen in two direct clashes: the affair of the *princes possessionnés* of Alsace, and, despite all precautions, that of Avignon and the Comtat.

The first incident involved those princes of the Holy Roman Empire with domains – often large ones – in Alsace. They claimed in the Imperial Diet, that the abolition of feudal dues on 4 August 1789 had injured them. They were thus attacking the treaties by which Alsace had become French. The Assembly answered the protests, reiterated and supported by the Emperor, through its spokesman Merlin de Douai (one of its lawyers) who thus defined the basis of the new international law: 'The only legitimate claim to union between you and your brothers in Alsace is the social pact established last year (1789) between all French people old and new... The people of Alsace were united with the people of France because they wanted to be; thus, it is their will alone, and not the Treaty of Munster which makes the union legitimate.'

In May 1791, when the attitude of Avignon and the Comtat, with regard to the Civil Constitution of the clergy, precluded any chance of a compromise, it was in the name of these same principles that the Assembly decided to consult the inhabitants about the possibility of a reunion with France. This problem was resolved peacefully, but the new regime thus came into conflict with traditional law.

The 'émigrés'

Amongst the leading activists we must, of course, include the *émigrés*, but for the time being they were hardly in a position to implement their policy. We know that there was a first wave of emigration in the summer of 1789, instigated by the Comte d'Artois; the taking of the Bastille, the Grande Peur and the October 'days' all contributed to this first wave, which included a very high proportion of aristocrats. The flood increased in 1791, at the end of the winter, as a result of what we may call the military emigration of army officers. Small groups were formed: in London, Brussels, the Rhineland, Switzerland and Catalonia, and in Piedmont around Turin, where the Comte d'Artois had established his court. There was a certain amount of movement from one group to another, depending on the varying reception of the *émigrés*, as well as on the overall situation. The *émigrés* made a great stir, but they were not universally supported; according to the accounts still available to us, they hardly present a flattering picture of the French aristocracy. They were not the kind of men who inspired confidence; they displayed inordinate ambition, and the allegiance shown by the Comte d'Artois towards his brother was, to say the least, equivocal. None of this was likely to help them to be taken seriously. We can see this in the Count's own tribulations: in January 1791 his emissary, Calonne, was refused admittance by the Emperor, and in May he himself did not receive the welcome he had anticipated when he visited Leopold II in Mantua. He decided at this point to leave Italy, and by June the largest concentrations of *émigrés* were in the Rhineland: at Koblenz, around the Comte d'Artois and the Comte de Provence; and at Worms, where the Prince de Condé was trying to form a counter-revolutionary army from the officers (without troops) at his disposal.

In the spring of 1791 the problem of emigration was on the agenda of the Constituent Assembly, which had been discussing legislation on this matter since February. Anxiety had been increased by the emigration of 'Mesdames', the king's aunts (in February 1791), but it was now the king's own attitude that was causing alarm.

Today we know everything, or almost everything, about the secret negotiations, but we should bear in mind the important effect this climate of uncertainty had during these months on a public opinion which was already uneasy. The royal family had decided to flee, and from October 1790 made contact with foreign courts through various emissaries: the Baron de Breteuil, the Austrian ambassador Mercy Argentau, and the Swedish Count Axel de Fersen. In December Louis XVI wrote to the king of Prussia asking him to convene a 'European Congress backed up by an army' to re-establish him in his rightful position. The ways and means of enabling the royal family to flee to Montmédy were organised by the Marquis de Bouillé, who commanded the garrison at Metz. By February everything was ready, and any obstacles which arose merely increased the sovereign's determination to escape. On 18 April 1791 the king, who had just received the Easter sacrament from a non-juring priest, was prevented from travelling to Saint-Cloud by the Paris national guard. They were afraid that this journey was connected with plans for the flight that was already suspected. The king decided to resort to a ruse, and he wrote to the Assembly to declare that he considered himself a free man, and that the Constitution 'was to his liking'. At the very moment that preparations were being finalised, the minister Montmorin vouched for the fact that the king had never considered fleeing. All the same, at the beginning of June, Marat insisted that an escape was imminent. He was right: the royal family fled during the night of 20–21 June 1791.

The flight to Varennes and its aftermath

We must be allowed to have recourse to the 'history of events' when the narrative requires it.* The royal family escaped from the Tuileries through an unguarded door; with assumed names and borrowed clothes, they took a berlin carriage in the hope of getting to the Imperial border at Montmédy. Armed detachments posted by Bouillé were to escort the convoy, but progress was slow and the relay system broke down. When the king stopped with his family at Varennes, on the night of 21 June, he had already been recognised at Sainte-Ménehould by the son of the postmaster, Drouet. Drouet alerted Sauce, the *procureur* of the commune of Varennes, and the king was obliged to reveal his identity and to remain where he was until three emissaries of the Constituent Assembly arrived to accompany the royal cortège (a royal 'convoy') back to Paris. They travelled through an enormous crowd, who had gathered on the plains as a result of waves of panic, and who, in Paris, expressed their disapproval in icy silence. This mute scene was one of the most important stages by which the paternal king of the *cahiers de doléances* gradually 'died' in the eyes of his subjects.

This did not concern everyone: the period after the Varennes incident, until the separation of the Constituent Assembly at the end of September, witnessed the development of two opposing forces which were to put an end to the unity of the bourgeois Revolution.

The reaction of the people can be analysed into several phases. In the first place came fear; it was thought, not unreasonably, that the king's attempt at flight would be followed by a military invasion. The massive arming of the national guards and the raising of 100,000

---

* Fernand Braudel and other leading figures of the 'Annales School' dismiss the history of events as superficial and concentrate on the history of structures. [Trans.]

volunteers are a reflection of this wave of panic, but they also show
how the danger had become exaggerated. It has been emphasised that
the Varennes incident was a significant moment in the maturing process
of 'national fervour'.[15] But it was more than this: whole sections of
the popular masses and the bourgeoisie were now won over to the
democratic ideas whose progress was revealed in the previous phase.
There was a spectacular upsurge of interest; surprisingly, this was just
as true in the provinces as in Paris. Petitions arrived from the Midi,
which was highly politicised, demanding that the king should be
dethroned; their demands were in no way more moderate than those
of the Cordelier club which, declaring that the monarchy was
incompatible with liberty, wanted France to become a republic.

No doubt there were some who took advantage of this collective
demand and exploited it for their own purposes: Condorcet and a few
others, for example, tried to propose a republic which they clearly
intended to be led by the hero of the Old World and the New, but
this Fayettist manoeuvre did not succeed. Others, in particular Danton,
suggested to the Jacobins the idea of a regency; this meant relaunching
the candidature of Philippe d'Orléans, who had considerable active
support. We can see how, in this uncertain climate, the most clear-sighted
leaders of the 'patriots' came – without being faint-hearted – to adopt
an attitude which appears cautious, and perhaps excessively so, in
comparison with the initiatives coming from the Cordeliers: Marat was
inclined towards the idea of a dictatorship which would serve the
people; Robespierre still rejected the alternatives of monarchy or
republic (12 July 1791), and insisted only that it was necessary to depose
the king. The democratic movement, which was in the process of
becoming a republican movement, was still uncertain which direction
to take, just as it did not have a clear idea of the means available to
it. This gave the bourgeoisie – who had been disconcerted by the
incident, certainly, but who were nevertheless very sure of what they
wanted – an opportunity to regain control in an organised manner. As
Barnave exclaimed in the Assembly on 15 July: 'Are we going to end
the Revolution, or are we going to start it again? To take one step
further would be a disastrous and culpable act. One step further in the
direction of liberty would mean the destruction of the monarchy; in
the direction of equality, the destruction of the concept of property.'

This was a very clear analysis of the political situation. We need to
do no more than mention the scheme which was devised to restore

[15] Soboul (14).

the credibility of the monarchy after the attempted flight. The plan proposed by Bailly on 21 June was to put it about that the royal family had been kidnapped, so that the king could emerge innocent: this was a very weak ploy, since the written declaration left by the king at the time of his flight had been unequivocal; but the statements made by the Marquis de Bouillé allowed this legend to spread, even if they could not make it plausible.

The king had been suspended and his prerogatives (the veto) withdrawn; if the *de facto* republic was not to be perpetuated, the king had to be restored, at the price of a limited revision of the Constitution. This was the policy adopted in the National Assembly at the session of 15 July 1791, when the king was declared inviolable. He would not be brought to trial, and his functions would be restored as soon as he had sanctioned the Constitution. All that remained to be done was to get this solution accepted by two stubborn parties: the king and his circle on the one hand, and the popular movement on the other. The king was not indifferent to this suggestion. According to Mathiez, the king and queen had 'done some serious thinking'; and although this might be overstating the case, they at least had the sense to put off a premature invasion by foreign troops.[16] The idea was not abandoned, however: 'armed force', wrote the queen, 'has destroyed everything, and only armed force can restore everything again'. In the meantime, 'It was just a matter of lulling them to sleep and giving them confidence, all the better to outwit them later.' The royal family appeared to be accommodating, if not humble. They broke with La Fayette and renewed the links they had previously established with the triumvirate, who were in control of the situation. However, the royal family laid down their conditions from the beginning: they wanted the Constitution to be revised so as to make it more authoritarian.

To satisfy the monarchy, the electoral qualifications were raised and two bills in July and in September 1791 attempted to restrict recruitment to the national guard to 'active citizens'. (See p. 154 below.) Although these measures were vigorously opposed by the democrats in the Assembly, this compromise was not too difficult to achieve, possibly because in the eyes of the king it was only a decoy, and a temporary solution. He was able to accept the revised Constitution (13 September) without too many qualms, and he swore to be faithful to the nation.

16 Mathiez (6).

The Champ-de-Mars massacre

In fact, the Revolution, far from coming to an end, was taking a new turn at this point. The bourgeois Revolution and its popular supporters were divided by bloodshed on 17 July. Let us recall the facts: in the middle of July, just when the Assembly was deciding that the king was above the law, the Paris movement inspired by the Cordeliers, and followed at a distance by a section of the Jacobins, reached its peak. On 15 July the Cordeliers circulated a petition, drafted by Robert, demanding a republic. It had 6,000 signatures and was to be deposited on the altar at the Champ-de-Mars: a grim contrast to the unanimous rejoicings of the Festival of the Federation. When the petition was lodged, two *provocateurs* were killed; the Assembly ordered the mayor, Bailly, to disperse the crowd, and martial law was declared. La Fayette gave orders to fire on the crowd: according to the most commonly accepted estimate 50 people were killed, which shows what a bloody fusillade this must have been. This was not all. At the end of July the leading figures of the fraternal societies became the victims of repression: Danton had to flee to England, the democratic press was attacked, and Marat was driven underground once more. This period of repression lasted until the amnesty which was declared in the middle of September. The granting of an amnesty did not mean that all was forgotten: the rift between the popular movement and a section of the bourgeoisie went deep.

In this crisis the bourgeoisie in the Constituent Assembly lost the appearance of unity that the 'patriot' party had managed to retain up to now. The split appeared amongst the Jacobins: on 16 July almost all the deputies deserted the club, with the exception of Robespierre, Pétion, Antoine and Coroller. They were followed by three-quarters of the Paris members (1,800 out of 2,400). These secessionists were to establish themselves at the convent of the Feuillants, which was to give its name to the new club as well as to the conservative tendency it represented: that of a bourgeoisie for whom 'the Revolution is over'. The Jacobins, who remained faithful to the Revolution, seemed to be a minority group, at least in Paris, but – and this was very important – they retained the confidence and control of most of the affiliated societies.

On 30 September the Constitution was completed and promulgated by the king. The Assembly broke up and some thought that the Revolution was over. Even in Paris, in a deceptively stable climate, there were plenty of demonstrations in support of the king: he was rediscovered and acclaimed ('The good people, they ask only to be allowed to love me'). There can rarely have been a more misleading impression: at the instigation of Robespierre, the members of the Constituent Assembly agreed that they should not be eligible for re-election to the Legislative Assembly. This voluntary self-effacement left a clean slate and revealed the fact that relations between the classes were distinctly more strained, in a population which had, in the course of one year, become much more politically conscious.

There was now a wave of new demands, and the compromise which had seemed to triumph proved to be short-lived. It was only to be expected from then on that these demands would come from abroad: the king of Prussia, the Emperor and the Elector of Saxony, together with the Comte d'Artois, met at Pillnitz and on 27 August 1791 issued a declaration which was both prudent and tactless. It presented the situation in France as 'a matter of common interest for all the sovereigns of Europe', but stated that they would not intervene without the unanimous agreement of all the powers.

5

Revolutionary France (1789–92)

Following the narrative of the events of the Revolution makes one feel all the more acutely the need to adopt a thematic approach to its discontinuities with the past.

It would be not only arbitrary but also impossible to attempt to draw a static picture of these incessant changes. On one side, there was a dream of a Revolution which would be complete and would take institutional form, and, on the other, revolutionary praxis and an appeal to change; and both these ideals were opposed by counter-revolution in its various forms. This leads us to present the new programme formulated by a Revolution which was becoming radicalised as a reaction to these conflicts, and so to discuss the system that the Constituent Assembly had hoped would be definitive.

A NEW FRANCE: INSTITUTIONS IN 1791–2

Revolutionary proclamations

The Revolution was a dazzling reality: '*Fiat, fiat*, yes, all this good will come about, yes, this process of regeneration will be accomplished, there is no power on earth that could prevent it. It is the sublime result of philosophy, of liberty and of patriotism. We have become invincible.' These are the words of Camille Desmoulins in 1789 in *La France libre*. We know what ambiguities lay beneath these acts of faith; had the Revolution happened, or was it still to come?

In any case, the dominant idea involved the repudiation of the past and the affirmation of a new principle, that of national sovereignty. Sieyès had remarked that: 'The will of a nation needs only to be real to be always legal – it is the origin of all legality.' At a time when some – including Sieyès himself – were tempted to play down this explosive principle, others very quickly sought to exploit it to the limit. In August 1789 those who frequented the Palais-Royal put forward a motion declaring: 'This veto does not belong to one man but to 25 million.' What was to be done about the king? 'Public liberty', wrote Marat (*Ami du peuple*, 4 October 1789), 'should never depend on the virtues of the prince, but on the legal controls imposed on him to prevent him abusing his authority'; and more brutally a year later: 'The king of the French people is less use than a fifth wheel on a cart.' Was this the savagery of an orator who was said to be violent? Let us listen to Robespierre, speaking about Avignon: 'Who dares to speak to me here of the rights of the popes?' (to the Jacobins, 25 April 1791).

What about national sovereignty? Those who wanted from the outset to channel the forces which had been freed realised the necessity for codification: 'The Constitution is our guide, the National Assembly our rallying point', declared Barnave to the Jacobins in June 1791. Another recurrent theme was that the Constitution revealed the effect of philosophy on manners and customs; it was Marat again who said (in terms that Barnave would certainly not have accepted!): 'Thanks to philosophy, the National Assembly could dismiss the monarch... without causing the least disturbance to the State.'

The Constitution was the concrete expression of the fundamental ideas of a new world. There was Liberty: 'Know for once the price of Liberty, know for once the price of a moment' (Marat, *Offrande à la patrie*, February 1789); then there was Justice: 'Remember that humanity is the chief virtue and justice the chief law' (Marat, *Plan de législation criminelle*), and also Happiness: 'Brothers, let us swear in the chief temple of the Empire... let us swear that we shall be happy' (Claude Fauchet, *Troisième discours sur la liberté française*, delivered in Notre Dame in Paris on 27 September 1789). However, order was also necessary: 'In our zeal we need the fire which invigorates and conserves: we should avoid the fire which devours' (Vergniaud to the National Assembly, 21 July 1792).

The lyricism of these fine phrases shows that the Revolution was perceived by the élite as well as by the common people as 'good news', to take up an expression of Georges Lefebvre.

However, the bourgeoisie in the Constituent Assembly were faced very early on with the problem of codifying the principles of the Revolution: the *Déclaration des droits de l'homme et du citoyen* (the Declaration of the Rights of Man and of the Citizen), adopted on 26

August 1789 as a preamble to the Constitution of 1791, developed this text with universal significance and indicated how it could be put into practice. We do not find in it the breadth of some of the expressions which have just been quoted, but the attempt has been made to use it as evidence of the Revolution's own view of its bases and limits. In this period of 'Atlantic' Revolutions there had been other proclamations; no new declaration, however, had ever had such force or such universality.

Equality

'Men are born and remain free and have equal rights; social distinctions can only be based on a common interest.' The *ancien régime* had had its own liberties, which were not the absolute liberties proclaimed by the Revolution. The *ancien régime* was founded on the structures of a society of orders and was essentially inegalitarian. This is what makes this declaration of the bourgeois Revolution so significant in the transition from a feudal society to the liberal, capitalist societies of the modern world.

Equality of civil status did not pose any major problem; the world which was emerging needed the idea – whether it was reality or fiction – of an initial equality of opportunity: all occupations were declared open to everyone. Revealing examples of obstructiveness or reluctant compliance were no doubt quick to appear. From the spring of 1791 the problem of slavery in the Antilles shows – in spite of Robespierre ('the moment you pronounce the word "slave", you pronounce your own dishonour', 13 May 1791) – the limits that certain of the revolutionary leaders intended to set for civil liberty. As a corollary to the liberty of thought proclaimed in another context, the equality of all citizens firmly integrated into the community those who had been excluded from the *ancien régime* on religious grounds: the Protestants and the Jews.

However, we know the limits that the bourgeois Revolution imposed on the equality it proclaimed: these were glaringly obvious in the domain of politics. The distinction introduced by the Constituent Assembly between active and passive citizens excluded, on financial grounds, from a half to a third of the population. The franchise qualification of the 'mark of silver' would, it has been noted, have prevented Rousseau from sitting in the Legislative Assembly. These political restrictions were in fact social restrictions; in the revolutionary triad of Liberty, Equality and Fraternity (which was to become classic), we are well aware that the third term was only added later. Security and Ownership came first.

Liberty

Of all the ideas launched into the world by the Revolution, the most popular was the idea of the conquest of liberty. The facts surrounding the taking of the Bastille were to be quibbled over for a long time, but the symbolic and historic significance of this collective gesture was unambiguous. The whole arbitrary system of the *ancien régime* collapsed with this citadel: it was the beginning of Year I of liberty.

Personal freedom was the first, and the least controversial, of the gains made by the Revolution. The Constituent Assembly did not go as far as introducing the principle of habeas corpus in the strictly defined English sense; but at least it introduced a whole series of measures to prevent arbitrary arrest and detention. The citizen who was pursued by the authorities was no longer gratuitously maltreated. Following the humanitarian lines of the Enlightenment, which had insisted on the abolition of torture, the Revolution made an effort to put an end to all pointless cruelty in the treatment of the guilty: before it was regarded as an instrument of repression, the guillotine was seen as a reaction against the barbarity of the punishments of the *ancien régime*. It is unfortunate that it has become a commonplace to smile at the 'humanity' of Dr Guillotin, or at the proposal of one member of the Constituent Assembly, Robespierre, that the death penalty should be abolished.

Freedom of opinion seems to be the natural extension of personal freedom, and the group which David placed in the centre of *The Oath of the Jeu de Paume*, in which Abbé Grégoire and Dom Gerle embraced the minister Rabaut-Saint-Etienne, symbolises the new equality as much as the hoped-for end to centuries of conflict. This is not to say that the law, and still more, social practice, adjusted themselves immediately to this ideal; and if the full equality of Protestants was proclaimed from the beginning, the delays and the difficulties involved in granting equality to the Jews show how revolutionary the principle really was. The ending of the Catholic Church's monopoly of the cure of souls, which was an implicit consequence of the proclamation of the freedom of conscience, was one of the factors alienating the Church from the Revolution. Conversely, by making priests into civil servants who had taken an oath of loyalty, the Constituent Assembly went against the separation of Church and State which may seem to us now like the natural consequence of the secularisation of the regime. We should not be surprised by this: to be so would be to lack historical understanding of a period which could proclaim: 'No one may be persecuted for his opinions, *even* religious ones.'

For the Constituent Assembly, freedom of expression, which was the corollary of freedom of opinion, was one of the most 'precious' – and the most feared – victories of the Revolution. 'Every citizen has the right...to speak, write and print freely, apart from being held responsible for the abuse of this freedom': that this qualification was incorporated into the law is evidence of an ambivalent attitude to freedom. However, the rise of the revolutionary press, vigorous and polemical as it was, is proof enough that a new force had become organised.

Not only personal freedom but also political freedom, the foundation of liberal society, was established at this time. The major themes of the Declaration of the Rights of Man adopted by the Constitution of 1791 were the sovereignty of the people, the principle of election in all spheres, and a representative system founded on the separation of powers. Some of these freedoms did not survive the Revolution. The return to centralisation under the Consulate encouraged an attitude of amused condescension towards a regime which dreamt of electing its judges and even its parish priests and bishops. However, the idea of the sovereignty of the people together with the idea (inherited from Montesquieu) of the separation of powers as the foundation of political liberty were to remain central to political liberalism in France and elsewhere, despite subsequent qualifications and vicissitudes.

Those who piously celebrate the achievements of the French Revolution have more difficulty in fitting economic freedom into their paradigm. The nineteenth century was to reveal the ambiguities of this concept, which would be defined more and more closely between August 1789 and 1791, although it was not mentioned in the Declaration of the Rights of Man.

Property and economic freedom

For the Constituent Assembly one of the most precious forms of freedom was property: in other words, freedom to dispose of one's goods. The turning-point came with the decrees of application of 5 and 11 August 1789. It is well known that freeing land, like individuals, from all forms of subjection and affirming a bourgeois view of individual property did not prevent the negotiation of a compromise with the world of the past. The new definition of property redeemed, as it were, part of the traditional heritage by maintaining the distinction between personal servitude, which was abolished without compensation, and rights stemming from a supposed contract, which were declared capable of being bought out. Equally well known is the bitter struggle waged by the rural communities, which succeeded in imposing the abolition of property rights without compensation.

When they were negotiating with the aristocracy, the Constituent Assembly had to take account of the peasants. Freedom of property would have meant the division of the common lands, which is what the richer peasants wanted. No one dared do anything about it till the summer of 1792. Freedom of property would also have meant the legitimation of agrarian individualism by the granting of the right to enclosure. In the end, this 'freedom of the countryside' was not achieved in the rural code (27 September 1791) which allowed land to be enclosed but did not suppress the right to pasture beasts on it.

In the case of freedom to produce, as in that of freedom to own, there were some revealing legal hesitations. In theory, the *maîtrises*, *jurandes* and corporations were abolished during the night of the 4 August and made no further appearance in the decrees of application. It was more than a year later, on 2 March 1791, that the 'Allarde law' (so called from the name of the chairman of the committee that drafted it) made freedom of contract the basis of future social relations by suppressing not only corporations but also privileged enterprises. Add to this the abolition of all state control of production (inspection of manufactures) and one sees the importance of the change. Yet it was not enough. The freedom of enterprise was matched by the freedom of work, a demand formulated by the Parisian bourgeoisie in 1791: 'liberty ought to exist for everyone, even the masters', in other words, they wanted a free market in employment. The Assembly responded to this on 14 June 1791 by voting the famous 'Le Chapelier law', which banned all assemblies or associations, whether of journeymen or of masters, and forbade them to 'discuss or decide on their so-called common interests'. When the freedom of association came into conflict with the freedom of work, the Assembly decided in favour of the freedom which best suited the bourgeoisie.

In the end, *laissez-faire* won. If the Assembly allowed itself to grant a few concessions on this point to the powerful – protectionist pressure groups – it did not respond in the same way to the spontaneous

demands of the masses about the control of the grain trade: in the
summer of 1789 free trade was re-established, then price controls were
lifted. This measure was extended to other products between 1790 and
1791, by the abolition of internal customs barriers.

Foreign trade was treated with greater circumspection. Monopolies
were gradually abolished in these two years, starting with the India
Company (April 1790). However, a system of moderate protection was
retained for both imports and exports, notably for grain; and, most
important of all, the powerful plantation lobby was successful in
preserving the 'exclusive' system which tied the colonies to the
metropolis.

France reconstructed

Once the foundations for a new society had been laid, it was time to
think about new institutions. Was there a clean break, or was there
continuity with the past? Historians used to debate this dilemma. In
fact, both answers are correct. In favour of the continuity thesis is the
fact that the Constituent Assembly were not levellers – as the new
administrative system reveals – and that, like the lawyers they were,
they remained influenced by legal traditions, as in the case of their
'Gallican' religious policy. However, innovation was still more
important and, if one were to focus on the features common to the
whole system, the most obvious one would be rationalisation. The
monarchy had allowed institutional structures to be built on top of one
another in an uncoordinated fashion, while the Assembly tackled the
problem at its foundation.

This action of theirs was more than a mere remodelling; new
principles were put into effect. Liberal principles underlay the separation
of powers at the top, the extreme decentralisation at the bottom, and,
above all, the general application of democracy. This bourgeois
liberalism was modified by the primacy of wealth. The shift from the
traditional hierarchy to the new meritocracy was tempered by a new
voting system based on property qualifications.

Secularisation and the affirmation of humanitarian values were the
remaining principles of a system which claimed to be guided by the
light of reason.

The constitutional monarchy

The king remained at the summit of this system, for until spring 1791
hardly anyone thought of doing without him. The future leaders of

the democratic party, such as Robespierre, had not yet travelled the path that would lead them to a republic. Even Marat saw some use in a 'King Log'.

However, he was no longer the same king. His political personality had changed, like his powers. In October 1789 the 'king of France' had become the 'king of the French'. He was now said to reign 'by the grace of God and the constitutional law of the State', which meant that supreme authority belonged not to the monarch but to the law. 'In France there is no authority superior to the law, and it is only by means of the law that the king reigns.' The monarchy remained hereditary, but the sovereign was obliged to swear an oath to the Constitution. He had become the supreme civil servant, with an annual 'civil list' income of 25 million *livres*. The image of the monarchy had changed radically, although its holder continued to inspire respect. The powers of the sovereign were transformed more radically still.

As head of the executive, he now had only very limited direct authority. He was in charge of the diplomatic service and appointed ambassadors, generals and senior civil servants. But the central government no longer had any direct agents in the country: the royal prerogative could only be exercised through government channels. The king was free to choose his representatives and he was not obliged to select them from the majority party in the Assembly; quite the contrary, since a deputy was not allowed to be a minister. But this did not mean that he was independent of the executive: the king was dependent on his ministers, needing their signature for any decision. The ministers, for their part, were not responsible to parliament in the English manner, but charges could be brought against them and they were accountable to the Assembly. There were six ministries (the Interior, War, Navy, Justice, Foreign Affairs and Finance). The king, who was personally unassailable and could not be called to account, had become dependent indirectly, via his ministers.

It has been claimed that he still retained one part of the legislative power. There were, indeed, very heated debates on the royal 'veto'. What did this involve? The Assembly had the right to introduce legislation, but it still had to be sanctioned by the king. There was a split between the right and the left of the Assembly, between those who supported an 'absolute' veto – whereby the king would have the right to reject a decree without appeal – and those who favoured a suspensive veto, which merely gave him a delaying power and in the end left the Assembly free to reaffirm its decision. What is more, the suspensive veto could not be applied to constitutional matters, nor to laws concerning finance. The king was also dependent on the Assembly as far as foreign policy was concerned, since he needed its consent before he could declare war or sign a peace treaty.

In other words, there was a 'bourgeois' compromise: this monarch was not a nonentity, and he had some real influence. All the same, the Assembly clearly held the political initiative.

The legislative power

Royal power had been restricted, with the result that the wider legislative body became more important. It was in fact responsible for the government of the country.

This explains the significance of the clashes between the 'anglo-maniac' monarchists and the 'patriots'. Those who favoured a system of the English type wanted two chambers, an elected Assembly on the lines of the House of Commons, and an upper chamber which the most open-minded thought should be recruited from an élite based on wealth and success as much as on birth. Perhaps they saw this as a way of realising the conservative compromise they dreamt of, or at least of buttressing the monarchy by introducing a further check on power.[1]

In the end it was decided to establish a single chamber: this was the National Legislative Assembly, with 745 deputies, elected for two years. It had absolute power with regard to financial matters, since it both drew up and voted the budget. In other spheres — matters of diplomacy or war — it shared power with the monarchy, or at least tempered royal decisions. Apart from these specific areas it had the right to introduce legislation. The royal veto could hamper the Assembly, but not paralyse it. This indicates the tone of the Assembly's relations with the executive. The government could not dissolve the executive; and although the ministers were not accountable to it, the Assembly could impeach them. Who exactly held this considerable power? It is not exaggerating to say that the bourgeoisie had delegated it to itself. Adult men (they had the vote at 25) were divided into two groups: 'passive' citizens who were excluded from voting and who only had the right to 'protection of their person, their property and their liberty', and 'active' citizens who were the real shareholders in the great social enterprise. These men had to have a permanent address, and could not be servants or bankrupts. Above all, they had to pay a direct tax

[1] Egret (68).

equivalent to three days' work. We should take local circumstances into account, especially since the problem has been controversial. We know that altogether there were about 4,300,000 active citizens compared with 3 million passive ones, a clear majority. However, the national total disguises some important variations. In the country it appears that very often the great majority of citizens were active; in the towns, on the other hand, the opposite was true: very often little more than about a third of the men were eligible to vote.[2]

This was still only the first round of a voting system with several tiers. The 'active' citizens nominated the electors, one to every hundred, from amongst those who paid a tax of ten days' work: there were thus about 50,000 electors throughout France. It was these electors, in their electoral assemblies, who chose the deputies and also those who were to be elected to public office. To be eligible, one had to own land and pay a contribution of a 'silver mark' (52 *livres*). The spokesmen of the democratic party protested vehemently against this 'silver mark', which distinguished those who belonged to the 'new aristocracy': they won their case eventually, but too late for it to be effective; the 'silver mark' was abolished, but the property qualifications for the electorate were raised substantially (in the end the elections to the Legislative Assembly were conducted on the basis of the 'silver mark').

Thus the bourgeoisie carefully established the framework of its new power, and defined its own new élite.

Local government

What was involved here was more than a reorganisation. The *ancien régime*, which, paradoxically, had contained both the centralised system of the *intendants* and the often anarchical complexity of age-old institutions, was replaced by a system based on decentralisation and rationality.

Between November and December 1789 there was an attempt to divide France in a new way. Thouret, following Sieyès, proposed a plan to divide the country geometrically – American-style – into 80 *départements*, each 18 leagues square. Each of these was to be divided into 9 equal communes or districts, which would themselves be subdivided into 9 cantons. In the name of tradition, and of geographical and historical realities, Mirabeau asked, on the other hand, for 'a

[2] Godechot (10), pp. 306–9.

division which does not seem too great an innovation', and it was in accordance with this that the final division was established, on 15 January 1790. This resulted in 83 *départements*, subdivided into districts, which were themselves made up of *cantons* formed from several communes. This was a standardised hierarchy, which as far as possible respected the old framework of the provinces, but which did not hesitate to carve up or regroup areas in accordance with the requirements of collective life. To examine these negotiations for a particular region is to be struck by the bitterness of the struggles, which reveal an extreme parochialism, and which were sometimes dominated by successful pressure groups. However, from the point of view of an inhabitant of another planet, the overall success of this solution is striking.

The new areas required new organisations, which were broadly similar at every level of the administrative hierarchy. At the level of the *département*, which had 36 members, 8 of whom were nominated the almost total disappearance of the central power, which was represented only by a *procureur général syndic*. Power devolved upon an elected deliberative assembly, the general council (*conseil général*) of the *département*, which had 36 members, 8 of whom were nominated to a permanent executive, the *directoire*. The district authorities, though on a reduced scale, were organised along similar lines, with a council, a *directoire* and a *procureur syndic*. Their powers were largely fiscal and not as wide as those of the *département*. The *canton* remained an almost empty framework. The municipalities also created in December 1789 were quite a different matter: they also had a deliberative assembly or *conseil général*, from which was drawn the *corps municipal*, or in other words, the mayor, the municipal officers and the *procureur* for the commune. The *ancien régime* had mistrusted the municipal corporations, but the Revolution raised their status and entrusted them with the major part of the administration.

Let us pass over the old controversy between 'federalist' and Jacobin historians; was this system of extreme decentralisation a viable one? It certainly suited the notables, whose triumph was assured by the Revolution. However, this system undoubtedly took for granted the fact that the 'victorious and peaceful Revolution' had been achieved, and the regime was very soon embarrassed by the excessive powers it had granted to local oligarchies, who were not necessarily supporters of the Revolution.

The judicial system and the army

Each of the major organs of government posed its own specific problems of reorganisation. The most decisive progress was undoubtedly that made in the judicial system. The Revolution reveals its human face in the reforms of the law and legal procedures, and its talent for reorganisation in the reform of judicial structures.

Although it did not last, the new philosophy of the Revolution was applied to the law (Penal code, September 1791). Several solutions were offered to the problem – so dear to the Enlightenment – of crime and punishment.* Offences were reclassified and 'imaginary offences', such as lese-majesty or heresy, were eliminated. The rest were arranged in a hierarchy from minor offences to crimes carrying serious penalties (penal servitude, the death penalty). There were standard penalties for all citizens. Above all, penalties were seen in a new light: there was to be no more gratuitous cruelty, and punishment was to be determined in accordance with what was 'strictly and obviously necessary'. Similarly, the Revolution laid down the conditions necessary for detention, for appearance before a court and for the presence of a lawyer. The essential guarantee remained the way in which justice was dispensed: now that the sale of offices had been abolished, there was a more equitable system of elected judges, assisted, English-style, at least in criminal cases, by a jury composed of citizens.

In the new pyramid of judicial authorities, one magistrate per *canton*, the *juge de paix*, elected by the active citizens, had the task of dealing with civil cases. He combined arbitration with jurisdiction in minor conflicts. In the district five elected judges assisted by an appointed official heard appeals for the more important civil cases, the appeal taking place before the tribunal of another district. The less important criminal cases were heard in a magistrates' court, and then, at district level, in a court of summary jurisdiction. Serious cases fell within the province of the criminal tribunal of the *département*. Under the new system the accused would face a president, three assessors, a public prosecutor and a representative of the king, but also a double jury (one for the trial, one for the sentence) composed of active citizens. Historians have recently begun to study how these tribunals functioned, what kind of cases they dealt with and how justice was dispensed. It is generally agreed that they worked well and that they made the

---

* *Des délits et des peines*: an allusion to Cesare Beccaria's essay on law reform, *Dei delitti e delle pene*. [Trans.]

judicial system considerably more flexible and also — to judge from the sentences imposed — more lenient.

This new system appears to have been an almost unqualified success. The army, however, represented an unsolved problem, if not a defeat. It is true that the organisation of the *ancien régime* army, officered for the most part by the nobility, meant that it was particularly disrupted by emigration. There were also problems at the level of the troops. Although certain members of the Assembly, like Dubois-Crancé, felt from the start that a new nation needed a national army, the ruling bourgeoisie could not make up its mind to undertake such a total reorganisation as the one we have described in the case of the judicial system. This meant that when dealing with officers suspected of counter-revolution, and with troops suspected of excessive commitment to the Revolution, the Assembly constantly wavered between the recourse to old-style disciplinary measures and the desire to make the life of the soldier more humane. What was the result? The most recent enquiries into the structure, as well as the renewed recruitment of the regiments of the line, tend to show that the description of the chaos of these troops in 1792 has undoubtedly been exaggerated: recruitment had improved and the gaps caused by emigration had been partially filled.[3] All the same, the *malaise* of these troops of the line could only be increased by the fact, that, since the spring of 1791, they had existed side by side with battalions of national volunteers who were better paid and better treated, and who elected their officers. Because these battalions were recruited on a departmental basis they gained a certain cohesion and, though they were obviously less well-trained, it is generally agreed that their lack of discipline was a myth exploited by hostile officers. After this came the second levy of national volunteers in 1792, and these men, it seems, were rather different. The coexistence and heterogeneous nature of these troops, which were to be merged after the Revolution, show clearly that the ruling bourgeoisie never really knew what to do with this army which remained very alien to it.

Financial reforms

The reform of finance and the reorganisation of the Church of France — which were linked by a common denominator, the *assignat* — represent the most serious failures of the policy of the Constituent Assembly: the failures which were to pose the most serious threat to the course of the Revolution.

[3] A synthesis in Bertaud (72).

However, at first sight the reform of the fiscal system, which rectified one of the basic problems of the *ancien régime*, seems to have been conducted with the same clarity and the same concern for rationalisation, standardisation and justice that we have encountered elsewhere. The old system was swept away almost entirely: it was in such a mess that hardly anything could be done with it. The traditional indirect taxes, which were particularly unpopular, were nearly all abolished: only *enregistrement*, stamp duty and external customs duties were retained.

Direct taxation became the main source of revenue; it underwent a symbolic change of name since it was henceforward referred to as the 'contributions'. Between November 1790 and March 1791, documents were drawn up establishing the new structures. The central element was a land tax which was to be levied on real estate: this was a natural attitude for a society which still regarded the land as the source of all wealth, in accordance with the ideas of the physiocrats. There was also to be a tax on personal property, but this was very difficult to assess. This *contribution mobilière* also included a personal tax (that of the active citizen's three days' work), a tax on luxury goods and, in particular, a tax on the estimated rent paid by those liable to contribute. Finally, a specific tax on revenue from trade and industry was introduced. This was the *patente*, or trade licence, which was also based on the estimated rent of those liable to pay these categories of tax. We should not be too ready to condemn these reforms; this was a simple system, and not a bad one. It must have been convenient, since it lasted such a long time: it included three of the 'four old taxes' of contemporary France.

The temporary failure stemmed from the difficulty of administering these new taxes: the land tax presupposed the preparation of land registers for each commune, based on a cadastral survey of the area.[4] This could be done quite quickly in areas where there had already been a cadastral survey, especially in the Midi where in about 50% of the cases the 1791 *états de sections*[*] were still available. Further north, however, this figure dropped to 10% or sometimes less; here, everything remained to be done. The Constituent Assembly sought to reduce to a minimum the agencies involved in collecting taxes, so in accordance with their liberal, decentralising principles, they handed this

---

[4] On this technical problem there is an important monograph by R. Schnerb, *Les Contributions directes à l'époque de la Révolution dans le département de Puy-de-Dôme* (Paris, 1933).

[*] A subdivision of a cadastral survey. [Trans.]

function over to the municipal authorities. There was provision for only one collector (*receveur*) for each district and one general payments officer (*payeur général*) for each *département*. Having eliminated the *percepteur* (tax-collector), the system was at the mercy of ignorance and ill-will. The regime saw its resources fall to almost nothing; the expedients by which it had survived since 1789 (the patriotic contribution of a quarter of income) had been failures; the State lived off money borrowed from the Caisse d'escompte. The venture of the *assignat*, which we have already described, stemmed in part from this failure.

The Church and the State

The nationalisation of Church property inevitably led to a complete reassessment of Church–State relations. However, this was not the only religious problem facing the Constituent and the Legislative Assemblies. The members of the Constituent Assembly found it quite natural to be concerned with these problems. Although a number of them were unbelievers, the idea of a secularised State hardly occurred to them: steeped in Gallicanism, they felt justified in modifying the structures of the Church of France and its relations with Rome; and having grown up in the generation of the Enlightenment, they shared its attitudes towards the 'parasitic' nature of the monastic life. The standpoint of nineteenth-century historians, who have made us accustomed to seeing this attitude to religion as the profane gesture of the ungodly, is not a suitable one from which to view the events which occurred in the early days of the Constituent Assembly. It is not surprising that the clergy, like other organisations, had its structures completely overhauled. This was done through the Civil Constitution of the clergy, voted on 12 July 1790 and promulgated on 24 August. Geographically, the Church was reorganised to correspond with the new administrative divisions. The old dioceses were abolished, and provision was made for each *département* to have a bishop. Like other civil servants, he was to be elected by the electoral assembly of the *département*, whereas the priests were to be appointed by the district assemblies. Intermediary bodies, notably the chapters, were abolished and replaced by a *vicaire général*, whose function was to assist the bishop in the running of the diocese. It was accepted that appointment by election alone was not enough; priests were therefore installed in their parishes by the bishop, and bishops themselves by one of the ten 'metropolitan' bishops who were at the top of this hierarchy. Metropolitan and diocesan synods were also to be established. The bishops received a comfortable stipend (from 12,000 to 50,000 *livres*), and the plight of the lower clergy was considerably improved. It goes without saying that in exchange these civil servants were required to perform a number of services; there was a plan to have them read the decrees of the Assembly from the pulpit, but this was abandoned. In December 1790, however, they were required, like all civil servants, to take the oath of loyalty to the Constitution, and this triggered off the schism between Church and State. We have already seen that problems had been building up as a result of the indecisiveness of the papacy; the open conflict now forced the Constituent Assembly to establish the constitutional Church, whatever the cost, during the winter of 1791. Elections were held to replace the non-juring bishops with men who were prepared to take the oath; there was a crisis over the consecration of these new bishops since, of the constitutional bishops already in office, only Talleyrand was prepared to perform the ceremony. Amongst the lower clergy it was relatively easy, except in certain areas, to fill the gaps with men who had previously been monks. By the time the papal briefs condemning the Civil Constitution of the clergy were made known, a new Church had already been set up.

The consequences of the schism

It was immediately obvious that this crisis would have serious consequences which went beyond the religious sphere. Faced with this problem, the policy of the Assemblies was indecisive, as we have seen. They took a hard line in the spring of 1791, after the papal condemnation, but later became more accommodating and allowed the non-juring priests to celebrate mass in private buildings and even in the parish churches. This policy of tolerance was ephemeral: it could hardly be acceptable to the constitutional clergy. In the summer of 1791, in the provinces as well as in Paris, there was open conflict between the two groups of clergy and their followers.

The climate had now deteriorated still further, and the Legislative Assembly decided to take repressive measures against the non-juring priests. A decree was issued in November 1791, followed by another on 27 May 1792 according to which any non-juring priest could be deported from France if twenty citizens demanded this. On the eve of 18 August 1792, when the Assembly abolished the last remaining congregations, a number of non-juring priests were arrested: like the aristocrat, the non-juring priest had become a figure of suspicion.

Like the Constitution itself, this catalogue of new institutions began on a triumphant note, but it ended with an image of tension and confrontation. This is because the Constitution of 1791 presupposed a stability which was simply not established. Society was in a state of flux, as we shall now see, before contrasting the institutional structure with the dynamism of revolutionary practice.

A NEW EQUILIBRIUM OR A BOILING POINT?

It is when one tries to portray the new society that one is most acutely aware of the difficulty of making a static study of a period when everything was in flux. We must not evade the issue, all the same, because it is essential to a crucial problem. Can the Revolution be considered to have come to an end by 1791–2? This is what the Constituent Assembly believed, like the historians who have tended to think that everything which happened after that date was contingent.

This question can be approached on two levels. There are what we may call economic pressures and, on a deeper level, there is the redistribution of property and social roles which resulted from the Revolution.

Economic pressures

Let us look at the trends: at the movement of prices and population, and at the redistribution of property. Only these statistics can tell us whether this 'fortunate year' was an illusion at a time when many problems were making their appearance.

The period of high prices lasted until the middle of 1790, and in certain places, right up to the harvest which brought back abundance for one year. Elsewhere, as in the case of the Nord and the Orléans region, both studied by Lefebvre, prices began to fall in the autumn of 1789, following a decent harvest. (See Fig. 19.) In any case the fall in prices became more noticeable and more general between 1790 and the summer of 1791. In the towns, however, agitation for higher wages replaced anxiety over the high price of bread. Strikes of a virtually modern type had taken place in Paris in the summer of 1789 (among the journeymen tailors and shoemakers). In 1790 they began again in Lyons, Marseilles and Caen. In April 1791 the strike of Paris carpenters was brutally repressed by the municipality. In the latter part of 1791 the cycle started again. A poor harvest, especially in the Midi, was followed by a rise in food prices at the end of the winter, in the spring and again in the summer, in June and above all in July. The crisis varied

in its impact from place to place, and it was not as severe as that of
1789, but it was sufficient to explain the revival of food riots. All the
more because the French economy was beginning to suffer in other
ways. The economic crisis had begun to affect the value of the *livre*
from 1789 on, and it fell by nearly 10% at the end of 1791 and by
50% in May 1792. The value of the *livre* in terms of gold followed
the same trend, with a slight delay. *Assignats* followed a similar pattern.
On 1 January 1791 a 100-*livre* note was worth 95 *livres*; six months
later it was worth 88 *livres*; on 1 January 1792, 69 *livres*; and in July,
just before the fall of the monarchy, 61 *livres*. The fall in the value of
the *assignat* was another factor increasing inflation, and thus the cost
of living. This was aggravated by the fact that for a while *assignats* were
issued only in large denominations (of 100 *livres* or more) and were
thus beyond the reach of wage-earners. Hence entrepreneurs and
municipalities issued their own paper money or struck their own copper
coins. These were sometimes forged, and were not always accepted and
bankruptcies resulted. The crisis of paper money loomed large over the
winter of 1791–2.

The price-curve is not all-important, or more precisely, it is
ambiguous. Does the price rise following the 1789 cycle, together with
the *assignat* adventure, really reveal a crisis? Was the Revolution
responsible for this crisis? Specialists in economic history encourage us
to be cautious. On one side, as contemporaries knew to their cost, there
was unemployment in the urban luxury industries as well as in the
service sector. On the other side, historians who have analysed the
more prosperous sector of international trade by counting the number
of ships arriving in French ports are sceptical of a general picture of
economic decline: in Marseilles, for example, the 'glorious eighteenth
century' lasted until 1792.[5] It was the war which caused the ports to
decline.

Population movements

Like the study of prices, that of population movements leads only to
qualified conclusions. The Revolution was a period in which there was
considerable movement, and in many ways it was a major turning-point
in demographic history, but most of its effects were still to come. We
should not underestimate the importance of emigration, but at the
beginning of 1792 the two waves of emigration already recorded in

[5] C. Carrière, 'Le Mouvement des navires dans le port de Marseille', *Provence Historique*
(1957).

1789 and 1791 added up to no more than 20,000 people, less than 0·1 %
of the French population.[6] The emigration of summer 1789, led by
the Comte d'Artois, was spectacular but small-scale. In spring 1791,
about the time of the flight to Varennes, the movement became more
obvious and also somewhat more diverse. The split over the oath to
the Constitution forced Churchmen into exile along with the aristocrats.
In the summer of 1792 the rate of emigration increased still further as
fighting encouraged officers to desert. However, emigration was at once
important and marginal. It was not the most important element in the
movement of population caused by the crisis. In his study of brigands,
Georges Lefebvre pointed out that one of the major features of the crisis
of the summer of 1789 was the fact that a substantial part of rural society
took to the road.[7] These wandering bands, who were recruited from
the section of the rural population that was most at risk, could be found
at the time of the troubles of 1791–2. However, there was an apparent
respite between the outbreak of the Revolution in 1789 and the 'great
winter', as the vagabonds called the crisis of Year III. The other major
factor in population shifts, so important and yet so rarely looked at
from this angle, was the recruitment and the movement of troops,
whether volunteers or *fédérés*; but these movements had hardly yet
begun. It is possible to follow their trail, all the same, and the men
of Marseilles of 10 August left more behind them than the memory
of 'La Marseillaise'. This may all seem rather superficial and without
lasting consequences. However, the demographic data collected for
certain towns or quarters show that considerable changes were taking
place. In some towns, such as Nancy and Toulouse, a fall in population
was an index of crisis. Even before the climax of emigration the nobility
of Toulouse had left town, no doubt for their châteaux. In other towns,
though, such as Strasburg and Orléans, the population began to rise,
while at Chartres the proportion of newly-weds who were not born
in the town rose from 25 % to 50 %. It is extremely likely that these
figures conceal a changing reality; in the Faubourg Saint-Germain,
which had been deserted by part of its noble population and had become
the Fontaine-de-Grenelle section, the social composition became less
exclusive as the vacancies were filled by outsiders.[8] The behaviour of
this population also began to change. Even before the introduction of
divorce and the 'marriage mania' (Mathiez) consequent on conscription,
the marriage rate was increasing. This increase, which would soon

[6] Vidalenc (35).   [7] Lefebvre (71).
[8] See *Contributions* (77).

become a characteristic of the period, was already noticeable in Strasburg, Chartres and elsewhere. It is difficult to explain why this happened: perhaps the change in society brought with it a change in values? This leads us to the second level of this approach. We have to ask ourselves whether there had been time enough for a new society to be built on the foundations laid by the Constituent Assembly.

A redistribution of roles?

Here, too, it may be premature to draw conclusions; it is traditional to do this only at the end of the period. However, on closer inspection it becomes obvious that a number of changes had already occurred. Apart from the general economic trend and its consequences, a redistribution of roles and of property had already taken place.

As far as the redistribution of roles is concerned, it could be objected that the social structures had not visibly changed. One could hardly claim that decisions as important as the suppression of the guilds and the atomisation of the labour supply imposed by the Le Chapelier law radically modified the living conditions of the urban masses. It no doubt fuelled the popular movement in 1791–2, but the rhythms of life and of production remained the same.

It was amongst what would today be called the tertiary sector, as well as amongst the notables, that the changes were most obvious. On the side of the losers, there was the former nobility. At this point, it had been only marginally depleted through emigration, since the families remained behind. The nobles have often been described as withdrawing to their country houses, but their reminiscences and account-books show that the country was not an entirely peaceful place either: there were outbreaks of unrest, for example in the form of the Grande Peur or peasant revolts. On the whole the nobles managed to preserve most of their estates: they sometimes participated openly in the first sales of Church property. What affected them most directly was the loss of income from the dues which had been abolished, or which the peasants refused to pay. Not all members of the nobility conspired against the Revolution, but they tended to retire into themselves and deserted the army.

What would replace them? In what we would call the public service sector, a major change had taken place. It was the end of the *officiers*. What became of them? It would be rather simplistic to suggest that they slipped imperceptibly into the new groups – which largely merged into one another – of the civil servants and the political notables. All the same, the supply of posts was enormous, as Godechot emphasises.[9] There were 40,000 municipalities, 600 district councils and 83 *départements*, together with all the posts associated with the new judicial system. It cannot be said that the *officiers* rejected these opportunities, for they can be regularly found taking advantage of them during the first years of the Revolution. Not all of them, however: for a fair number of them this was the moment to capitalise on the income from land which was already essential to them. This was true for those who, like the *parlementaires*, were closest to the noble 'caste', but also for many of the former *conseillers secrétaires* to the king. In this way a group of landowners began to form, including *officiers*, bourgeois and former nobles, a group which was to play the leading role in French society for half a century. The supply of new posts in the administration was to correspond to the aspirations of the men of the law – solicitors, barristers, notaries and lawyers' clerks – a group which had tended to proliferate at the end of the *ancien régime* and which, it has often been said, made the Revolution. They were still recruited in a fairly selective way, but the social type of the civil servant or the bureaucrat who played an important part in the Revolution was already taking shape. We should not yet see him as a character from Balzac: he was elected, an innovation of the period. In this sector two groups changed most of all. It would doubtless be premature to emphasise the new officer class which had not yet had time to prove itself or make a breakthrough. However, if we look at the former order of clergy as a social whole, we shall find that they had changed radically. In the first place, the religious orders had apparently disappeared into thin air. The consequences of the dissolution of the monasteries and the abolition of religious vows were evoked, with broad humour and some wish-fulfilment, by the popular imagery of 1791. Monks and nuns were supposed to have thrown off their habits and veils and made good use of the freedom they had regained. The later careers of this group were extremely varied, ranging from a religious life in a secular framework in the case of some nuns, to secularisation pure and simple in the case of a number of monks, or, frequently enough, to parish work in the ranks of the constitutional clergy. This last group of secular clergy was reduced by emigration and split by the conflict over the oath to the Constitution, though the situation was extraordinarily fluid and also varied from one place to another. The curé who had taken the oath to the Constitution and thus become a civil servant appeared in some

⁹ Godechot (75).

places like an intruder who was maltreated or even driven out, while in others he participated actively in the Revolution at village level or even acted as its spokesman.

At the other end of the social scale, it was doubtless the peasants who were most affected by change. The transformation of this group was reflected in changes in the way in which they were described, with the old local labels, such as *laboureurs* or *ménagers*, being replaced by standardised terms, such as 'farmers' (*cultivateurs*) or 'peasants' (*paysans*).[10] The alteration in vocabulary was an indicator of much more profound changes. Between 1789 and 1792 rural life was transformed. In the first place, the burden of taxation became much less heavy. The reform of the fiscal system reduced the peasants' share of taxes, all the more so, if we may put it like this, because they did not pay at all. Seigneurial dues were also abolished. The importance of the change is well known, and so is the disappointment of the peasants when they discovered the limitations of the decrees passed between 5 and 11 August 1789. However, most if not all of the peasants refused to accept the commutation of seigneurial rights over land, just as they refused from now on to pay *champarts* or tithes. This collective refusal to pay led to serious tensions and on occasion to violent confrontations. The peasants were to have the last word, and the Legislative Assembly, at the suggestion of Couthon, resigned itself to the abolition of seigneurial rights without compensation. Serious problems remained unresolved, such as that of the common fields which the better-off coveted, while the others wanted them to remain undivided. In the aftermath of 10 August 1792, in fact on 14 August, the Legislative Assembly passed a law relating to the division of these common lands, thus giving rise to another series of problems. However, by far the most important of the changes was the enormous amount of land which came on the market as a result of the expropriation of the clergy and the sale of the *biens nationaux*. This was one of the great turning-points in French agrarian history. This sale of land was largely achieved in the few years with which we are concerned.

Redistribution of the 'biens'?

We have a more precise idea than contemporaries of the extent of these lands, which were thought to be immense. They amounted to 6–10% of French soil, though it is true that they were very unequally

---

[10] A recent study of this change is in M. Agulhon, *La Vie sociale en Provence intérieure à la fin de la Révolution* (Paris, 1971).

Biens nationaux

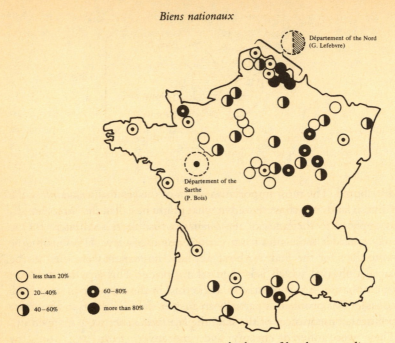

Fig. 19. Variations in peasant gains on the basis of local case studies

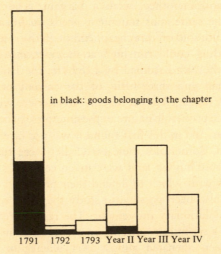

in black: goods belonging to the chapter

Fig. 20. The rush to buy: the rise in price of the *biens nationaux* coming on the market in the district of Chartres

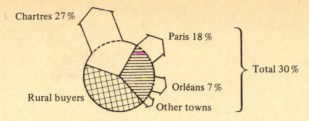

Fig. 21. The beneficiaries of a windfall: the dispersal of the farmland of the cathedral chapter of Chartres. The percentages refer to the value.

distributed. The most important section of the *biens nationaux* were the Church lands which were sold in what might be called the 'first round', as opposed to the lands of the *émigrés*, which were sold later.[11] One may consider these sales from various points of view. How profitable were they for the State? Above all, how important were they in the social upheaval which was then taking place? This is what we wish to emphasise. Is it too early to assess this, in the summer of 1792? To consider this problem is partially to answer the first question about the political consequences of the sale: the *biens nationaux* were snapped up. They were offered cheaply and, moreover, from 1791 on, the depreciation in the value of the *assignat* made them a particularly attractive proposition: they were a bargain, from which people profited. All the same, this statement needs qualification: the *biens nationaux* were not sold off dirt cheap. Although the reserve prices were quite low, bidding could run high at the auctions. Overall, in the *département* of the Nord studied by Lefebvre, the lands were sold at between one-half and three-fifths of the current price, where the peasants had not managed to get together to interfere with the auctions. It is clear that the profitable nature of the enterprise generally overcame political scruples, and in this first round it was not rare for the nobility to acquire land. Sometimes these early sales were turned into civic festivals, and those buying land were given crowns as tokens of their merit and guns with which to defend their property. In certain areas (Alsace) it has also been possible to study the effect on these sales of the counter-revolutionary movement. The results are clear: between 1791 and 1792 a significant proportion of the lands in the first round had already been alienated almost everywhere. In the district of Strasburg the figure was one-third in 1791, in the *département* of the Nord, two-thirds by the end of 1792, and in the district of Chartres,

[11] Lefebvre, 'La Vente des biens nationaux', in Lefebvre (73) remains fundamental.

more than three-quarters in the same period. However revolutionary the later stages of the transfer became, it may still be said that the essential arrangements had been sketched out by the middle of 1792.

The decree of 14 May 1790 which laid down the methods of sale for the whole of our period stipulated that it should take place by public auction, in the chief town of each district, on the basis of a tender for the whole amount. It is true that there was a possibility of auctioning the land piecemeal in certain places because of regional variations in legal arrangements. Above all there was the possibility of the peasants getting together, as Lefebvre has shown in the case of the Nord, whether they did this officially or unofficially in the name of an individual. On the other hand, professional speculators also entered the market, although this did not happen in every region to the same extent as it did in the Paris basin.

A statistical analysis of the purchases shows that the sales were very much to the advantage of the bourgeoisie. In these two years it was complete farms which were sold, and it was the rich who profited from it. However, this needs qualifying: some peasants were richer, and some rural societies more aggressive, than others. If we translate the information provided by the monographs into a distribution map, we shall find contrasts.[12] The proximity of towns was an important factor. In the Paris region this was noticeable in Seine-et-Oise, where the peasants did not do very well. However, this was also true in the Midi, near Bordeaux, Toulouse, Montpellier and Montauban and in the west, even around a small town like Vire. Away from the towns, the peasants acquired a larger share: more than half the total sales in Burgundy, in upper Normandy, in the east (Alsace and Lorraine) and in the Midi from Gers to lower Languedoc. Yet there were whole regions, such as Brittany, where the peasants got only a very small share. In this jigsaw which we are trying to reconstruct, one of the most obvious features is the existence of frontiers. Lefebvre has made this clear in the case of the *département* of the Nord, where the peasants acquired a very large share in the interior of the *département*, but only a very small one in the districts of maritime Flanders. Bois has found a similar frontier in the *bocage* of the Sarthe.[13] An average for the whole *département* blots out the contrast between two zones: the south-east, where the peasants took a fair share of a booty which, it must be admitted, was rather poor, and north-west, where the bourgeoisie captured virtually nine-

[12] The map in Fig. 19 is derived from Lefebvre, with additions from more recent research.
[13] Bois (36).

tenths of much more desirable land. These details would not be so important if they had not led Bois, the author of the *Paysans de l'ouest*, to calculate the lasting effect of this episode on collective behaviour during the Revolution. In the zone where the peasants saw themselves deprived by the bourgeoisie of the land they had counted on acquiring, their hostility to the aristocracy of the *ancien régime* was transferred with interest to the victorious bourgeoisie. The frontier described by Bois distinguishes the area which would support the Chouans from that which would remain republican. Such a case study is doubtless helpful for drawing provisional conclusions about this new and still unstable society.

A redistribution of roles had taken place. Is it possible to speak of a new equilibrium supporting the institutional edifice of 1791? What we see is tension and incessantly renewed conflict, which encourages us to turn to an analysis of the revolutionary dynamic, the practical politics which remain one of the most salient features of the Revolution.

THE REVOLUTIONARY DYNAMIC

The France of this period can be described on several levels. As a link with the preceding section, we shall briefly describe the practical politics of the assemblies and other deliberative bodies, and then attempt to analyse the different levels of revolutionary practice, from the most spontaneous to the most highly organised. We shall conclude with a discussion of collective attitudes revealed above all by the festivals of the Revolution. We shall see the contrast between the rigid France of the 1791 Constitution and that of the 'fires of sedition'.

The Assembly and its deputies

The formal structure of institutions has already been described, but it remains to be seen how they worked and who made them work. This sounds a simple enough ambition, but one which the present state of research makes it difficult to satisfy. The attempt leads to extremely divergent interpretations. As far as the summit is concerned, we need to know what the parties created at this time represented. Were they simply rival 'teams' composed of similar social elements, or were they the organs of specific social groups? As for the political base, in other words the level of local administration, we need to adopt a quantitative approach and ask ourselves what proportion of the people acted out the Revolution; we need therefore to study elections and also the kinds of people participating in revolutionary meetings. Only the sociologists can tell us the composition of the French 'political class' during this phase of the Revolution, and whether the traditional pressure groups had been displaced.

To begin at the top: thanks to the English and American historians (even if the conclusions they draw about the 'bourgeois Revolution' are sometimes doubtful), we now have a systematic investigation of the social structure of the revolutionary Assemblies.[14] For the 1789–92 phase we have two samples which are extremely diverse, owing to the conditions in which they were formed: the Constituent and the Legislative Assemblies. The former was the result of the spontaneous transformation of the Estates General into a National Assembly; the latter was the result of elections under the regime of the Constitution of 1791. In other words, in the first Assembly, top-heavy relative to the second, we find a massive group of the privileged orders, nobility and clergy. We also know that after the Constituent Assembly had been formed, the proportion of nobles within it declined because some emigrated, while others simply returned to their own provinces. However, the priests in the first estate, together with the monarchist nobles, continued to play an important part. From this point of view the shift from the Constituent to the Legislative Assembly marked a real watershed, since the privileged groups disappeared almost completely from the body of deputies. This was at once a process of standardisation and a revelation that the majority of the aristocracy had now taken up a style of politics of which the most anodyne form was playing a waiting game and the most committed form conspiracy in favour of counter-revolution.

There remains the group of deputies from the third estate, which stayed constant, or rather grew stronger, between the first Assembly and the second. Let us begin by defining them in terms of what they were not: there were no 'true' peasants, no wage-earners or urban craftsmen. From one Assembly to the next the importance of the notables remained constant, and, following Godechot, we may remark that in 1792 the different social groups had their own forms of political life. The aristocracy turned in on itself and went its own way, while ordinary people, excluded from the start, created their own marginal political forms. Shall we therefore say that only the bourgeoisie belonged to the political class? This would be to lay ourselves open

[14] For these conclusions, see Cobban (16), and Palmer (58).

to the charge of overextending this term; and the Anglo-American school has pointed out how the productive bourgeoisie, manufacturers and businessmen, are underrepresented, while the lawyers are over-represented. This was even more true of the second Assembly than of the first. Let us not go over all this old ground again. The point is that these Assemblies contained representatives of the bourgeoisie such as it existed in late-eighteenth-century France, and not teams of profes-sional politicians.

So much for the selective recruitment of this political body 'at the top'. As for its organisation, we have already remarked that it would be anachronistic to describe the groups which formed in these Assemblies in terms of modern political parties. They were more like clusters which came together and sometimes split apart again. There was no real organisation and *a fortiori* no control of the organisation by Paris or the provinces, and the deputies were not delegates. This explains how in order to co-ordinate their actions, the deputies joined parallel structures, such as the clubs (for example, the Breton club, out of which the Jacobins developed). In any case, each of these groups found its own kind of support: salons or exclusive clubs suited those who feared contact with the public. Patron–client networks were also important, and we immediately think of the La Fayette 'lobby' or that of the Duc d'Orléans. We should not underestimate the role of efficacious pressure groups, such as the planters and dealers involved in trade with the West Indies. Thus the solidarity among deputies from the same province visible in the Estates General was replaced by new forms of association.

Local political life

It seemed best to start from the better known or more visible Assemblies, and move on to what should logically have come first – political life in the provinces. It is the crucial moments when elections take place that reveal the temperature of political life. The analytical procedures of psephology are coming to be applied to these elections, but technical problems stand in the way of a study of this 'prehistoric' period.

The most open electoral system in our period was that obtaining at the time of the formation of the Estates General. The historians who have tried to calculate the rural turn-out, whether in Normandy, Maine or Gascony, have put it at just under 25%.[15] This is at once a small

[15] Figures from Godechot (10), following Bouloiseau, Bois, etc.

proportion and one which was to be expected. It is likely that some voters were not recorded, at this moment of rupture with the *ancien régime* in which only the 'wiser part' could express their opinion. The need for this political apprenticeship has to be borne in mind, but it remains true that the electoral system established by the Constituent Assembly narrowed the electorate considerably.

Another controversy among historians, on which we have touched already, is the relative importance of active and passive citizens. What distinguished them was the two-tier electoral system, with its different criteria for voters and for candidates. Besides the property qualification, we have to take account of the effects of the conditions in which electoral assemblies were held in the *départements*: the length and complexity of the operations, which lasted for days. The eagerness to vote for local officials in 1791 was genuine, but the context was that of a particularly select body of notables.

Who were these notables? In the cases in which an analysis has been made of the recruits to official bodies, the social boundaries of the group can be seen quite clearly. It includes men of the robe, *rentiers*, members of the professions, businessmen and wealthy merchants, and former *officiers*; a cluster of types which was not restricted to the closed world of the traditional municipal oligarchy, but completely excluded popular or semi-popular participation. It is easy to understand how this political group, which had sealed itself off too quickly, could appear, at the end of 1791, and still more 1792, ill-adapted and irrelevant to the needs of the politically conscious section of the population. It is not difficult to explain the strong reaction against the notables in the spring and summer of 1792.

It is perhaps possible to attempt a contrasting sample survey to discover the social composition of the revolutionaries themselves. A reliable indicator is the frequentation of *sociétés populaires*. Godechot suggests that on average some 2% of the adult male population of the towns (and rarely more than 8%) frequented these societies, compared with 8% in the countryside (and occasionally over 15%).[16] In Marseilles in the summer of 1792 the proportion varied between 10% and 15%, but it is true that passive citizens had already made their appearance at these meetings, that the distinction between the 'political' and the 'revolutionary' was disappearing, and that the group of revolutionary militants was widening, although it was still in the minority.

[16] Godechot (75).

Revolutionary practice

Political practice 'at the top' changed together with the institutional framework, and this leads us back to the dynamic realities of a Revolution which was on the move, even if not fast enough for those who, like Marat, believed that liberty was the product of the 'fires of sedition' which had to be kept burning.

It is impossible to ignore the insurrections, which have attracted the interest – if rarely the sympathy – of the earliest writers on the Revolution, from Michelet to Taine, who asked questions about the crowd and the revolutionary days. At the end of the last century, positivist historians turned from narrative to analysis, and offered the first interpretations of these events in the light of the sociology of the day. Dr Lebon, for example, studied the revolutionary crowds, describing them as a collective entity, but an infantile one, with its impulses, its tropisms, and its pathological features: being of low intelligence, not far removed from the animal. In fact, Taine had already seen it in this sort of way, in a celebrated passage which compared the crowd to a man who is drunk, unable to see, euphoric, who then turns restless and violent, and finally breaks loose. However, in a well-known article Lefebvre brought us back to earth by distinguishing two sorts of crowd.[17] There is the kind which has collected by chance, which offers the ideal testing-ground for these electric shocks, and there is the much more common type of the 'semi-voluntary' assembly at harvest-time, at the church door after mass, at the market, queuing at the baker's or crowding outside the Palais-Royal. It is also possible to find voluntary, organised groups right from the start, and we may say that the increasingly revolutionary situation from 1789 to 1792 gave such groups a more and more important place, from the 'spark' of 14 July to the organisation of the happenings on 10 August. On the basis of these suggestions, systematic studies of revolutionary crowds have been undertaken, notably by Rudé, which attempt to classify their actions, to determine their social composition (followers as well as leaders), and to analyse the ideas and the slogans which mobilised them for action.[18]

[17] Lefebvre, 'Foules révolutionnaires', in Lefebvre (12).
[18] Rudé (24).

The revolutionary 'days'

To begin with, it is doubtless necessary to distinguish urban from rural movements. To limit ourselves to the case of Paris, which has been studied most thoroughly, we may suggest the following typology of collective action. At the most spontaneous level we have the food riot, or, more generally, the disturbance with social motives. This is the case in the movements which Rudé has studied. The Réveillon affair in April 1789 is almost too neat an example of a conflict between wage-earners and their employers. Spring 1792, with its demands for bread, and for sugar and coffee as well, offers a similar example of people forming small groups, of a diffuse agitation which could easily transform itself into a riot, with the looting of stocks of wholesalers.

Even in these cases, where the original stimulus seems to have been economic or social, it would be extremely difficult to reduce the events to one component. A political demand prolonged them. The 'days' of 5 and 6 October 1789 are an example of this mixed type, which was the most common type in the provinces as well as in Paris. The point of departure was indubitably economic, and the demands of the women of Paris were concerned with shortages and dear bread. However, the denunciation of the conspiracy of the aristocrats and the return of the king to Paris were superimposed on this movement and then associated with it.

It is in the strictly political riots that, following Lefebvre, we can best observe the sudden shifts which led to the genuinely revolutionary groupings. To return to his distinctions, the 'semi-voluntary' group was generally predominant at the start. On 14 July, it was a group which was already looking for arms that was transformed into a revolutionary crowd by the resistance they encountered outside the Bastille. As political consciousness developed, the element of improvisation or surprise in the 'days' was reduced. In the period covered by this study there was still a recognisable measure of spontaneity in the incidents of 20 June 1792 – this in fact accounted for their failure – but there was already an organised procession, led, to some extent, by the national guards. The taking of the Tuileries on 10 August 1792 apparently marked the end of a cycle; the action was no doubt sparked off by an isolated incident (the Swiss guards charging the *fédérés*, an action which was seen as treachery), but this was a planned revolt, anticipated on both sides and involving organised leaders, *fédérés*, 'patriotic' national guards, and the people in arms.

It would be an oversimplification to claim that all the revolutionary crowds followed this model. However, there is a lack of other evidence: what Mousnier would call the 'furies' have not been studied in as much detail for the provinces as for Paris. We can at least say that the model put forward by Lefebvre, and adopted by Rudé, does seem to fit the outbreaks of revolutionary activity which multiplied at local levels in the summer of 1792: outbreaks which, though inspired by socio-economic considerations, now had an added political dimension. However, at the risk of sounding naïve, it should be emphasised that there were some revealing differences between Paris and the provinces, especially the fact that in Paris, until 10 August 1792 and beyond, the revolutionary crowd had never been opposed by counter-revolutionary forces. This was not the case in every province. In the Midi there were confrontations which were at once serious and confused, sometimes involving both religious and social divisions. This was the case, as we have seen, in the bloody incidents at Montauban and Nîmes in 1792. However, these were not the only patterns of conflict. There were often struggles between different social groups (very clearly the case in Avignon), but there were also 'vertical' conflicts between factions, when each side had its own bourgeois leaders and popular supporters. Once again it is the Midi which provides an example of this, in the *chiffonistes* and the *monnaidiers* of Arles.

The revolutionary crowds and action in the countryside

The forms of disturbance just described were all urban, and it may seem artificial to link them to the manifestations of revolutionary activity in the countryside. The first outbreak in rural areas was a panic movement: the Grande Peur. We have already discussed the importance of this episode. However, following Lefebvre, we may recall some of its specific features. Its very title tells us that it was a movement of 'fear', in other words, it was undeniably an expression of collective feeling of the old type. It was a false alarm, spread throughout the kingdom by word of mouth. Although certain aspects of the behaviour of the urban crowds have seemed disconcerting, the impression of strangeness is even stronger in the country. All the same, we must not exaggerate its impact; it has been said that the Grande Peur did not live up to its name, and that the 'fear' did not really lead to panic: the spontaneous, collective response was defensive and organised.

We can see, however, how the idea of a peasant Revolution which

took the form of the Grande Peur and was then pushed into the
background by the urban revolutions (to reappear later in the
counter-revolutionary form of the Chouan risings) could give the
impression that the rural world was indifferent to, or only marginally
concerned with, the Revolution: as if it was fighting only to protect
its own interests. This is no doubt to fail to appreciate the intensity
of the Revolution in the countryside in 1791 and 1792. This failure can
be explained. Despite what Mathiez and Soboul have had to say about
it, the fragmented nature of that silent struggle (refusal to pay dues,
pillaging) obviously makes it much less accessible than the urban
explosions.

   All the same, regional studies are beginning to show the extent to
which the peasants were involved, and to disclose the existence of
'crowds' and if not of 'days' of action, at least of periods of heightened
activity and of outbreaks which were sometimes impressive. The timing
of the Revolution in the countryside was not simply derived from the
towns; it was no doubt more sensitive to the pressures of poverty and
famine. This accounts for the lull in 1790 and at the beginning of 1791:
a period of good harvests and a fall in food prices. It is tempting to
identify two types of peasant uprisings: those in the plains of northern
France and those in the Midi.[19] In the spring and autumn of 1792, in
the plains of intensive cultivation (Beauce) and the surrounding areas,
itinerant assessors were sent from market to market to fix maximum
prices for grain and for bread. At the same period the whole of the
south-east was caught up in a revolt in which the level of popular
involvement was on the whole much lower, but in which political
considerations and aggression against the nobility became essential
features.

Ideas and actions

Would it be possible to draw up a list of ideas which prompted action?
Such a reductionist approach would be impossible and no doubt
artificial as well; like Lefebvre, and after him Soboul, all we can do
is to offer some suggestions about the crowd's fundamental motives.[20]
The crowd was inspired by both fear and hope. This hope was an act
of faith on the part of those for whom the Revolution, in Lefebvre's
phrase, was a piece of 'good news' in the old millenarian tradition.

---

[19] M. Vovelle, *Les Taxations populaires de 1791–2 dans la Beauce* (Paris, 1958); *Les Troubles
    sociaux en Provence de 1750 à 1792* (Paris, 1971).
[20] There is a great deal packed into one section of *La Révolution française* (15).

This hope found concrete expression in more precise demands, whether economic ('To plenty', as we find inscribed on painted plates), social ('We knew our turn would come') or political: the dream, for a time at least, of stability and equilibrium ('the Nation, the Law, the King'). Fear, which provoked conflict, found a thousand and one means of insinuating itself, and this made it perhaps an even more powerful motive force.

Once again, it is Lefebvre and his followers who have pointed out that more often than not the revolutionary violence was defensive, even where this seems most paradoxical: this was the case on 10 August 1792. It was to defend the Revolution that the people took action. A whole cluster of themes connected with the idea of fear emerges. It is perhaps not necessary to orchestrate them into a 'symphony of fear' as some have done (Palou), but we should try to identify their components.[21] The first stages of the panic reactivated the old image of the brigand or the mythical invader. We know that this type of panic returned in 1790 (around Laon, Verdun and Rouen) and was strong at the time of the Varennes crisis, in Champagne and as far as Queyras. Here, the fear of invasion was more important than that of brigands, a fear which was to be expressed after 10 August in 'La Carmagnole':

> Madame Veto avait promis
> De faire égorger tout Paris...

(Mme Veto had promised / to cut the throats of the whole of Paris)

The brigand turned invader thus became one of the characters in the mythology of a constantly changing 'plot', one of whose villains was the grain hoarder. At the top, these included Bertier de Sauvigny, the Paris *intendant*, and his father-in-law Foulon de Doué, who were accused of being agents in a plot to starve the people. At the lower levels, the suspected hoarders ranged from the municipal officials who defended free trade in grain to the *laboureurs* who stockpiled food and preferred private sales to public ones. Very soon, however, the plot came to be seen in essentially political terms: the first wave of emigration in the summer of 1789, and certain incidents such as the banquet of the *gardes du corps* (lifeguards) at the beginning of the October 'days', helped shape this image into the 'aristocratic plot'.

In the following years this notion – which was sustained by articles written by journalists who were often well informed – became stronger and more diverse: its different stages are marked by such decisive

[21] J. Palou, *La Peur dans l'histoire*.

episodes as the flight to Varennes and the Brunswick manifesto. Linked
with the *émigrés* and a potential traitor, the aristocrat became an object
of suspicion; after the constitutional schism he was joined on the list
of the infamous by the non-juring priest.

These widely shared attitudes for the most part account for the
violence of the crowd during these revolutionary 'days'. We would
be wrong to ignore this behaviour because the old-style historians were
interested only in this violence, and got a lot of mileage out of it. The
'repressive will' which prolonged and surmounted the fear of a plot
took the form of a spontaneous exercise of popular power, which
involved, according to Marat, not only deliberations but also the power
to massacre. The myth of the lamp-post,* evoked in the images of the
time, symbolised this popular justice whose bloody episodes – including
the murders of Launay (governor of the Bastille) and Flesselles (mayor
of Paris), Bertier and Foulon – were the forerunners of the first days
of confrontation. The provinces were not lagging behind – they offered
a more varied picture from which we may perhaps conclude that
revolutionary violence was strongest in areas where there was counter-
revolutionary activity – from Nîmes to Montauban and Avignon.

If the revolutionary crowds were haunted by the notion of a plot,
was it not because this idea was universally accepted? They were paid
back in their own coin, for there was a certain vogue for explaining
rural or urban uprisings in terms of a plot inspired by the Orléans
faction, or even by Marat.

The sociology of the participants

Who took part in the revolutionary 'days'? A simple question, but
one so distorted by traditional answers that it needs reformulating.
According to Michelet, it was the 'people': much more of a myth than
a collective reality. Others, writing after the Commune, projected their
own fantasies on to the Revolution: from Taine onwards we have
become accustomed to the image of a Revolution perpetrated by the
unskilled working classes, the unemployed and the habitual criminals.
After Jaurès, Jacobin historians rejected these myths; since Rudé we
have learnt to study the participants in the Paris 'days' one by one.[22]

It is possible to describe the typical Paris insurgent between the
pre-revolutionary 'days' and 10 August. Not surprisingly, this group

* For hanging aristocrats and others. [Trans.]
22 Rudé (24).

was preponderantly male: on an average 'day' barely a tenth of the participants were women. However, this figure was not constant: on the bloodiest occasions (the Bastille, 10 August) the proportion of women was lower, but on the other hand it rose considerably during the unrest provoked by economic factors in the October 'days' of 1789 or the food riots in the shop doorways in 1792. The crowd was young, but, if one may put it like this, not excessively so; the average age was between 29 and 38 years. They were young men, but mature: a Revolution of fathers of families. Overall, between two-thirds and four-fifths of them could sign their names: a relatively high proportion, but not surprising for Paris. Similarly, the proportion who were not born in the area (about two-thirds) is about what one would expect amongst the people and the petty bourgeoisie of Paris. If we go straight to the heart of the problem – the analysis of the participants according to social class and occupation – we can at once lay the ghost that troubled Taine: the unemployed, the habitual offenders and those without fixed address did *not* form the bulk of the crowd. The proportion of habitual criminals was always lower than a sixth and was generally minute (2% in the shooting at the Champ-de-Mars); those living in lodgings never accounted for more than a quarter, and the unemployed represented a fifth at the most. The most important group, the core of these troops, appears to have been composed of artisans: independent producers (shopkeepers and craftsmen) of the kind to be found in Paris in large numbers. They brought their journeymen with them; but these days of revolt were not led by the 'working class' (an expression which is anachronistic). Although in some precise cases, such as the Réveillon riot, wage-earners were in a majority, they accounted for only a quarter to a third of the participants in the revolutionary days between 14 July and 10 August. The *sans-culottes* were to emerge at the end of the period from this group in which small producers formed the majority and wage-earners a strong minority. It should also be noted that the better-off groups – officers, professional men, *rentiers* – also participated in the movement, but only in a small minority. The relative homogeneity of the group of revolutionaries was often reinforced by their recruitment from the poorer quarters of Paris, notably from the Faubourgs Saint-Marceau and Saint-Antoine, where there was massive participation. Recent research confirms the impressions of contemporaries: 'Yes, we shall always remember the *sans-culottes* of the faubourgs.'

Limited in numbers, the bourgeois element was disproportionately high among the 'leaders' of the movement: Maillard the *huissier* (usher), Huguenin the advocate, Santerre the brewer, Varlet the clerk, Jacques Roux the priest, Legendre the butcher, Hanriot the customs official. This social gap between the crowd and its spokesmen has been emphasised by Rudé in the case of Paris, and it has also been found in provincial towns and in the countryside.

The studies which we have supervised, following Rudé's methods, on the sociology of crowds in Provence (an area very much involved in the Revolution), reveal a pattern similar to that of Paris. In Marseilles, the proportion of independent producers involved varied between 60% and 85% in the years 1789–92. These participants were generally in their thirties, married, and fathers of families. Suitably qualified to take account of local variations, the same pattern can be found in Toulon, Arles, Tarascon and Avignon.

In the countryside, the analysis of the insurgents of 1791 or 1792 inevitably reveals a greater diversity. Behind this diversity, however, recurrent features may be observed, such as the massive participation of the small peasants (*manouvriers* in the north, *travailleurs* in the Midi, wine-growers everywhere); and the important 'provocative' role played by some minorities, including foresters and rural craftsmen such as nail-makers, glass-makers, and, everywhere, weavers. Conversely, certain groups, such as the *laboureurs* from the large farms of the plains, are absent altogether. They were associated with the enemy. Between the two camps, thus defined, the rural petty bourgeoisie (notables in their own social world) of *huissiers*, notaries, schoolmasters, priests who had taken the oath to the Constitution, and sometimes businessmen, played an important organising role. Examples abound in what might be called the leadership of the local *enragés*.

With these leaders, officers or spokesmen, we pass from the level of revolutionary activity as it came into existence – 'crowds' or 'days' – to the forms of organisation which it developed.

The clubs

The Constitution was the means by which the revolutionary bourgeoisie tried to institutionalise the victorious, peaceful Revolution. However, a parallel network of unofficial institutions, groupings and hierarchies also came into existence, and thus exerted an important influence on the course of events.

It is well known that the 'clubs' antedate the Revolution, and that from the 1770s on, discussion groups (*sociétés de pensée*) had multiplied.[23] These societies were in more or less direct contact with the Masonic lodges and were in any case recruited from the same people, but this is not to say that they derived from the lodges. There was a deeper but indirect connection between earlier forms of sociability and the success of the new organisations.[24]

The Jacobin club in Paris, which was to acquire branches throughout the provinces, developed out of the Breton club, a society of deputies to the Estates General. This group, which was led by men like Le Chapelier, very quickly attracted new members from amongst the leaders of the 'patriot' party. The removal of the Assembly to Paris in October 1789 gave the club its base and its title, since it met in the convent of the Jacobins; it also gave it its structure. It was now open to men who were not deputies, though they were still usually prominent figures: the club remained very exclusive, as we can see from the annual subscription of 24 *livres*. The Société des amis de la Constitution ('Society of friends of the Constitution') – the official title of the Jacobins – did not remain unanimous for long. In April 1789 several of the most important Jacobins (Sieyès, Mirabeau, La Fayette, Bailly) founded the '1789 society', though they did not initially make an open break with the Jacobins. This society had a restricted membership. Its aims and its prestige were higher, which meant that it had no direct influence on public opinion. It was more like the English-style club that the aristocratic party was to favour: like the so-called 'Impartial' club with right-wing members (Malouet or the journalist Mallet du Pan), which was replaced, after it broke up, by the Club des amis de la constitution monarchique ('Club of the friends of the monarchical constitution'), which was led by Clermont-Tonnerre and was to last until 10 August 1792.

In the ever-increasing list of clubs that could be compiled for 1790, it was certainly the Jacobins who had the strongest influence on the course of the Revolution. It is true that they were only relatively homogeneous and that their debates were sometimes ineffectual: Michelet called them a 'great society of inquisitors and glib talkers'. However, this glib talk was by no means fruitless. It involved explaining themselves: 'Writing and speaking openly, professing their principles in a straight-forward manner, giving an honest account of their actions, their views and their experiences' and, as a result, making

---

[23] The relatively old study by Cardenal (79) remains of great value.
[24] M. Agulhon, *Pénitents et Francs-maçons dans l'ancienne Provence* (Paris, 1968).

converts and 'providing a centre (for the societies) which are being set up throughout the kingdom'.

This pledge, given early on, led to the expansion of the club: in Paris, it already had 1,200 members by July 1790; this involved a revision of the original structure of the club, which had been a body associated with the Parlement.

Above all, the club spread throughout the provinces to form a dense network of affiliated societies which were to be its strength. These clubs, which often sprang directly from discussion groups or Masonic lodges, had a great variety of names, but the preponderance of Sociétés des amis de la Constitution ('Societies of friends of the Constitution') reveals the influence of the Jacobins. The first of these appeared in the last six months of 1789: in Dijon, Grenoble, Strasburg and Lille, but also in Bayeux, Dax and Castres; middle-sized towns sometimes acquired a society before the regional capitals. There were 152 societies in August 1790, 227 in March 1791 and 406 in June 1791. After this, the crisis of Varennes and in particular the split in the club reduced the number of affiliated societies to about 100, but a new campaign meant that from September 1791 there were again about 1,000. The numbers continued to grow during the period of increased commitment the following year, from September 1791 to August 1792. By the time the monarchy fell, the numbers cannot have been far short of the 2,900 to 3,000 which is the minimum estimate for the peak period which was to come. These are high figures; at this period the chief town of every district – and even of every *canton* – had its popular society, though the distribution of these clubs was far from even. The local style of social life and above all, certain social factors (the urban structure of the village in the Midi), account for the fact that a certain part of the Midi – which includes Languedoc and Provence, and stretches northwards up the Rhône valley and westwards probably as far as Aquitaine – had an exceptionally high concentration of societies: from 60% to 80% of the communes, sometimes even more, were involved, whereas the average level of participation drops to 10% in neighbouring areas (the Alps or the central plateau), which were closer to the national average.

A whole network of connections and communications was established, which could sometimes be used for the purpose of denunciation; one of the essential features of the system was the communication between the societies. The system did not depend on Paris: affiliation to the mother society in Paris was accompanied by numerous other affiliations between various branches. Thus, clusters or networks were formed which played a very important role in activating political commitment in the regions, just as they defined the areas served by the great provincial clubs, like those of Grenoble and Marseilles, to take just two examples.

Some profound changes affected the aims of these popular societies. The stages in this process can be characterised by the following simple schema: in Paris, until the middle of 1790, clubs which reflected the various revolutionary and counter-revolutionary options made discreet progress. Recruitment was still highly selective. In the provinces at this period, societies composed of civil servants and local notables met twice weekly when the post and the newspapers arrived from Paris. This was the phase of apprenticeship.

An early upsurge in activity can be identified roughly between July 1790 and July 1791. This was when the Jacobin club separated itself from the moderate majority in the Constituent Assembly. It was also the period when it experienced not exactly competition but indirect pressure from the fraternal and popular societies which were then multiplying in Paris. They were being set up in every section of the capital; there was even one in the premises of the Jacobins, the Société fraternelle de l'un et l'autre sexe ('Fraternal society for both sexes'), founded by a schoolteacher, Claude Dansart. This was typical of the movement in its early days: it was concerned with literacy and the reading of decrees and official documents, and its members, citizens recruited without discrimination, were addressed with the familiar 'tu'. One of these fraternal societies was to assume a significance much greater than that of a local club: this was the society of the Amis des droits de l'homme et du citoyen ('Friends of the rights of man and of the citizen') which very quickly became known as the Club des Cordeliers ('Cordelier club'). Its members were largely drawn from amongst the people but this did not mean that it was not brilliantly led: Marat, Desmoulins, Hébert and, above all, Danton. The Cordeliers were in the forefront of the movement which turned against the monarchy after the Varennes crisis. They led the central committee of Parisian fraternal societies, and they were the instigators – and the victims – of the Champ-de-Mars petition on 17 July 1791.

This crisis in the summer of 1791 was followed by a period of repression which affected the clubs fairly severely: not only the Cordeliers but also, indirectly, the Jacobins. The Constituent Assembly denied the societies any public existence and forbade them to exert any pressure on established authorities. In fact, however, if the attacks on the clubs continued into 1792, this was because these groups had recovered their momentum and were more important than ever, in spite of the repressive measures. By the end of 1791 the Jacobins had recovered from the crisis caused by the secession of the Feuillants. The parent society preserved almost intact its network of affiliated societies in the provinces; after a short period of uncertainty, the Feuillants were unable to maintain any hold over them. It would be an oversimplification to say that this indicated that the provinces were more 'patriotic' than Paris; rather, it revealed the two conflicting conceptions of the nature of the popular society held by the Jacobins and the Feuillants, who did not attach the same importance to mass participation. In any case we can, with Gaston Martin, identify the triumph of the Jacobins as occurring in the winter of 1791 and the spring of 1792. This triumph was symbolised by the intensity, the scope and the spectacular popular success of the great clashes between Brissot and Robespierre over the question of war. This upsurge of the Jacobins throughout 1792 reflects the general increase in strength of the popular societies in a period of increased commitment. The great debates of the spring, however, seem somewhat academic. In the events of July, it was essentially the Cordeliers, together with the other fraternal societies, who took the initiative in preparing for revolt, although the Jacobins still retained an important role. At this point, at the end of our period, we should try to place the influence of the clubs in a wider context, outside Paris. In the Midi, the 'dictatorship' of the great clubs, like those of Montpellier or above all Marseilles, had never been as well accepted. The local authorities were afraid to act counter to these parallel structures.

The national guards

Finally, we should try to see these clubs and popular societies in the context of the other organisations which developed spontaneously, on an experimental basis, one after another. The clubs represented spontaneous organisations arising outside the framework of the new system of institutions; but another possibility was to make use of certain elements of the new system. This was what happened, from the beginning, in the case of the national guards, who had developed from the bourgeois guards or militia during the crisis of July 1789, and had later become the official militia of the new regime. Their role was undoubtedly ambiguous: the bourgeois militia which showed its repressive side in certain incidents in the provinces in the summer of

1789 (Mâcon) found itself taken over, at the very moment it was becoming the national guard, by the revolutionary dynamism of the streets. This moment is illustrated by the bizarre assembly of the 1789 October 'days': first the women, then the men making a feeble attempt to marshal the demonstration but falling into step with them. In the summer of 1790 these guards of the new order scored more than a passing victory during the movement of the federations and its highpoint, the Paris festival of 14 July. This was also the moment when they came closest to having a direct influence on the course of the Revolution: when La Fayette was tempted to become a new Caesar. The national guard was an organised, structured and hierarchical body, especially in Paris where a 'paid national guard' had been established. At this period it could be seen virtually as the force which defended the new bourgeois order against the fury of the people: the fusillade at the Champ-de-Mars in July 1791 was to illustrate this danger clearly. During the following winter this trend was reversed. In the disturbances of the winter of 1791–2, and the following spring, and in the countryside rather than in the towns, we see the position of the national guard changing: their attitudes ranged from complicity to active participation, which led them to furnish the rioters with officers and arms.

This pattern can be seen in the riots in Paris in the summer of 1792: the Feuillant national guards from the rich quarters of the city were no match for the enthusiasm of the national guards from the popular and Jacobin sections. Amongst the various popular organisations into which popular feeling was channelled, the national guard appears to have followed revolutionary dynamism rather than inspired it.

The birth of the section movement

For the final phase of the period we are studying we can assess the role of another organisation: we refer to the urban 'section' movement which was a typical example of an institution which turned into a bastion for revolutionary activity. In the towns the previous administrative divisions had been replaced by 'sections', in the hope that these new divisions would be less vulnerable to revolutionary infiltration. In practice, in 1792, in other cities as well as in Paris, these local assemblies were held more often and involved a wider section of the community; in the graph drawn up on a day-to-day basis for the sections in Marseilles, this becomes clear from the winter of 1791–2, and between

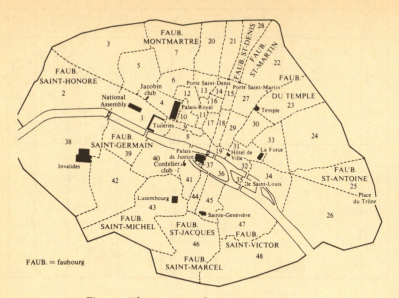

Fig. 22. The sections of revolutionary Paris

the end of June and August there was a spectacular upsurge: the number of people attending 'section' meetings (which were now held every day) rose from under 100 to 200 or 300.[25] This development, which occurred between the beginning of 1792 and the summer of that year, provided the popular movement with a new and essential structure.

The popular movement had its own hierarchy, from the crowd in the street to the formal revolutionary organisations. In a similar manner we shall move from the panic transmitted by rumour to the most elaborate forms of expression of opinion.

Public opinion

In the early stages, in the 1789 campaign for the Estates General, public opinion was expressed in brochures, pamphlets and essays: but also in the Grande Peur, a panic movement in the old style but still very effective. In order to illustrate the coexistence of various levels of collective awareness, we should like to introduce a comparison here. Our example shows that news was spread in two different ways. Let us look first at the Grande Peur which was spread orally, in an

[25] See Fig. 23, which is based on my own research.

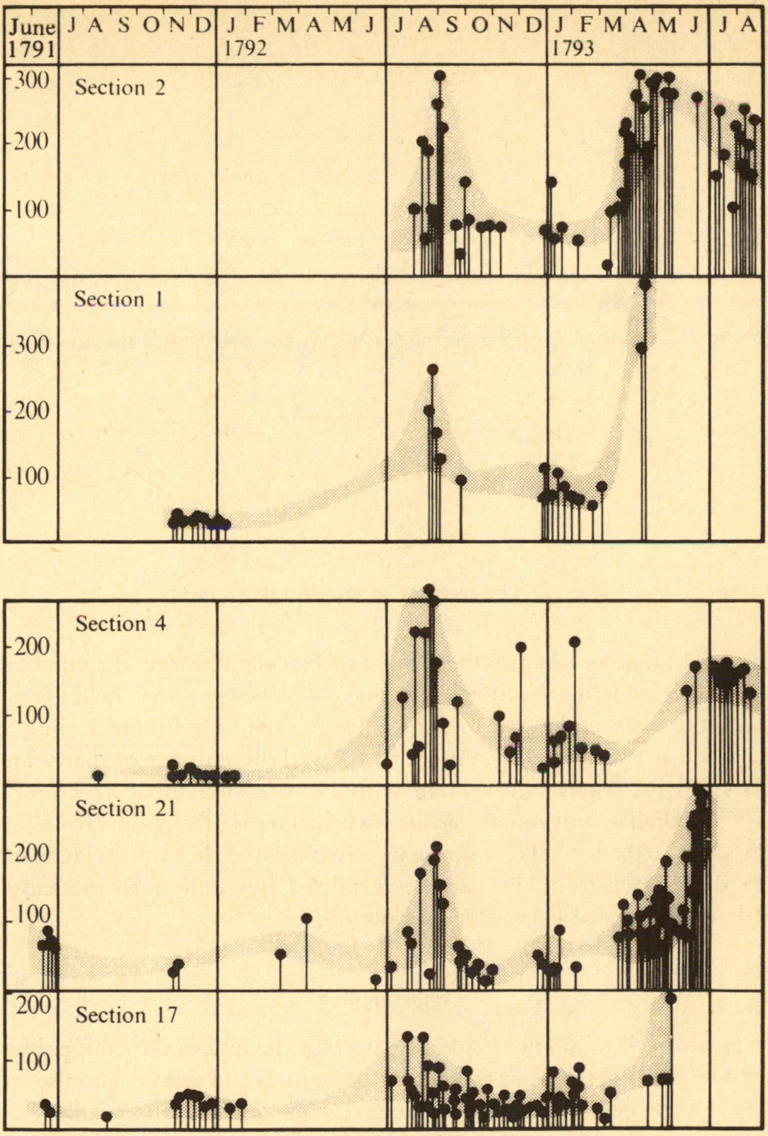

Fig. 23. The rise of the sections: the participation in the sections of Marseilles

uncontrolled manner. Let us follow one of these channels of diffusion in the Alps. The rumour sprang up around 25 June in Bresse, by the 28th it was in Valence; it had reached its farthest point, Cannes and Antibes, by 3 August. In ten days it had covered an astonishing amount of ground: from Livron to Die, to Veynes, Gap, Seyne-les-Alpes, Digne, Castellane, Roquestéron and Vence. On the other hand – although the paradox is only an apparent one – recent work has shown that three years later, in the same areas of the south-east, news speeches and resolutions could take much longer to reach the Assembly: in this case, towns and main roads were again at an advantage.[26] To reach Paris, it took on average approximately 5 to 6 days for papers from Lyons, 9 from Valence, 10 from Marseilles, and 15 from Montpellier. Outside the large towns, the situation was even worse: only the *département* of the Rhône could transmit news in less than a fortnight; the whole of the Rhône valley needed at least a fortnight, and in the interior of the *département* of the Loire, in Ardèche, Lozère, Gard and, on the other bank, in the interior of Isère, eastern Vaucluse and Var, it took about three weeks. News from the Haute-Loire and the Hautes- and Basses-Alpes was seldom received in under a month. Whereas the panic was transmitted instantly, the propagation of orders and news to and from the provinces encountered obstacles and delays, for which the slow pace of the transport system was not the only reason. This impression is no doubt in need of qualification: we have used as an example a 'centripetal' movement spreading from the provinces to Paris. However, if one looks at the maps Reinhard has drawn up to show how the news of the king's flight to Varennes on 20 June 1791 was spread, one can see that even such an important piece of news shows a distinct, if less dramatic, delay: it was a week before the news was known in Montpellier or in Digne.[27]

After these examples it should not be surprising that we should make distinctions between levels of opinion and of news, true or false, transmitted by oral channels. There was the news of the arrival of the brigands in July 1789, of the invaders (in later panics); and in the rural troubles of 1791–2 there was the idea, or the rumour, that the Assembly had passed a decree authorising taxes on grain and bread. The news, true or false, was the converse or the complement of surprising ignorance. In our examination of the attitudes of the masses, we now pass on to its more elaborate and explicit expressions. Songs, plates and playing-cards have their place in the mass diffusion of simple key ideas,

[26] This point is also based on my own research.   [27] Reinhard (84).

and we shall return to them as expressions of a new sensibility. However, at the level of the most elaborate forms of public opinion which was just coming into existence, we have to consider printed matter: books, newspapers and periodicals. To insert them into this context will allow us to appreciate both the significance and the limits of their influence.

The revolutionary press

The first phase of the French Revolution is dominated by the discovery and the quite spectacular exploitation of the possibilities offered by the freedom of the press. The call for the Estates General involved a general invitation for people to express their opinions; they were not slow to do this, as the pamphlet programmes testify, from the best to the least known. In this way the periodical press came into existence. Brissot, who founded the *Patriote Français*, and even Mirabeau came up against the obstacle of the censorship; but this censorship became more and more difficult to impose as the letters which the deputies wrote to their constituencies became diffused in manuscript and in print. The freedom of the press became inevitable.

We need to remember, as has been pointed out, that the journals which could be found in such profusion in Paris at that time cannot be compared to those of today, even from the material point of view.[28] The newspaper industry was still at the craft stage, the work of small printers who sometimes edited the paper as well, the most famous case of this combination being, perhaps, that of Hébert and his *Père Duchesne*. In general, however, the printer worked with a journalist or a team. The case of the journalist who took complete charge of his paper is not unusual. Marat is the most spectacular example: he not only kept up an almost daily production of 1,000 copies of his *Ami du peuple*, but doubled it on occasion. However, editorial teams already existed, organised round one individual, such as Mirabeau, who ran his *Courrier de Provence* with the aid of a brains trust which also helped write his speeches. Even in this case, however, information was unevenly distributed and it was not always communicated immediately either: Marat waited over a month before commenting on the events of 4 August. In any case, information only reached the paper from the provinces thanks to the help of a network of correspondence. In the case of foreign news, the situation was even worse, and the editors contented themselves with reprinting articles from foreign papers. This

[28] Walter (82), and Godechot (81).

incomplete and partial knowledge was better than nothing; friendly co-operation made up for the absence of news agencies. Even when he was in hiding, Marat kept up his contacts by means of a house in the Rue des Canettes. It was possible to be very well informed in this way, and Marat, who was also remarkable for his foresight, reported the treason of both Mirabeau and La Fayette, and even predicted the king's flight; two years before its discovery, the Tuileries' strong-box held no secrets for him.

So much for information. There were similar problems for the editor with regard to the format. Apart from *Le Moniteur*, a newspaper was a small octavo or duodecimo pamphlet, clumsily produced and rarely illustrated (apart from the woodcuts in the *Révolutions de Paris*, a precious source). They appeared irregularly, usually two or three times a week. The print run seems to have been small. It has been estimated that certain issues of the *Révolutions de Paris* reached 200,000 copies, but this was an extremely exceptional case, and the 'average' maximum, if we can call it that, was around 15,000. Mirabeau thought that 10,000 copies was a success: Marat's *Ami du peuple* reached only 2,000. One might smile to see some curé from the Ardèche write to him in the name of thousands of readers from the *département*, but this information, although exaggerated, is a reminder that the journal was read collectively in the popular clubs of Paris, and also in the provincial clubs which used to hold their meetings when the mail arrived from Paris.

The content of these papers was more or less as follows. There was often a sort of long editorial, which was an expression of opinion as much as a commentary on current events. The news was followed by a correspondence column. The only concessions to practical matters in these papers were news about the weather, shows and sometimes a rudimentary form of advertising. People subscribed to these papers, as in the case of the provincial clubs we have just mentioned, but the evidence of prints suggests that copies were also sold by auction or from stalls. No doubt the two methods of diffusion involved different publics and different journals, and the most 'patriotic' section of the press was for a long time virtually confined to Paris.

In this press the extreme counter-revolutionaries were quite well represented. It is true that they inherited some already existing papers (such as the *Gazette* and the *Mercure de France*) and also – still more important, perhaps – some able pamphleteers, of whom the best known is doubtless Rivarol, editor of the *Actes des apôtres*. These men did not lie low: this section of the press expressed itself with violence until 10 August, and journals such as the *Ami du roi* or *Le Petit Gauthier* were weapons in their struggle: journals like these thought that even the Brunswick manifesto did not go far enough.

The most numerous and weighty journals were those of the centre, as we would call it. They included some semi-official journals, such as *Le Moniteur*, which published laws and decrees, *Le Journal logographique*, which reported debates verbatim, or *La Feuille villageoise*, a journal of large circulation in the tradition of the almanacs. In between the journals specialising in information and those specialising in commentary came the open forum of *Le Journal de Paris*. At the beginning of the period the so-called 'patriot' press still seemed undifferentiated: Mirabeau's *Courrier de Provence*, Brissot's *Patriote Français* or Carra's *Annales patriotiques*. As the Revolution progressed, differences appeared, and Gorsas's *Courrier de Versailles* was quickly taken over and paid for by a secret fund of the civil list.

Other papers, on the contrary, became more radical. Among the most incisive were *Les Révolutions de Paris*, a democratic paper edited by Loustalot until his death in 1790, *Les Révolutions de France et de Brabant*, edited by Camille Desmoulins, and Fréron's *L'Orateur du peuple*. Marat's *Ami du peuple* deserves a special place because of its success, its clairvoyance and also its violence, which was not in its style, but in the perpetual attempt to stir the people up. Hébert's *Père Duchesne* was a paper of another type, equally radical in its attitudes, but popular in its style in the racy tradition of the fairground.

The press spread to the provinces: *Le Journal de Marseille*, *Les Affiches de Rennes*, *L'Abeille de Lille*, the *Strasburgische Zeitung* and *Le Courrier de Lyon*. Many of them were to become more and more politically committed under the influence of the clubs, whose opinions they expressed.

This league table of the revolutionary press may hide the intensity of the fight for freedom of expression. In practice, nothing is more revealing than to follow the career of a journalist like Marat step by step. Although Marat was on the run in October 1789 and in June 1790, and again in the summer of 1791, he was protected by the district of the Cordeliers. His life underground should remind us not to speak without qualification of the freedom of the press as one of the successes of this liberal phase of the Revolution. This would be to forget that this bourgeois liberty had strict limits.

The revolutionary festival

The revolutionary festival would seem at least to be the polar opposite of the crowd: a ritual and a celebration of the recovery of unanimity.

In autumn 1789 the spontaneous generation of the festival could be seen; the calm, reassuring festival of the blessing of the flags of the national guard of Paris at Notre Dame on 27 September, but also the unofficial or spontaneous festival of the processions on 5 and 6 October, between Paris and Versailles, when a crowd of women who had gone to Versailles formed themselves into a procession on the way back with improvised emblems: branches, loaves on pikes (symbols of the return of abundance), or the heads of the royal lifeguards (symbols of the defeat of the counter-revolution).

At the end of 1789 a ritual could be seen in the process of creation in the spontaneous movement of federations in the provinces. Imposing assemblies of national guardsmen, from the formal point of view they illustrate another style, which might be called the festival attached to one place and organised around a point of assembly, the 'altar of the fatherland'.

The Festival of the Federation, in Paris, on 14 July, was a synthesis of these new forms. The search for unanimity was expressed in the massive participation of every class (at least this was the official image) in the construction of the earthworks at the Champ-de-Mars. The layout was determined by the taste for the large-scale, for grandeur in the manner of antiquity: the triumphal arch, the terrace and, raised up, the altar of the fatherland, the setting for an open-air show, or rather, for a religious ritual.

Part of the ritual of the festival was invented in the summer of 1790. Henceforward there would be festivals which we might describe as repeat performances of earlier ones, an important fact because it shows that a liturgical calendar had been created, a secular liturgy based on the constitutional Revolution. Thus the anniversary of the oath of the Jeu de Paume was celebrated on 20 June 1790; but it was 14 July, which had become the symbol of the fall of the *ancien régime*, which became the national festival in the annual cycle of festivals of the federation. This is not to say that the ritual had become fixed. There was a significant evolution from the movement of willed unanimity of 14 July 1790 to the 14 July of combat in 1792, in which a prostrate Louis XVI took part in the symbolic *auto-da-fé* of the emblems of the *ancien régime* and of feudalism, hanging from the branches of a giant tree of liberty.

The anti-festival could be found in the march back from Varennes, a reminder in reverse of the return to Paris on 6 October 1789: there was not a word to be heard in this improvised march of mourning: 'Anyone who cheers the king will be beaten, anyone who insults him will be hanged.' In the same way, without looking systematically for a reversal, the imagery invites us to contrast the Festival of the Federation of 14 July 1790 with the dramatic episode of the Champ-de-Mars petition of 17 July 1790. The distinction, which is partly one of convenience, between the 'crowd' or 'revolutionary days' and the 'festival' should not be allowed to deceive us; one passes naturally into the other, preventing the pattern of the festival from becoming a formal one at least at this stage of the Revolution. The massacre of the Champ-de-Mars? A procession which went wrong. Conversely, the sometimes horrible drama which ended in a festival can be found not only in the Parisian 'days', but also in the multifarious provincial episodes which echoed them. At Marseilles, for example, when the local bastille, the Fort Saint-Jean, was taken, the murder of its commander, Major Beausset, followed by his mutilation, ended in a *farandole*.*

The great official liturgies of the period began, in the tradition of the Festival of the Federation, by trying to impose the myth that the Revolution was over. Thus on 4 February 1790 the royal promise to maintain the Constitution was celebrated in Paris and in the provinces, like the solemn proclamation of the Constitution on 18 September 1791. However, the Revolution was already creating and celebrating her guardian heroes, just as she honoured her first martyrs. Some were imposed by events: the funeral of Mirabeau, who was considered a genuine hero, was celebrated in the provincial towns as well as in Paris. The adaptation of the church of Sainte-Geneviève into the Panthéon, destined to receive the ashes of these great men, legitimated this movement. On 11 July 1791, the transfer of the ashes of Voltaire illustrates an art of festival which had already reached its peak: a procession–parade, in which the theatrical element was supported by floats designed by David and by the choirs of Gossec. New in its form, the funeral of Voltaire also marked the end of the illusion of unanimity. In its context – the political crisis following the return from Varennes, and the religious crisis as well – it had the significance of a manifesto.

* Provençal dance. [Trans.]

This breach of unanimity would be felt still more deeply in the months to come, when two series of festivals confronted one another at virtually the same moment. On 15 April 1792 another solemn march celebrated the liberation of the 'patriot' Swiss guards of Châteauvieux, victims of the repression of the Nancy affair. The bourgeois supporters of the Feuillants replied on 3 June by celebrating its martyrs: Simonneau, the mayor of Etampes, killed in the course of a popular riot, and Lieutenant Desilles, an officer who had tried to interpose himself at Nancy. Like the Revolution itself, the festival fell apart, and ended in the tragic ritual of the proclamation of the threat to the fatherland in July 1792, to the anguished rhythm of the salvoes of the warning cannons.

New forms of expression, aural and visual, were thus elaborated, expressing a sense of crisis and suitable for a wide public.

Revolutionary symbols

The festival represents a privileged moment of a diffuse sensibility which permeated everyday life.

Is it already possible to speak, as Godechot does, of new revolutionary 'cults'?[29] The term may be too strong for this particular phase of the Revolution, but there was certainly a new religious sensibility.

There were outward signs of the new revolutionary symbolism. On the one hand, iconoclasm (the burning of the papers and the symbols of the *ancien régime* in the *auto-da-fé* of 14 July 1792). On the other hand, there was the new revolutionary system. Its Ten Commandments was the text of the Declaration of the Rights of Man, which was, significantly, set up in place of the Tables of the Law. There were other visual symbols. The erection of altars of the fatherland, an individual initiative at the beginning of 1790, spread rapidly, helped by the festivals of the federation. The altar was generally associated with the tree of liberty, planted first in the centre-west in 1790 (Périgord, Poitou), and then becoming general: it is said that there were over 6,000 such trees in France in 1791.

These new 'temples' in the open air were symbols of collective decisions. Individual loyalty to the Revolution was expressed, soon after the taking of the Bastille, by the wearing of the tricolour cockade, which was made compulsory for men by a decree of 8 July 1792. The spread of the red Phrygian cap legitimated another stage in the progress

[29] Godechot (20).

of the Revolution. It was already known as a symbol in 1789, but from the summer of 1791 onwards it became the normal headgear of the *sans-culottes* and those who claimed kinship with them. It was only in 1792, when the term *sans-culotte* spread, that trousers and the *carmagnole* (a short jacket worn by the lower classes) acquired a revolutionary significance. The weapon of the *sans-culotte* was the pike, appropriate for hand-to-hand fighting in the street.

Thus a system of revolutionary symbols was elaborated, which drew on Freemasonry (the eye, the compass, and the carpenter's level) and on antiquity (the lictor's fasces) as well as on current events (the Bastille).

A new aesthetic sensibility

The revolutionary sensibility did not express itself in these specific forms alone. It might be said that it impregnated all aspects of life and all forms of culture, whether élite or popular culture. The French Revolution has been described for so long in terms of artistic sterility that it is tempting to go to the other extreme and insist on the impression of abundance which it gives. Of course there was a relative decline in whatever could be linked to the former aristocratic market. Again, its very brevity did not easily allow the Revolution to leave permanent monuments behind it. The buildings of the future remained on the drawing-board of visionary architects like Boullée, and the designs of David lasted no longer than the festivals for which they were intended. On the other hand, the revolutionary climate was a stimulus to a number of aspects of collective production, which was liberated. Freedom of expression opened up two virtually new frontiers, one oral (parliamentary speeches), and the other written (newspaper articles and pamphlets).

More traditional sectors also profited. The theatre was freed from censorship by a decree of 19 January 1791, but already in November 1789 Marie-Joseph Chénier had been able to put on a play directed against tyrants, *Charles IX*. More popular than ever, the theatre vibrated in time with all the main episodes of the Revolution. The public was educated to pick up all the possibly topical allusions, even in the most classic speeches, and it reacted appropriately. It will easily be understood that it was the most unorthodox sectors of expression and communication which were given greatest emphasis. Public speaking has already been mentioned. It found its most noble expression at this time from Mirabeau to Vergniaud, and later in the winter of

1791–2 in the great duel between Brissot and Robespierre concerning the war. The same point can be made about the press if we look at it not as a means of conveying opinions but as a form of expression. In the best articles of Desmoulins or Marat it is not difficult to find passages which are much more important than the events with which they deal.

A duality of language, popular and cultured, is found not only in the press but also in other forms of expression, without really breaking the continuity of an art which for the first time spoke of the Revolution to the élite and to the masses, each in their own language. As for the graphic arts, in their many forms they expressed both the symbolism and the events of the Revolution, and went from the updated playing-card to the allegorical plates which the most popular factories, such as Nevers, put on the market. There were also the popular woodcuts which diffused and interpreted images of the major scenes of the Revolution. Educated people also had their images. The admirable engravings of Prieur, and the pictures of Monnet engraved by Helman, evoked the revolutionary 'days' with a boldness of perspective like that of the great landscape painters and often with an almost pre-Romantic *frisson*, which imbued them with the grandeur of the events themselves.

A similar gradation can be found in music which was also creating a new language. The old tradition of the poetry of protest of the *ancien régime* was easy to modify to fit the needs of the Revolution without losing its freshness:

> Aristocrate, te voilà donc tondu
> Le Champ de Mars te fout la pelle au cul
> Aristocrate te voilà confondu...

(Aristocrat, you have been skinned, / the Champ-de-Mars has kicked you up the arse, / Aristocrat you've had it)[30]

As the Revolution progressed, the songs had more and more bite to them. It was towards July 1790 that people began to sing *Ça ira* to the tune of the national chimes, and the crisis of 10 August in its turn popularised 'La Carmagnole':

> Madame Veto avait promis
> De faire égorger tout Paris
> Mais son coup a manqué
> Grâce à nos canniers...

[30] Barbier and Vernillat (25).

(Mme Veto had promised / to cut the throats of the whole of Paris, / but thanks to our artillerymen, / she failed)

Classical music too had the aim of being 'at once noble and popular' to use the phrase of Méhul's librettist. These new aims were to be found in the *Marche lugubre* (1790) and in the *Peuple, éveille-toi*, which Gossec composed in 1791 for the transfer of Voltaire's remains to the Panthéon. The method employed was a massive recourse to brass and large choirs. Halfway between this orchestral music and the popular song which it quickly became, 'La Marseillaise', composed in April 1792 by Rouget de Lisle, remains the most successful example of the impact of the Revolution on art.

This revolutionary climate seemed to have changed the whole existence of the French. However, it is important to be aware of the limits of its success, or we shall not be able to understand how revolutionary aspirations became more extreme, and how a new programme was formulated very far removed from that of the triumphant and peaceful Revolution.

OBSTACLES: AN IGNORANT OR HOSTILE FRANCE

As we have seen, it is tempting to present a picture of a France reconstructed on the new basis of the power of the bourgeoisie, and, side by side with this, a France in a ferment of social change, its continuous revolutionary dynamism organising itself in parallel hierarchies, and expressing itself in a new sensibility. But it would be unjust to interpret the shift from the first to the second Revolution as no more than a response to these repeated stimuli. It also derived from the obstacles and conflicts which had revealed themselves, and which must be described so as to produce a balanced picture of France at the turning-point of the 'two' Revolutions.

Ignorance

Among the obstacles to the progress of the Revolution, contemporaries would have given first place to what might be called 'ignorant France'. It is possible to trace its contours, with the help of the map of barriers preventing the spread of news (see Fig. 18). The picture which emerges is one of contrasts, firstly between Paris and the provinces, secondly between the towns and the countryside, and still more important, between 'zones of activity', where news was constantly arriving, and zones which were 'inert' or off the beaten track. The presence or absence of roads was very important, but so was the difference in the receptivity of the local inhabitants. Even in the towns there was a split between the active and the passive population. A document like the published account-book of Madame Hamel, a member of the bourgeoisie of Nantes, shows how it was possible to live one's life and take very little notice of the Revolution. This was the equivalent, for the petty bourgeoisie of the towns, of the rural chronicles (many records of the deliberations of the communes take this form) which express complete indifference to everything which is not a threat to man, beast or crop. In spite of this, it seems that one of the moments of most intense concern and participation everywhere was (roughly speaking) that between Varennes and 10 August, although it varied somewhat from place to place. The provinces were on the march, and far from showing themselves to be behind or less dynamic than Paris, as they would do a year later, they were in the vanguard. We are thinking, for example (unprejudiced by local patriotism), of the Midi, which was intensely politicised, and gave an example to Paris by sending men and manifestos.

The obstacles of ignorance had not been removed, but they had never been less important. France had come a long way since the Grande Peur. On the other hand, ignorance had sometimes turned into hostility.

A map of rejection

It is important to trace the contours of the France which rejected the Revolution, on the eve of the decisive challenge which the monarchy failed to meet. In this phase, in which it is not yet possible to study the evolution of public opinion through the polls, it is necessary to have recourse – taking infinite precautions – to documents which offer a snapshot of opinion about a specific issue, and to draw out its implications.

Take the case of the constitutional oath imposed on the parish clergy. It is possible to draw a map showing differences in the percentages of adherences according to region. Sagnac started to do this at the beginning of the century, and local studies have carried on his work for most *départements*.[31] It will be objected that these figures are unreliable, and the point is a fair one. The local administrations rounded off the figures, and passed over many individual reservations and, still

[31] Sagnac's article in the *Revue d'Histoire Moderne* (1906) has become a classic.

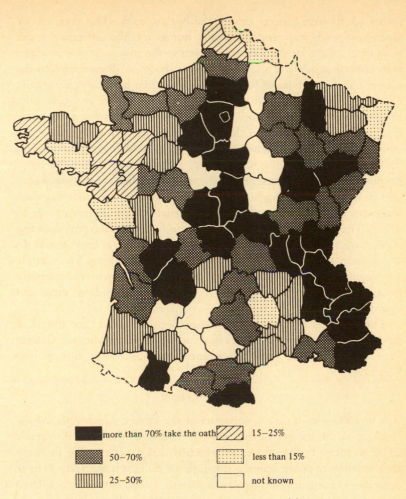

Fig. 24. The constitutional oath: success and limitations

more important, a flood of later recantations. However, if we treat this document as a snapshot, not so much of the secrets of individual consciences but of a state of local opinion (clerical and lay) in 1791, it has considerable value. There are areas dense with rejections, just as there are zones where the vast majority of priests took the oath. The areas where it was rejected most strongly stand out clearly: not only Brittany, Maine and the Vendée, Alsace and Lorraine, but also the

● 10 letters   ⬤ 100 letters

Fig. 25. The French who proposed themselves as 'hostages for the king'

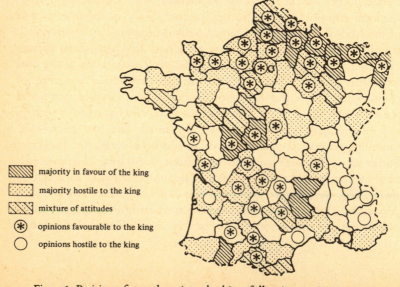

Fig. 26. Petitions for and against the king following 20 June 1792

northern plain, and the Midi (Lozère, Haute-Loire and the Ardèche). Conversely, the oath was accepted most frequently around Paris, followed by a horseshoe shaped region in the south which took in the central Pyrenees, central Aquitaine, and the western side of the Massif Central (Périgord, Limousin, Berry and the Nivernais). Via Burgundy and the Lyons region, this zone was attached to the mountainous area of the south-east Alps, from Dauphiné to Provence. The split is clear, but what does it mean? It is obvious that it reflects the influence of major crises, as in the case of the south-east, where rejections ripple out from Nîmes. Does this mean that the map reveals the split between revolutionary and counter-revolutionary France? Yes and no, for other snapshots both confirm and qualify the impression given by the first one (Reinhard's maps for 1791 and 1792 are extremely valuable in this respect).[32]

If we take each of the moments of most intense activity in these years and study the local responses which reached Paris, we will discover the zones of real revolutionary commitment (congratulatory addresses after the Varennes arrest, the events of 20 June and 10 August 1792) or, conversely, of conservatism (disapproval of 20 June, or lists of citizens who offered themselves as 'hostages' in the place of the king in the spring of 1792). Of course, it all depends on where the document comes from. If it comes from a club it is much more likely to be revolutionary than if it is filtered through local government. We also have to take account of the close and sometimes paradoxical relationships between elected bodies and the rest of the population: in poor areas, in the west, the local authorities were strongly Jacobin, while in the Jacobin area of the Midi they sometimes lagged behind the popular movement. It is only by taking account of these paradoxes that a balanced picture can emerge. Certain regions were decisively hostile, such as the area south-east of the Massif Central, already known as a centre of counter-revolution, and the Breton peninsula, which should soon reveal itself to be the same. Then there were the zones of what we may perhaps call 'disciplined conservatism', in the north and the north-east: unwilling to take the oath, full of would-be hostages for the king, hostile to 20 June and unenthusiastic about 10 August. The remainder of France supported the Revolution. The southern plains, although far from Paris, were highly politicised and expressed a firm attitude. The Alps and the heart of the Massif Central were faithful to the Revolution but distant and thus laconic. The Paris basin followed the metropolis,

[32] Reinhard (84).

and there was a Jacobin zone from Nivernais to central Aquitaine which
turned the flank of the Massif Central and penetrated it from the west.
Attitudes had already set and would long survive the Revolution.
However, we should not be surprised by their ambiguities. Extreme
revolution and counter-revolution often seem to coexist in the same
places, or to dominate them in turn. These regional variations lead us
to ask the same questions about different social groups.

Who are the aristocrats?

Was this a divided society? It would not be artificial, or even
paradoxical, to begin an examination of this question by looking at the
division between the sexes. In a society — even a revolutionary
society — which retained all the prejudices of male superiority, women
play a significant role at various levels: the study of crowds has shown
that the participation of women was particularly strong where
economic demands were predominant. However, the female revolutionary was beginning to move away from the role of housewife;
although she was not always readily accepted, she began to attend
meetings at the clubs, and sometimes founded her own (Claire
Lacombe's clubs for 'patriot' women). The counter-revolutionary
attitudes stirred up by the religious schism were also strongest amongst
women: the street disturbances at the end of 1791 ('dévotes' spanked
under the jeering eyes of the 'patriots') are not just a good story.
However, the split between the sexes was not the most important
division; nor can we say that this Revolution of 30–40-year-old men
represented a revolt of youth against the more mature. Social factors
were clearly important. Who were the enemies of the Revolution?
They were defined by the Revolution itself: 'aristocrats'; but the list
of adversaries grew, so that the non-juring priest and sometimes, by
extension, the clergy who had taken the constitutional oath became
objects of suspicion.

On the other hand, the real supporters of the new regime, so Marat
informs us, were the ordinary people (*petit peuple*), who did so much
for a Revolution which gave them so little in return. By 'ordinary
people' we mean that group which was recruited partly from amongst
the wage-earners but mostly from master craftsmen in small workshops
and from shopkeepers. This group was to give rise to the *sans-culotte*
movement. Between these two opposite poles there are two important
unknown quantities. First, the attitude of the peasantry. It is the country

areas that account for the marked contrasts we have seen on the maps of revolutionary activity in France. The peasants have been accused of being profoundly indifferent, obsessed with their own particular aims, or even fundamentally hostile to the Revolution. In fact the opposite was often true: the peasant population supported the Revolution in so far as this put an end to the seigneurial regime; this is clear from the struggle which was pursued until the summer of 1792: the peasants who participated in the violent actions of the spring of 1792 were genuine revolutionaries. However, the unequal distribution of land during the sale of the *biens nationaux* accounts for local variations in the degree of support for the Revolution: where the bourgeoisie frustrated the expectations of the peasants, conditions were ripe for a counter-revolutionary backlash. In the period with which we are concerned the decisions had virtually been made, but the outcome remained uncertain.

The bourgeoisie appears to have been just as ambivalent, or rather, divided in its attitudes, even though, as we have seen, it had total control over the organisation of the new system. A section of the provincial notables had already become frightened and deserted the cause of the Revolution: notaries, bourgeois and professional men were now to be found amongst the members of the counter-revolutionary movements. The bourgeoisie was essentially split: a shifting but in the end a clear division emerged between those for whom the Revolution had gone far enough, and those for whom this victory implied an alliance with the 'people'. However, this process follows the general pattern of events already described so that there is no need for us to tell the story again.

It is preferable to describe the social bases of all the different groups which rejected the Revolution, and ideally to define the counter-revolution in terms of 'doctrine and action' – to quote the subtitle of a recent study[33] – just as we defined the theory and practice of the revolutionaries.

The ideas of the counter-revolutionaries

The doctrine became more elaborate and more precise in the course of these very years. A hostile interpretation of the Revolution took shape first in the press and then among the *émigrés* and also certain foreign writers. Some of them defined their position in terms of a

[33] Godechot (34).

complete rejection of innovation, like Mirabeau's brother, known as the 'Barrel', the thundering voice of the extreme right. Others retained an ideal which was rather like that of enlightened despotism, except that they wanted to preserve the traditional social hierarchy: these are the ideas which can be found among the orators of the right, like Cazalès, Montlosier and Abbé Maury, as among the first of the *émigrés* like the Comte d'Antraigues, Rivarol the publicist, Comte Ferrand and the former *intendant* Sénac de Meilhan. Some of them had little sympathy for the *ancien régime*, and indeed for the responsibilities of the nobility, while others, forerunners of the 'ultras'* of 1815, claimed to be sympathetic towards the true 'people'. Most of them denounced the bourgeoisie, rejected the very principle of revolution and set store by tradition. Many of them became bogged down in their own mythologies, like Abbé Barruel who launched, although he did not invent, the idea of the Masonic Orléanist plot as the essential cause of the Revolution. Not all of them were so short-sighted, but we have to recognise that the most profound thinker from whom the philosophy of the counter-revolution derived was not born in France but in Britain. Burke was a former liberal whose *Reflections on the Revolution in France*, published in 1790, was immediately translated into French and became the bible of the anti-Jacobins. Jacques Mallet du Pan also deserves a place of his own. He was of Swiss origin, worked as a journalist under the Constituent Assembly and then returned to Switzerland. His *Considérations sur la France* resemble Burke's reflections because their critique of the Revolution goes far beyond the event and looks for the deeper causes.

If the French theorists sometimes seem rather poor stuff by comparison, this is essentially because the true counter-revolution, for them, was a matter of deeds rather than words, expressing itself in conspiracies, networks and attempted insurrections. Without returning to a narrative account we may still distinguish between a counter-revolution of conspirators, dominant at the start, and a more experienced version which attempted more or less skilfully to gain mass support. An example of the first type was the movement directed from 1790 by the Turin committee, a movement which can be seen at work in the conspiracy of the south-east. It was only really successful when it eventually joined up, on the basis of popular slogans, with mass movements in the towns and countryside, typical cases being the urban

---

* Name given to the most conservative group after the restoration of Louis XVIII. [Trans.]

risings of Montauban, Nîmes and Arles, together with the camps of Jalès in the Vivarais. Can we conclude that the real turning-point came at the end of 1791, at the time of religious conflict on a massive scale which gave the counter-revolution, as Furet and Richet put it, 'the infantry it lacked'? This would doubtless mean underestimating the importance of earlier episodes. However, it is certain that new possibilities were opened up from then on by the popularisation of counter-revolutionary slogans.

Generally speaking, the main themes of the counter-revolution at village level were as follows: the defence of the good priest, that is the non-juring priest, and so the persecution of his replacement; a refusal to pay the new taxes; hostility in some places to the new municipal authorities, or if they were on the same side, to the administrators who came from the world of the bourgeoisie of the towns; and finally the beginnings of hostility to the purchasers of the *biens nationaux*. All this led to a vague sense of hostility which sometimes erupted into open conflict. At the end of 1791 only a few zones in the south-east had so far made this transition from the first to the second stage of the 'counter-revolutionary war', and the slow pace of this development reveals the difficulty that there was in combining the aristocratic and conspiratorial counter-revolution with the popular one. Elsewhere, thinking of a shift in collective attitudes which took place in some areas between 1792 and 1793, we spoke of a certain fluidity of rural opinion: in the Catholic Ardèche, for example, where they burned the châteaux in the spring of 1792 but turned counter-revolutionary in the following year; or in Maine, where one thinks of the hideouts of the extremists at the point where the plain and the *bocage* meet. The paradox, we are told, is doubtless a verbal one, and it was not in fact the same people who were to be found in the two camps.[34]

In any case it is easy to understand how the double stimulus of the fall of the monarchy and a foreign war could complete the process of political maturity. In response to the rising danger of counter-revolution, a new revolutionary programme was formulated, with which we will conclude our description.

New revolutionary proclamations

On the eve of the fall of the monarchy, we must listen once more to the language of the Revolution as it was expressed in speeches and in

[34] Bois (36).

the press, for this reveals the atmosphere of the moment. We find that another form of discourse has developed, quite different from that of earlier years. There was no abrupt change: as early as 1789 certain theorists of the Revolution had used this language which seems to be new; but what had originally been the expression of individual opinions had now become the language of a changed, collective sensibility.

To illustrate this, let us follow the development of two typical revolutionary notions: 'the people', and 'violence'. Initially, we only come across 'the people' in the abstract context of national sovereignty. Now the idea has caught on and become part of a collective, unanimous vision: 'The people in a state of revolution are invincible', declared Isnard to the Assembly in November 1791. He was echoed at almost exactly the same moment by Robespierre addressing the Jacobins: 'Tremble, traitors, the people are stronger than tyrants.' A binary opposition was established between the isolation of the oppressive tyrant and the collective strength of the people. A distinction now began to emerge, and the idea of 'the people' developed. Almost from the start, Marat had used the term in a restrictive sense: 'In the state of war in which we find ourselves, it is only the people, the common people, who matter' (*Ami du peuple*, 13 June 1790). He explained: 'What would we have gained by destroying the aristocracy of birth if it is replaced by an aristocracy of the rich?' (30 June 1790). Thus orators who would not always use the same terms joined in the chorus: in January 1792 Maximin Isnard declared that 'The most dangerous class of all is made up of a large number of people who have lost by the Revolution, and in particular a vast number of big landowners and rich merchants, in short, a whole host of wealthy, proud men who cannot stand the idea of equality.'

On 9 July 1792 Robespierre declared to the Jacobins: 'I was tempted to say: liberty has been lost. Then I looked towards the people and I said: liberty has been saved.' Even if it is not spelt out, we can sense a development in the idea of 'the people', defined in a restrictive sense, as custodian of revolutionary authenticity. This discovery was then 'imposed', as it were, by more popular spokesmen; without beating about the bush, Hanriot expressed the views of the common people of Paris in the name of the Finistère section on 31 May 1792: 'For a long time the rich have been making the laws, now it is the turn of the poor, and the rich and the poor should be equal.' In the name of the peasants, curé Dolivier, on 27 April, had defended the *taxateurs*★

★ Rioters who forced bakers and other sellers of food to accept what they considered a
  fair price, as opposed to the market price. [Trans.]

of Beauce in the following terms: 'It is revolting that the rich man and all around him, servants, dogs, horses, want for nothing in their idleness, while he who earns his living by labouring, man or beast, sinks under the double burden of too much work and not enough food.' The poor against the rich, the common people against the landowners: there was perhaps a danger to the Revolution in these conflicts. In the winter of 1792 Jérôme Pétion, who represented the attitudes of a section of the bourgeoisie in all its mediocrity, declared in his famous letter to Buzot that 'The bourgeoisie and the people together made the Revolution: only their united action can preserve it.' This notion was to become one of the main themes of the next few years.

At the same time a new theory, that of necessary violence, was being elaborated, a translation into theoretical terms of the experience and practice of revolution. Once again, this idea was expressed very early on by Marat; in September 1789 he explicitly stated that 'The political machine can only be wound up by violence, just as the air can only be cleared by a storm.' His declaration after 10 August 1792 was directly in line with this: 'Do not be alarmed by words: it is only by force that we can make liberty triumph and assure Public Safety.'

Marat was, perhaps, no more than an orator, isolated from the revolutionary struggle. However, the theme of violence became stronger during 1792 and Vergniaud, who was later to change his mind, expressed it just as emphatically: 'In former times, in the name of despotism, alarm and terror often emerged from that notorious palace: let them re-enter today in the name of the law' (to the National Assembly, 10 March 1792). The Revolution had hardened: it was no longer the moment for sincere professions of faith, as Robespierre pointed out: 'Patriotic legislators, do not condemn suspicion. Whatever you may say, it is the guardian of the rights of the people: it is to the profound sentiment of liberty what jealousy is to love.'

Violent upheavals, terror, suspicion, public safety: a whole new ideological arsenal was being assembled in the course of 1792: a year which takes us straight to the heart of what has been called a 'second Revolution', even if it was only the prolongation or the culmination of the first.

6

The second Revolution

The Legislative Assembly lasted scarcely more than ten months, from 1 October 1791 to 10 August 1792. However, if it were not inevitably subjective and in the long run tedious to seek to identify the phases of least and most intense revolutionary activity, we might well say that these ten months were amongst the most lively and the most decisive of the whole period. They ended dramatically, leaving us with an image of the fall of the monarchy and the taking of the Tuileries by the people in arms; of all the revolutionary 'days' these were the most tense, the ones with least place for spontaneity and improvisation, the ones with the most important consequences. If one examines the day-to-day attendance at local revolutionary assemblies, there is a rising curve of popular participation in the militant revolution stretching from the winter of 1791 to the summer of 1792 – an active period. The year 1792 was one of intense revolutionary activity, which does not mean that the Revolution changed course at this point, or that it took a turn for the better or for the worse. However, it was taking on a new shape: the experiment of constitutional monarchy had soon proved itself to be a failure, and the foreign war helped to make the conditions in which the struggle was taking place even harder. Whether they liked it or not, the bourgeoisie, which was already split into Feuillants and Girondins, was thus forced to accept the increasing importance of the popular movement, with whom one section of the bourgeoisie felt it was essential to collaborate: names such as *sans-culottes* on the one hand, and 'Montagne' on the other appeared at the same time during the crisis of winter 1791–2.

The first six months of the Legislative Assembly were dominated by
the question of war against counter-revolutionary Europe. Traditional
historians – Parisians with a taste for oratory – were understandably
carried away by the great clashes between Brissot and Robespierre. The
decision to wage war, which was desired by some but feared by others,
was to have serious consequences later on. This desire for radical
measures on the part of a certain section of the bourgeoisie reflects above
all a crisis which was both political and social. The drama took place
in France itself.

The Legislative Assembly

It is not difficult to guess that the experimental nature of the new
relations between an uneasy legislative power and an executive kept
on a tight rein was going to pose some serious problems. This was all
the more true because at least one of the partners had no desire to
co-operate at all.

At first sight the Legislative Assembly might appear to be the more
flexible: it consisted of 745 new men, since the decision had been taken
that the members of the Constituent Assembly would not be eligible
for re-election. We should remind ourselves of a few facts about the
Assembly: it was the first modern-style elected assembly in France.
Unlike the Constituent Assembly, it had not inherited the division into
orders characteristic of the Estates General: as a result the aristocracy
was much less strongly represented, and so was the clergy. The fact
that these men were new did not mean that they were inexperienced;
although half of them were under 30, many had all the same risen
through the ranks of the new local authorities. The same 'bourgeoisie'
was again to be found represented: many men of talent, about 20%
of them lawyers, plus some doctors and some military officers. These
groups greatly outnumbered the authentic representatives of the
productive bourgeoisie; however, we are accustomed to this apparent
paradox.

The political shape of this assembly had been established in outline
towards the end of the Constituent Assembly; the right was represented
by the Feuillants, who had more than 250 deputies at the beginning
of the Legislative Assembly. Membership of the Feuillant club signified
an identification with certain common attitudes: attachment to the

Constitution, which they considered to be of their making, and also to the monarchy, though no doubt not in the manner of the aristocrats – those unconditionally nostalgic figures of the *ancien régime* who hated these bourgeois legislators. The Feuillants were above all afraid of any popular questioning of the newly established order; for them the Revolution came to an end in 1791. We again encounter the old split between the Fayettists, who had perhaps become more independent of the king since the disgrace of La Fayette, and the Lamethists, named after one of the members of the 'triumvirate', which flattered itself – presumptuously – that it had the ear of the sovereign in the person of Barnave.

There were distinctly fewer Jacobins: 136 deputies were members of the club. However, they included some of the most talented men: Brissot, a journalist who had been poor for a while but was now successful; Condorcet, the ultimate representative of the philosophy of the Enlightenment; and also the men from the provinces: Guadet, Gensonné and the brilliant orator Vergniaud. These last three were deputies for the Gironde, which gave the group its posthumous name; but at this period they were known as the Brissotins. Amongst the Jacobins there were some who had more marked democratic tendencies, such as Lazare Carnot, Robert Lindet and Couthon (who was paralysed). Others frequented the Cordelier club: Merlin de Thionville, Basire and Chabot – the 'Cordelier trio' – represented what today would be called the extreme left. There were also 350 deputies who did not belong either to the Feuillants or to the Jacobins, but formed the centre of the constitutional party.

Various pressure groups, some more organised than others, emerged and the clubs played a crucial role in this: during this period the Jacobins, with their relatively democratic structure, regained the position in Paris that the Feuillants had taken away from them. The most influential speakers in the clubs were not always deputies – for example Robespierre at the Jacobins – while on the other hand many of the deputies did not frequent the clubs: the Girondins preferred certain salons, such as that of Madame Dodun or that of Madame Roland, who was soon to become one of the leaders and certainly one of the most forceful personalities of the group. As for the Feuillants, the Fayettists in particular found a welcome at the house of Germaine de Staël, Necker's daughter.

A body composed of these elements contained nothing to make impossible the collaboration with the monarchy which the Constituent

Assembly had supported, against the wishes of the king himself. What exactly was going on at court? Fundamentally, the royal family remained categorically opposed to the new order and indulged in considerable duplicity; apart from occasional moments of hesitation, they waited with increasing impatience for order to be restored by the hoped-for intervention from Europe. The clandestine correspondence, with Fersen and with Mercy Argentau, became increasingly important, and it is this which reduces the value of other expressions of the royal attitude. The members of the triumvirate, and in particular Barnave, flattered themselves for a while that they had some influence: this was never more than superficial. We are aware of it in Louis XVI's initial address to the Assembly: a veritable 'discourse from the throne' (Reinhard).[1] He had called for the 're-establishment of order', and here he made his views clear: the consolidation he dreamt of was expressed in terms of economic prosperity, 'social' measures, the education of the people, a programme for the physiocrats. He was in no position to bring this about.

The counter-revolutionary peril

While the attitudes of the politicians remained unclear, the country itself, the provinces as well as Paris, was moving in the direction of increased revolutionary activity. This may have been the result of the flight to Varennes (Reinhard has produced a thought-provoking distribution map of the shock-waves propagated by this incident).[2] In fact, in many places, this increased revolutionary activity was no more than an intensification of earlier clashes: new elements merely increased the bitterness of the struggle.

It was the same for the counter-revolution: in the winter of 1791–2 we find more intense activity in the settings we have come to recognise, while it also gained a hold in new regions, as a result of the religious conflict.

In the Midi, royalist conspiracies stirred up trouble again in the Vivarais, which had already been the scene of the first Jalès camp of 1790. In response to an appeal from the committee led by a noble, Malbosc, the Catholic national guards of the region held another assembly on the plain of Jalès in February 1791; it was broken up and Malbosc was killed, but the conspirators were not discouraged. They hoped that all the royalist areas on the east of the Massif Central would join together in an uprising; without anticipating too much, we can

[1] Reinhard (84).   [2] Reinhard (84).

say that the chances of success for a 'third Jalès camp' were significantly
reduced by the capture, in February 1792, of a number of the leaders
of the south-eastern conspiracy. However, an armed gathering under
the direction of the Comte de Saillans took place at the beginning of
July 1792 at the Château de la Banne. It was completely routed before
it had a chance to take any action. The Jalès camps have attracted a
lot of attention; but it would not be difficult, in this south-eastern area
on which the royalists pinned their hopes, to find equivalent, if
smaller-scale, incidents during the winter and spring of 1792, in upper
Provence as well as in Dauphiné. But it is the urban centres which catch
the attention: in Arles in March 1792 an armed expeditionary force
from Marseilles reinstated the Jacobins and defeated their opponents,
the *monnaidiers*; in Avignon, the murder of the 'patriot' Lécuyer was
matched by the excesses of 'butcher' Jourdan (the massacre of the
Glacière). Stories about the events in Arles and Avignon spread
throughout the same area as tales of the clashes in Nîmes the previous
year.

The religious conflict was beginning to play a significant part in this
increase in revolutionary activity and in the hardening of attitudes; the
supporters of the counter-revolution were very quick to exploit the
split over the constitutional oath. New zones of conflict emerged, not
so much in the Midi, which had been politicised early, as in other parts
of the countryside. Not that the towns were spared: in Paris during the
winter of 1791–2 there were numerous and revealing clashes in which
the non-juring priests organised alternative services and the 'patriots'
responded by beating pious women on their way out of mass. These
are examples of increasing anti-clericalism, among the people as well
as the bourgeoisie, which was leading to the advocacy of the marriage
of priests.

In the towns clashes like these did not further the cause of the
counter-revolution. However, in certain provinces a more serious trend
was becoming obvious. At the end of 1791, the Legislative Assembly,
like the Jacobin club, discussed those areas of 'fanaticism' which were
emerging in the west of France, in Brittany, in the Vendée and
throughout the *bocage* – some of the areas where the non-juring priests
were in a majority. However, this was not the case in all such areas,
as Godechot has pointed out: the east and the north, though equally
hostile to the oath, nevertheless did not turn to counter-revolution.[3]
There were other factors involved besides religious ones, social factors

[3] Godechot (10).

and collective attitudes. We should also take account of purely political considerations; led by nobles like La Rouairie, the Breton association had been working since summer 1791 to create a network of conspiracies in the west. This had little impact in the cities, but was well established in the small towns. The fact that the government reacted by sending spies and then propagandists to this area reveals their growing anxiety at the discovery of an alien France, a France of fanaticism. In spite of Robespierre, who declared that 'we must not launch a head-on attack on the religious prejudices beloved of the people. The people need time to mature', the attitudes of the revolutionary bourgeoisie were hardening.

An economic and social crisis

On the map of this France where trouble was spreading, new centres of discontent appeared: the result of another powerful stimulus, anxiety over food supplies as the economic situation began to deteriorate again. The harvest of 1791 was not a poor one everywhere, only in the Midi. However, regional differences in the economic situation led to considerable resentment. The areas which did not produce enough for their needs raised the cry of famine, while those in surplus did not like to export their grain. Prices began to rise again from the winter of 1791–2 onwards and reached their highest point in the spring. This was not simply the result of the scarcity of food: the effects of inflation were beginning to be felt. Among the popular classes who did not have access to banknotes, the remedies for the scarcity of currency, such as *billon** and promissory notes, produced further problems. This was as much the case in the towns as in the countryside, but urban society, which had acquired new tastes in the course of the century, such as that for morning coffee, took the deprivation of sugar and coffee very hard. These were colonial products cut off as a result of France's changing relations with the rebellious Antilles (Santo Domingo). Some speculators were accused of hoarding these commodities in order to raise their price artificially. To cap it all, there was unemployment. It affected not only luxury trades and the building industry, which were hit by emigration, but also rural industries, such as metal-working in Normandy. Thus a number of factors converged and reactivated the social crisis, going well beyond its economic point of departure. The peasant masses became restive, and the whole agrarian question became

* Currency with a metallic value below its face value. [Trans.]

acute once more. Some problems had been left over from the liquidation of the feudal regime, such as the dues which had been declared redeemable, and were therefore still demanded, despite the conspiracy of the peasant communities to avoid payment. Hence there were repeated conflicts and a revival of hostility towards the nobles which now reached its highest point.

This was the essential pattern. Since the work of Mathiez, the general development of the crisis has been known; however, numerous later local studies have revealed its complexity. The troubles in Paris during the winter are well known, linked to the rise in prices: in January the grocers who hoarded sugar and coffee had their shops pillaged, and in February there was trouble over soap. However, agitation in Paris was of less importance than rural revolts. Here the common denominator was the grain riot. Gangs, sometimes large ones, would hunt for grain and when they found it on the market they would fix their own price. This price fixing seems to have been a spontaneous popular phenomenon but it was subject to considerable local variations which it may not be too arbitrary to divide into two groups.

In the plains of large-scale cultivation – like Beauce – armed bands would leave the poor villages, often situated in the forest, and make for the markets to fix the prices of corn and bread. In some cases the local bourgeoisie took the lead, in other cases they did not. On some occasions, several thousand men were involved. The pattern of the March revolts in Beauce was repeated, with nuances, in the plains of large-scale cultivation in the northern half of France: from Dunkirk to Noyon, to the central Loire region between Tours and Orléans. In southern France, on the other hand, affairs took a different turn. The bands divided into smaller groups and they moved much shorter distances, although this did not prevent the contagion from spreading to whole regions. In the north, the main target was the market; in the south, it was the château. Many of them were burnt as part of a massive movement against the nobility. This movement had a number of centres which are not equally well known but often continued a local tradition of revolt, as in the case of Quercy, followed by Lot, Cantal and Corrèze, and also Morvan, further to the north. The Vivarais, Languedoc, Provence and part of Dauphiné were the areas most affected. The peasant *jacquerie* was here combined with the confrontation between Jacobins and counter-revolutionaries without completely melting into it. On the right bank of the Rhône, the châteaux went up in flames in the southern Ardèche, and also, on a massive scale, in the Gard. Lower Provence was the scene of these troubles in the winter and the spring of 1792, from Arles to Grasse. In the following months, upper Provence and the Drôme region of Dauphiné were partly affected.[4]

It is difficult to draw up a balance-sheet of this winter and spring of agitation, since the data are still known only in part. In any case, the balance would certainly be a premature one, in the sense that the movement continued to gather momentum until the summer of 1792. In general there were two high points of peasant agitation, between February and March and between August and September 1792, while the urban movements reached their peak between May and the beginning of August. It does not follow from this time-lag that the two movements were independent of one another. The result of this series of shocks was a decisive step forward in the politicisation of the masses.

This step forward is revealed in the first place by the reaction of the politicians, Feuillants or even Girondins. Not that they understood everything: agrarian agitation was as alien to them as the discovery of the 'fanatics' of the west. It was a great temptation to lump together and to label 'counter-revolutionary' all those whose actions threatened the respect for law, property, free trade in grain, or the Civil Constitution of the clergy. The symbol of this defensive reaction was the celebration of the festival of the Law, on 3 June 1792, in honour of Simonneau, the mayor of Etampes struck down by the grain rioters, taking 'Liberty, Equality and Property' as its theme. Elsewhere, however, it was necessary to throw out the ballast and concede one of the major demands of the peasants, concerning the redemption of seigneurial dues. It was Couthon, in the spring, who demanded that the landlords should be required to produce their original title-deeds to land associated with these dues. This requirement was so difficult to satisfy that it amounted to the *de facto* emancipation of the peasantry. All the same, it was implemented only in part. It was accepted, on 18 June 1792, only as far as *droits casuels* were concerned.

The 'sans-culottes'

Parallel to this defensive reaction of the bourgeoisie which went from the Feuillants to Brissot, another gradual change may be discerned – the coming of age of the popular movement. In the towns (as in the village

[4] M. Vovelle, *Troubles sociaux en Provence de 1750 à 1792* (Paris, 1971).

risings, led by the national guard) a new political class may be seen
emerging, the *sans-culottes*. In the big cities the sections began to be
frequented by the lower classes and certain clubs such as the Cordeliers
were open to them while the Jacobins were more welcoming than they
used to be. A new leadership emerged from the bottom, in some cases
on the occasion of the spring troubles. The Simonneau affair at Etampes
revived the memory of Dolivier, the curé of Mauchamp, who defended
the grain rioters and put forward an egalitarian agrarian programme.
Curés, lawyers and petty bourgeois, these spontaneous leaders of the
nascent rural *sans-culottes*, had an equivalent in the towns. In Paris
Jacques Roux, curate of Saint-Nicholas-des-Champs, drafted a programme for the spontaneous economic and political demands of the
masses (such as price-fixing and violent struggle), while at Lyons, in
June, Lange in his *Moyens simples et faciles de fixer l'abondance* demanded
a nationally fixed maximum grain price. The programme and the
leadership of the group who were to be called the *enragés* were already
present.

Part of the Jacobin bourgeoisie were aware of these changes and
believed that it was more and more necessary to attract popular support.
It is scarcely surprising to discover that Marat saw matters in this light,
but so, more significantly, did Pétion who wrote a thunderous letter
to Buzot in February 1792 to denounce that section of the bourgeoisie
who were separating themselves from the people:

They place themselves above the people and believe themselves to be on the
same level as the nobility, who in fact despise them and are only waiting for
a favourable moment to humiliate them. They have heard so often that this
is the war between the haves and and have-nots that they cannot shake this
idea off. The people, for their part, are annoyed with the bourgeoisie, are
indignant at its ingratitude. They are conscious of what they have done for
the bourgeoisie, and of the fact that they were all brothers in the glorious days
of liberty.

At the same time, Robespierre delivered to the Jacobins a famous
speech on 'the people...the only support of liberty' suggesting that
the peasants be taken seriously, and that the ordinary people of the
towns should be armed with the pike, 'this as it were sacred weapon'.

Let us not read too much into these declarations. There remained
many silences and misunderstandings. Because these Jacobin leaders
were still attached to the dogma of free trade and market forces they
chose to pass over the spontaneous demand for a maximum grain price.
Even so far as politics were concerned, they remained divided over the
means of ensuring the triumph of the Revolution. This was the moment

of the meeting between Marat and Robespierre, who had a high regard but little affection for each other and did not manage to come to an agreement over the question of violence in the Revolution. The next step was not altogether certain, but all the same new words and realities were making their appearance. At the beginning of April people began to speak of the 'Montagne'. This new trend was expressed symbolically in a festival which was in a sense a response to the fusillade of the Champ-de-Mars: the ceremony of 15 April 1792 in honour of the liberation of the Swiss guards of Châteauvieux, victims of the suppression of the Nancy affair, a ceremony which had greater popular success. However, the new trend was more than purely symbolic. Père Duchesne wrote 'To your pikes, good *sans-culottes*! Sharpen them up to exterminate the aristocrats.' It seems that the Jacobins of Marseilles took him literally, for in March they launched armed expeditions (pre-emptive strikes) against the centres of counter-revolution in the Midi. The renewed bitterness of what Lefebvre has called 'the defensive and punitive reaction' is also to be explained by a change in the political climate which made war the order of the day at home and abroad.

The coming of war

The problem had in fact existed almost since the beginning of the Legislative Assembly. It became obvious in October 1791 at the time of the first clash between the king and the Assembly over a series of decrees which called into question the whole orientation of French politics. The first two of these were already concerned with matters outside the French borders: the decree of 31 October summoned the Comte de Provence to return to France within two months, on pain of forfeiting his rights; this measure was then extended to include all the *émigrés*, who were ordered to return to France by 1 January, otherwise they would be suspected of conspiracy and have their property sequestered. The decree of 29 November seemed to be directed against enemies at home: this compelled the non-juring priests to take a civil oath, on pain of forfeiting their pensions, or even being deported if troubles broke out, at the discretion of the local authorities. Yet another decree (29 November) was aimed directly at the counter-revolutionary powers, since the king was invited 'to call upon the Electors of Trier, Mainz and other princes of the Empire who are harbouring fugitive Frenchmen to put an end to the assemblies and the recruitment which they tolerate on their border'.

This is the political background to one of the greatest debates in the history of the Revolution, second only, perhaps, to the trial of the king. Many were aware, correctly, that the whole future of the nation was at stake. It is understandable that historians of the Revolution have dwelt on these oratorical jousts in which the great men of the Revolution declared their positions. We are more reluctant than historians of fifty years ago to say that Robespierre was right or that Brissot was wrong: each appears to have played his role in a complex political game. Everyone was aware that this series of decrees was leading directly to external conflict, and they reacted accordingly.

Those who promoted the decrees wanted war, and first among them were the supporters of Brissot. The two intellectual leaders of the group at this time were Brissot himself and Condorcet. Brissot's adventurous career as a journalist had given him a favourable reputation and an aptitude for diplomacy; Condorcet, who was better established and had a calmer personality, had retained his connections with the business world from his days as director of the Mint. These men managed to express the ideas of the pressure groups which, as we have mentioned, surrounded them. One such group was composed of cosmopolitan refugees such as the Genevan banker Clavière; another was connected with the business world – commerce and finance – and was in close contact with the Girondin group. Connections such as these do not detract from the sincerity of the leaders of the Brissotins but they enable us to have a better understanding of the options facing the section of the bourgeoisie that the leaders represented. They wanted to fight for two reasons. At home, they no doubt expected that war would expose treason, even at the highest levels: 'Let us mark out a place for traitors, and let that place be the scaffold' (Guadet). They also thought that war would revive the economy, by increasing demand, and that this revival of business would be a stabilising factor. These various arguments appealed to different milieux. In addition to these reasons there was a deeper one, less dependent on the current climate: this was the idea that war was 'a national blessing' and that the Revolution would only have triumphed 'when it had offered Europe the spectacle of a free nation which sought to defend and maintain its liberty' (Brissot, 16 December 1791). We could, like Soboul, examine this Girondin notion of the national interest and observe, from the speeches themselves, how closely it corresponded to the interests of the French bourgeoisie in the face of the European aristocracies. Girondin romanticism was counting on the lack of unity amongst the powers and the readiness of the people to rise in the name of liberty to achieve an easy victory.

Brissot's policy was to receive unexpected support: in the first place from La Fayette and his group. We may suspect that their motives were different: General La Fayette, who was an odious figure to the court, had failed in the autumn to become mayor of Paris. The coalition between the Jacobins and the aristocrats who were attempting to turn disaster to their advantage had resulted in Pétion gaining this key post, which delighted the queen. 'Even if things are going too far, we can exploit the situation.' With an army on the frontier, La Fayette hoped that a victory in war would put him in a strong position: with an army behind him he would be able to assert himself *vis-à-vis* the king as well as the Assembly.

In this general climate of deceit, the court took a different line. The queen had pinned all her hopes on the intervention of foreign powers, and in her correspondence with Fersen she expressed her joy at the idea of conflict: 'The fools, can't they see that this is helping us!' Believing, as the king wrote, that 'the physical condition and morale of France is such that it will be unable to sustain even half a campaign', the royal family pressed for war; all the same, its very duplicity meant that it had to temper its apparent attitude, since it had at least to seem to be taking notice of its over-obliging counsellors from the Lamethist party.

The members of the triumvirate had made a realistic assessment of French forces and of the internal divisions, and as a result they were anxious not to risk military involvement. They were increasingly close to the Emperor Leopold, with whom they were secretly in correspondence, and they relied on him to stabilise the situation by peaceful means. The king pretended to follow their directions so as to deceive them, and it was at their instigation that he adopted a measured attitude towards the four decrees of the winter of 1791–2. In order to rally conservative opinion he vetoed the decrees relating to the non-juring priests and to the *émigrés*; so as not to clash head-on with national opinion, he agreed – without too much difficulty – to invite his brothers to return to France and to prevail on the Elector of Trier to break up the meetings of *émigrés*. However, whereas his ministers, like the members of the triumvirate, were hoping to defuse the international crisis, the king secretly hoped that the ultimatum would be rejected.

It is in this climate of uncertainty that the intervention of Robespierre should be placed, together with the famous oratorical duel in which he opposed Brissot in the Jacobin club. Robespierre read the situation in the light of the ambiguous attitude of the king: for three months, from December to February, he argued against his opponent. He pointed out that the army was in disarray and that the Revolution was in danger: it needed strengthening against its enemies before it could be spread. He did not share the optimism of those who hoped to see the people rise up in the name of liberty: 'No one likes armed missionaries.' He was disturbed by the suspiciously unanimous support for war: he did not think this was a good sign and, pursuing to the end the thankless task his clear-sightedness imposed on him, he predicted that even if France was successful in war, the country would be at the mercy of a victorious general. In his speeches of winter 1792, Robespierre emerged as the most lucid leader of the revolutionary avant-garde, but he remained isolated even in his own group, and his success was limited to a certain public.

The 'hawks' had the last word: we can agree with Lefebvre – who can hardly be suspected of sympathising with the Brissotins – that in this 'march towards war' the responsibilities were divided.[5] It is true that the Emperor Leopold put pressure on the Elector of Trier to comply with the invitation to disperse the gatherings of *émigrés*, but at the same time he made renewed threats; in particular he pursued negotiations with Prussia to launch a joint offensive. When he died, on 1 March 1791, agreement had virtually been reached; the new emperor, Francis II, who was said to be stiffer and less 'liberal', had only to move into action.

The Jacobin ministry

This was all the partisans of war in France needed. The note from the Emperor announcing that the gatherings of *émigrés* had been dispersed was met with renewed demands. Narbonne, the minister for War and a representative of the Fayettists, was pushed forward in opposition to Delessart who spoke up for the policy of the triumvirate at the ministry of Foreign Affairs, and Bertrand de Molleville, who was an unconditional supporter of the royalists. One side declared that the army was ready to take the offensive, while the other persisted in advocating peace. The bellicose Narbonne was dismissed, but there was a general outcry in the Assembly, from the Fayettists to the Brissotins. The minister Delessart was accused of 'cowardice and weakness beneath the dignity of a free people', and it was decided to arraign him before the High Court.

[5] Lefebvre (12).

In spite of the Lameth group who advised him to take a firm line,
Louis XVI did reach a compromise with the Brissotins. He dismissed
his Feuillant ministers in favour of a 'Jacobin' ministry. This contained
Girondins, for example the minister of the Interior, Roland, a former
inspector of factories, and the banker Clavière, who was Finance
minister; but the strongest member of the team was Dumouriez, who
was responsible for Foreign Affairs. He was a general who pretended
to support the Jacobins but who had offered his services to the court
in order to realise La Fayette's dream: a short, successful war, followed
by a return at the head of an army to restore the authority of the king.
Although no one could rely on Dumouriez, he had the advantage, for
the moment, of being liked by almost everyone. Certainly by the king
and the Girondins since he was pressing for war, and the Brissotins
toned down their attacks on the court. Only Robespierre denounced
them as 'intriguers' who had deserted the revolutionary cause.
However, this division which would lead to the split between the
Girondins and the Montagne was not yet particularly significant: when,
on 20 April 1792, Louis XVI proposed to the Legislative Assembly that
they should declare war on 'the king of Bohemia and Hungary' (a
stylistic device, and an illusory precaution so as not to involve the
Empire), they almost unanimously – with only twelve votes against,
either Lamethists or supporters of the Montagne – committed themselves enthusiastically to war.

This was to give the French Revolution a new dimension, and it
was also to change its course and its own internal dynamic. It is too
easy for us, with the benefit of hindsight, to say that none of those
who had advocated war got the war they had dreamt of.

FROM WAR TO THE FALL OF THE MONARCHY (20 APRIL TO 10 AUGUST 1792)

The period of setbacks

The most clear-sighted had realised that success could not be taken for
granted. Diplomatically, France was isolated, without the support of
her traditional allies. The negotiations conducted in London by
Talleyrand had come to nothing, and the most France could hope for
was that certain powers would remain neutral (Spain and Sweden, since
the death of Gustavus III).

The presence of foreign refugees – from Belgium, the Empire, Switzerland and Savoy – offered the possibility of conducting a subversive propaganda campaign against the kings. But the war of subversion needed to be initiated with an offensive.

We have discussed the disorganised state of the army of the *ancien régime*, and no new force had yet properly taken it in hand. What is more, there was a crisis at the highest levels: the officers – generals of the *ancien régime* and in the old style – could only conceive of a traditional war. The lack of organisation amongst their troops daunted them, and their political sympathies, which were at best Fayettist, made them cautious about the war and even more cautious about what was going on in Paris. The result was that they failed to exploit the apparently favourable situation in the north, where the Austrians had only about 30,000 men to defend Belgium, which was said to be ready to revolt. Under the command of Rochambeau, an old-style veteran from the American wars, Lückner, an old mercenary, and La Fayette, more of a politician than a soldier, the march of the French columns, which should have converged, went wrong: in the centre, the column which had set out from Lille to take Tournai fell back in disorder and lynched its general, Dillon, whose incompetence and equivocations had been patently obvious.

As a result, the generals suspended the offensive, and in May whole corps, such as the Royal-Allemand (Royal German corps), went over to the enemy. Rochambeau resigned, and La Fayette, who was moving closer to the Lamethists, went as far as open treachery: he secretly proposed to the Austrian ambassador, Mercy Argentau, that fighting should be suspended so that he could turn his army against Paris in order to disperse the Jacobins and establish a strong regime. As it happened, military operations were suspended by an agreement between the generals. In Paris, people felt that there had been a betrayal. They were quite right, even though they had no real evidence: the queen had handed the French army's campaign plans to the enemy. Those who spoke out – Marat and the Cordeliers – were forced to be silent. Robespierre, however, solemnly declared to the Jacobins: 'I do not trust the generals...I say that almost all of them are nostalgic for the old order of things...I have faith only in the people, the people alone.'

The failure of the Girondins

The attitude of the Girondins in power was much less clear-cut. At first they tried to negotiate with La Fayette, and they attacked all those, from Marat to Robespierre, who denounced the betrayal, just as they tried to strengthen military discipline. In these actions we can already see signs of that instinctive fear of the popular movement that was soon to dominate the outlook of the Girondins.

However, these overtures to the right were unsuccessful. La Fayette pretended to take no notice of Roland and his friends. They were therefore forced back towards the left and drawn into bitterly denouncing what Brissot and Vergniaud called the 'Austrian committee': an expression which referred to certain groups at court, and in particular the queen. Brissot and Vergniaud were even led to suggest that violent measures should be taken to deal with these traitors at home. They also emphasised the need for a patriotic commitment as described by Roland, in a truly grand manner, in a famous letter to the king on 10 June: 'The fatherland is not just a word embellished by the imagination, it is a reality for whom we have made sacrifices and to whom we become daily more attached as a result of the concern it causes; it has been created by great effort, and it rises up in the middle of our anxieties; it is loved as much for what it has cost as for what is expected of it.'

These moments of inspiration, panic, audacity or sudden withdrawal are a true reflection of the equivocal attitude of the Girondin bourgeoisie; as we shall see in a moment.

The fact that the Girondins had returned to a policy of intimidation was revealed by a new series of revolutionary decrees: on 27 May the Assembly issued a decree to the effect that any non-juring priest could be deported at the simple request of any twenty 'active' citizens; on 29 May another decree provided for the disbanding of the 6,000 men of the king's constitutional guard; finally, on 8 June, at the request of Servan, the minister for War, a further decree authorised the levy of 20,000 *fédérés* in the *départements* to attend the celebration of the Federation, and then to form a camp near Paris. This was an important measure, and no doubt an ambiguous one since many were suspicious of it: Robespierre, for example, who mistakenly saw it as an attempt by the *départements* to oppose the Revolution in Paris; and also the 2,000 Fayettist national guards from the bourgeois quarters of the capital who, with greater justification, petitioned against this proposed intrusion.

Future events, however, were to show that the Girondins themselves had misjudged these *fédérés*.

These decrees renewed the conflict between the Girondins and the king. Louis XVI accepted the disbanding of his guard, but vetoed the decrees relating to the non-juring priests and the *fédérés*. This was what earned him the fine admonition from his minister of the Interior from which we have already quoted the passage about the patriotic spirit. These were just words. Thinking he was safely supported by the generals, the king dismissed the Girondin ministers Servan, Roland and Clavière; he kept Dumouriez but he was clever enough to get out while he could and went off to join the northern army. The new ministry was composed of little-known Feuillants, whilst the Assembly decreed that the ministers who had been dismissed should take with them the confidence of the nation.

Had La Fayette's moment arrived? On 16 June he wrote to the Assembly from the frontier to denounce the anarchy that he claimed was being sustained by the Jacobins, 'sedition mongers at home' who were as dangerous as the enemy abroad. Faced with the threat of a *coup* from the royal family or the Feuillants, the Girondins were to try to utilise the popular dynamism evident in the Paris sections. Pétion, the mayor of Paris, was sympathetic to their cause, and helped them in their task, while Robespierre and the most active members of the revolutionary movement in Paris tried in vain to denounce what seemed to them a premature move.

The 'day' of 20 June

It turned out that they were right: on 20 June the people of the *faubourgs* took up arms, and, under the leadership of men like the brewer Santerre, they invaded first the Assembly then the Tuileries – though there was no bloodshed. With his own particular brand of passive courage the king submitted himself without flinching to the long procession of the people. He put on the Phrygian cap and drank to the health of the nation: this was perhaps a way of swallowing the bitter words of Legendre: 'Sir, you are a traitor, you have always deceived us and you are deceiving us again.' However, he did not withdraw his veto, nor did he recall the Girondin ministers.

This improvised day of action achieved nothing, and appeared to leave everyone in disarray. We must now look at the state of the various political factions involved in the contest which followed.

La Fayette left his army and appeared before the Assembly on 28 June, demanding that measures be taken against the Jacobins: the left did not manage to obtain a vote of censure for this act of indiscipline. However, the general was equally unsuccessful in what Massin has called his '18 Brumaire': he was not supported by the court (the queen informed Pétion of his plans), and the Parisian national guard from the bourgeois quarters did not turn up to the meeting he had arranged. He still did not give up. He invited the king, in vain, to flee to Compiègne where he had massed some troops, but the king, who was expecting something better, was not interested in putting himself under La Fayette's protection.

The Girondins were also in a state of confusion, or at least irresolution: their policy of intimidation had failed, Pétion had been suspended from his duties as mayor, and the leaders of the party, Brissot and Vergniaud, were oscillating between the denunciation of the royal treachery at the beginning of July and the attempt to reach an agreement with the king; when the Feuillant ministry was worn out by their attacks, Guadet, Vergniaud and Gensonné secretly made contact with Louis XVI. The king did not discourage an initiative which was useful to him; from then on the Brissotins modified their outlook and disowned the popular movement, which was increasingly calling for the removal of the king: they abandoned their recent attempt to gain popular support.

This survey might suggest that the king, too, made some serious errors of judgement, and that he let slip several opportunities. Let us say that he played his hand, which consisted of pinning his hopes on the success of foreign armies. This passivity, which had triumphed on 20 June over the demonstration by the people, was noticeable again on 14 July 1792 at the third annual festival of the Federation: the monarch, who was no longer acclaimed by anyone, had insisted on being present, it was said 'as if he were at a sacrifice'; but he had lost the initiative, and so had La Fayette and the Girondins. It was the turn of the popular movement.

The eve of 10 August

In July 1792 France looked like a country under arms. The rural revolt of March was more or less over in most places, although it would revive in August and continue into the autumn. When the countryside became quiet, the towns took over. Vergniaud was to write to Louis XVI on

29 July: 'A new revolutionary explosion is rocking the foundations of a political system which has not had time to consolidate itself.'

There are many signs of this upheaval. It was only on 25 July that the Parisian sections were made permanent. However, in the major provincial cities, as in the capital, these assemblies had begun to meet much more frequently. Their numbers were also increased by the participation of the 'passive' citizens, the *sans-culottes* for whom pikes had been demanded. This was the moment of the greatest influence of the major political clubs, both in Paris and in the provinces. It was not just a time of debate: the townspeople also took to the streets on a more massive scale than ever. In the Midi, which was then in the vanguard of the Revolution, people were hanged in both Marseilles and Toulon, often local administrators: municipal officials, *Conseillers généraux*, and members of committees running districts and *départements*. This reveals the split between the leadership, which was Feuillant or even openly counter-revolutionary, and the people, who set up their own parallel hierarchies.

The supporters of the Revolution were riding high, excited rather than frightened by the beginning of the war, as one could tell from the presence of the *fédérés* and others on the road. These armed troops, who were converging on Paris, were carrying out an order decreed by the Assembly and vetoed by Louis XVI. However, on 2 July the Assembly had bypassed the king's decision by ordering the *fédérés* from the *départements* to attend the 14 July festival in Paris and then to go to the camp at Soissons. This last precaution was almost superfluous since the troops were already on their way, despite the veto, as in the case of the 500 men of the Marseilles battalion, on 2 July itself. From all parts they converged on the capital. Some, such as the group from Toulon, arrived in time for 14 July, while the Bretons from Finistère turned up on the 25th and the men from Marseilles on the 30th. These last made their presence felt from the start by clashing with the pro-La Fayette national guard. This physical presence of the Revolution 'on the march' was marked by a new atmosphere. New ideological weapons were being forged in the fire of action.

Patriotic and democratic movements

Thanks to the war, patriotism became one of the mainsprings of revolutionary unity. This patriotism was expressed in the 'Chant de guerre de l'armée du Rhin' (War song of the Rhine army), a song composed in Strasburg by Rouget de Lisle which was to acquire its definitive name of 'La Marseillaise' in a detour to the south, and would then be popularised by the *fédérés* of Provence on their march and their entry into Paris. Soboul has noted the close association between the patriotic theme ('sacred love of the fatherland') and the revolutionary theme of war against 'vile despots' and 'ancient slavery'.[6] More topically, there was the theme of the plot, the denunciation of traitors, parricides, 'hordes of slaves' or 'accomplices of Bouillé'. However, Reinhard has also noted that this hymn of liberation is free from 'chauvinism', *avant la lettre*,* and is addressed to all peoples who are still subject to tyranny or enslaved.[7]

This patriotic impulse, which would lead to the rise of national consciousness, was formalised in the proclamation of the 'fatherland in danger'. This was discussed by the Assembly in the first days of July, and the political content of the measure allowed the Assembly to bypass the royal veto without breaking the law. However, the proclamation meant much more than that. It had what Roederer the *procureur syndic* of the *département* called a 'magical effect'. The proclamation itself helps us to understand what he meant:

A large force is advancing towards our frontiers. All those who hate liberty are taking up arms against our Constitution. Citizens, the fatherland is in danger! Those who wish for the honour of marching in the front line to defend what they hold most dear should never forget that they are French and free. Their fellow citizens should maintain the safety of persons and property at home. The magistrates of the people should be on the watch. With calm courage, the sign of true force, everyone should await the official signal for action and the fatherland will be saved.

Then, on 22 July, came the ritual of the reading of the decree in the public squares to the sound of the warning cannon, followed by the enrolment of volunteers – more than 15,000 in Paris alone. This amounted to a psychological conditioning which should not be underestimated.

This was of course a patriotic reflex, but it had definite political repercussions. Had not Louis XVI proved himself to be a traitor? Was a king necessary at all? Despite those in Paris and in the provinces who condemned the outrage to the king on 20 June, and despite Brissot's last speech denouncing 'the regicide faction which wishes to create a

[6] Soboul (14).
* The word is derived from Nicolas Chauvin, a nationalist of the Napoleonic era. [Trans.]
[7] Reinhard (84).

Republic...[while]...men attach to the name of "king" a magical virtue which preserves their property', the removal of the king became more of an issue than ever before. Petitions demanding it came not only from the sections and clubs of Paris but also from the provinces, whether directly or via the *fédérés* who had come to town.

Indeed, it seems likely that the first initiatives came from the provinces: from Marseilles on 27 June, then from Montpellier, from Angers on 18 July, and so on. The *fédérés*, who were very soon officered by the Paris organisations – at the Jacobins Robespierre was extremely concerned with this and a central committee of *fédérés* was set up – petitioned for the king's removal. Their initiative coincided with that of the clubs and sections. At the Cordeliers a motion demanded the convocation of a 'Convention' to give France a new constitution (15 July), while at the Jacobins on the same day Billaud-Varenne demanded the deportation of the king and the convocation of primary assemblies on the basis of universal suffrage. The Paris sections followed suit, the first being the section of Mauconseil which on 31 July declared that it no longer recognised Louis XVI as king. On 3 August Pétion, the mayor of Paris, went to the Legislative Assembly to demand the removal of the king in the name of 47 out of 48 Paris sections. On 9 August a majority of the Assembly rejected his demand. In the face of this dilatory attitude, the initiative passed to the people in arms.

The fall of the monarchy

Amongst the immediate causes of the 'day' of 10 August, what has become known as the 'Brunswick declaration' has an important place: however, it is clear that even without this trigger the situation was ready to explode. This manifesto was drawn up by an *émigré*, the Marquis de Limon, on 25 July 1792; it was thought preferable to the more political text that Mallet du Pan had written for the Feuillants, and the Duc de Brunswick who commanded the coalition agreed to sign it. The chosen text did not err on the side of tact, promising that if the 'least outrage to the royal family' was perpetrated, 'exemplary vengeance' would be exacted, by 'handing over the city of Paris to the soldiery, and punishing the rebels as they deserved'. This was all that was needed to complete the mobilisation of a public which was far from experiencing the panic expected by the authorities.

Both sides prepared for confrontation. Only the Legislative Assembly remained irresolute, failing to examine the petitions for the removal of the king and not committing itself, even as late as 8 August, to condemning the attitude of La Fayette. It lost the initiative: at the end of July a popular committee for insurrection, containing both 'patriots' and *fédérés*, was formed to organise the revolt. On 4 August the section of the Quinze-Vingts issued a final ultimatum declaring that if the Assembly did not comply with the wishes of the people the tocsin would sound at midnight on 10 August. It has been noted (by Lefebvre and by Reinhard) that this attitude, which in retrospect appears to have been aggressive, owes a great deal to the fear of an aristocratic plot, and not without reason.[8] The other side were also prepared for a struggle which they thought they could win. Noblemen gathered at the Tuileries where the Swiss guards were concentrated; they were also counting on the support of the Feuillant battalions of the national guard from the bourgeois quarters.

During the night of 9 August, when the ultimatum expired, an 'insurrectionary Commune' was set up at the Hôtel de Ville. It was composed of delegates from the Paris sections and replaced the official municipal corporation. Pétion agreed, without reluctance, to be kept out of the matter. In the morning the national guard from the 'patriot' *faubourgs*, together with the *fédérés* led by the men from Marseilles, marched to the Tuileries. They had an unexpected stroke of luck in the defection of the national guards who were supposed to be protecting the château, which was now defended only by the nobles and the Swiss guards. However, the men from Marseilles then encountered sustained fire from the Swiss guards; they were kept back for a while but finally made the assault, together with the *sans-culottes* of the *faubourgs*. At ten o'clock, on the orders of the king, there was a cease-fire, but not before many of those defending the château had been killed.

Roederer, the *procureur syndic* of the *département* and a man of Girondin sympathies, had early in the day taken the royal family to the Assembly, which was then sitting at the Manège. The king was received with respect, as a monarch, but when the success of the popular uprising became clear his functions were suspended. The Legislative Assembly recognised the insurrectionary Commune of Paris, which, for its part, allowed the Legislative Assembly to remain in being until the formation of a National Convention elected by universal suffrage which would decide on the fate of France and of the monarch, interned by the Commune in the Château du Temple.

[8] Lefebvre (11), and Reinhard (84).

A new era in the French Revolution began on 10 August: the events of the day itself show what a distance had been travelled since July or October 1789. This was a premeditated, organised uprising with common slogans and a precise, collective aim: it bore witness to the maturity of the popular movement.

In three years the monarchy had been destroyed and a new adventure was now beginning: the so-called Revolution of Equality which replaced the bourgeois Revolution of Liberty.

This does not mean that the social composition of the movement changed radically, but henceforth its control was gradually to be wrested from the fraction of the bourgeoisie whose vision had been of an impossible compromise between the notables and the aristocracy of the *ancien régime*. For the bourgeoisie of the Montagne, which was shortly to become dominant, 10 August was a test of the popular support which seemed to them to be one of the tokens of the Revolution's survival.

Glossary

Acquits au comptant	practice in the royal Treasury which allowed the king to take money for his personal needs without having to give an account of it
alleu	allod, freehold land involving no duties or restrictions
ancien régime	the political and social system of France before the Revolution
arrentement	tenant farming, see *fermage*
assignats	paper money issued during the Revolution
aveu et dénombrement	(literally 'avowal and enumeration'), declaration by a vassal, when he acquired a fief, of his obligations to his lord
bailliage	administrative division of northern France under the *ancien régime* (cf. sénéchaussée)
biens nationaux	property which was nationalised, i.e. appropriated by the State and sold off during the Revolution
bocage	(literally 'woods'), the small enclosed fields of western France
cahiers de doléances	lists of grievances for submission to the provincial estates or, after 1789, the Estates General
Caisse d'escompte	Discount Bank, founded in Paris in 1776
canton	administrative division (midway between an *arrondissement* and a commune), set up during the Revolution in 1790
cens	cash payment to a seigneur by a non-noble tenant
chambres des enquêtes	three chambers of the Parlement concerned with criminal cases
chambre des requêtes	chamber of the Parlement concerned with civil cases
chambre des Tournelles	chamber of the Parlement concerned with capital offences
chambrelan	craftsman who was not a member of a guild and worked secretly in his room (*chambre*) rather than in an open shop

champart	rent or dues paid in kind and calculated as a fraction of the harvest
chiffonistes	a counter-revolutionary faction in Arles
Chouans	Breton peasants who rose against the Revolution
commis, commissaire	administrator who held his appointment at the king's pleasure (cf. *officier*)
compagnons, compagnons du devoir	journeymen, associations of journeymen
Comtat (Venaissin)	part of Provence, under papal control 1274–1791
conseil d'en haut	the most important of the king's councils, which usually met on the upper floor at Versailles, hence its name
conseil d'Etat (or *conseil du roi*)	Council of State
conseil des dépêches	council concerned with reports from the *intendants*
conseil des parties	Supreme Court, rival of the Parlement of Paris
conseil privé	Privy Council
conseiller secrétaire	councillor secretary to the king; *conseiller* was a purely honorific title attached to a number of offices
Cordeliers	Paris club whose members, including Danton and Marat, were to the left of the Jacobins
corvée	forced labour, especially by peasants on road repairs
département	one of the 83 administrative units into which France was divided in 1790
dérogeance	custom by which nobles who engaged in trade or manual labour forfeited their noble status
dîme	ecclesiastical tithe
dîme inféodée	tithe which was 'impropriated', i.e. in lay hands
domaine proche (or *réserve seigneuriale*)	'demesne', that part of a manor administered directly by its lord
domaine utile (or *mouvances*)	the right to the use and profit of a piece of land
droit d'enregistrement	the right to payment when certain legal documents were drawn up; royal edicts, to be enforceable, had to be inscribed in the registers of the Parlement
droits réels	rights exercised over things as opposed to persons
élection	tax district (subdivision of a *généralité*)
élu	official of an *élection*
enragés	(literally 'the angries'), an extreme revolutionary group led by Leclerc, Roux and Varlet
états	(a) the 'three estates' or 'orders' into which French society was conventionally divided (the clergy, the nobility and the 'third estate') (b) a provincial assembly, in which the members were grouped by estates

états généraux	Estates General (1789); summoned regularly in the sixteenth century but not between 1614 and 1789
fédérés	local militiamen
féodalité	'feudalism' in the sense of seigneurial rights
fermage	(a) system of tenant farming which included an annual payment of a fixed sum (in cash or kind) for the length of the lease (b) the actions of a *fermier*
fermier	not a farmer but a steward or land agent
fermiers généraux	the men who 'farmed' the taxes, i.e. paid the government a lump sum for the right to collect them
Feuillants	a political group which separated from the Jacobins when its members refused to depose Louis XVI after the flight to Varennes
gabelle	the tax on salt, one of the most important taxes in France
gabelou	official of the *gabelle*
généralité	one of 34 administrative units of the *ancien régime*, each run by an *intendant*
Girondins	a group or party in the Legislative Assembly. Originally the supporters of Brissot, who came from the Gironde; later, the opposition to the Jacobins
gouvernement	provincial government or administration
gouverneur	(governor), great noble, the official head of provincial administration
Grande Chambre	a court of appeal, the most important chamber of the Parlement of Paris
Grande Peur	the rumour that bandits were coming, which spread through the countryside in the early days of the Revolution (July 1789)
huissier	usher in a law court
intendant	a *commis*, representing the central government, administering a *généralité*
Jacobins	Paris club to the left of the Girondins (but to the right of the Cordeliers), which met in a former convent of the religious order of the Jacobins, hence its name
journaliers	farm-hands paid by the day
journée	(literally 'day') an occasion when the crowds took to the streets
jurandes	group chosen to govern one of the *métiers jurés*
jurés	see *métiers jurés*

laboureur	(literally 'ploughman') a rich peasant or yeoman farmer
lettres de cachet	sealed letters from the king, especially those ordering the imprisonment of an individual
lit de justice	(literally 'bed of justice'), an official visit by the king to a *parlement*, sometimes necessary to make the magistrates register royal decrees
livre	pound (in weight or money)
mainmortables	tenants who were only allowed to transmit their holdings in a direct line; also *mainmorte*, the property of *mainmortables*
maîtrise	the position of master-craftsman
manouvrier	wage worker on a farm
ménager	southern term for share-cropper or *métayer*
métayage	(or *mégerie*) sharecropping, i.e. agreement by which the landlord stocked the farm and the tenant paid a proportion of the produce (usually half) as rent
métayer	share-cropper
méthivier	gleaner, agricultural labourer in a tied cottage
métiers jurés	sworn crafts
métiers libres	free crafts
monnaidiers	a counter-revolutionary faction in Arles
Montagne, (la)	the Mountain, the Jacobin deputies who sat in the upper seats of the National Convention
mouvances	see *domaine utile*
noblesse de cloche	(literally 'nobility of the bell'), those who acquired nobility via municipal office
noblesse de robe	(literally 'nobility of the gown'), those who acquired nobility through office in the *parlements* and other courts
nulle terre sans seigneur	'no land without a lord', medieval legal maxim
octroi	tax or toll on goods imported into a town
officialité	ecclesiastical court; tribunal of an *official* or ecclesiastical judge
officier	official, i.e. holder of an office which could be purchased (contrast the *commis*)
parlement	not a parliament but a law court; the Parlement of Paris was the most important, but some provinces, such as Brittany and Provence, had their own
pays d'élection	provinces which had their taxes assessed by the élus
pays d'états	provinces in which the *états* voted the taxes; regions incorporated relatively recently into France in the fifteenth century

philosophes	(literally 'philosophers'), a group of intellectuals critical of the *ancien régime*, including Voltaire and Diderot
portion congrue	clerical stipend
président à mortier	judge of the Grande Chambre of the Parlement of Paris
princes possessionnés	princes of the Holy Roman Empire with possessions in Alsace
procureur	attorney or prosecutor
procureur général syndic	high official ('Attorney General')
rente	not 'rent' but income (including income from annuities); hence the need to refer to income from land as *rente foncière*
réserve seigneuriale	see *domaine proche*
sans-culottes	(literally 'without breeches'), a militant Paris group composed mainly of wage-earners and shop-keepers, but including master-craftsmen
section	one of the 48 districts into which Paris was divided in 1790
sénéchaussée	administrative division of southern France under the *ancien régime*
subvention territoriale	land tax, intended as a substitute for the *vingtième*
taille	the main direct tax under the *ancien régime*
terres roturières	land held (even by a noble) on conditions applicable to a commoner or *roturier* (such as payment of the *taille*)
traitant	tax-farmer (see *fermiers généraux*)
travailleur de terre	farm-hand
tribunaux présidiaux	court of final appeal for less important cases
veillée	(literally 'wake'), an evening of work and entertainment, organised in turn in different houses in a village
vingtième	direct tax of a twentieth of revenue from profits and offices

Bibliography

This bibliography is deliberately selective and includes only a small number of articles from learned journals.

A. GENERAL

1. Surveys

1 Caron, P. *Manuel pratique pour l'étude de la Révolution française*, Paris, Picard, 1947
2 Walter, G. *Répertoire de l'histoire de la Révolution française* (work published between 1800 and 1940), 2 vols., Paris, Imprimerie nationale, 1941–5
3 Aulard, A. *Histoire politique de la Révolution française*, Paris, Alcan, 1901, reprinted 1926
4 Jaurès, J. *Histoire socialiste*, Paris, 1901–8, reprinted Ed. Sociales, 1968
5 Lavisse, E. *Histoire de la France contemporaine*, vol. 1, P. Sagnac, *La Révolution (1789–92)*
6 Mathiez, A. *La Révolution française*, Paris, 1922–7, reprinted A. Colin, 1959
7 Taine, H. *Les Origines de la France contemporaine*, Paris, 1876–93
8 Tocqueville, A. de *L'Ancien Régime et la Révolution*, reprinted 'Idées', Gallimard, 1964. Trans. M. W. Patterson, Oxford, 1933
9 Furet, F. and Richet, D. *La Révolution française*, 2 vols., 'Réalités', Paris, Hachette, 1965. Trans. S. Hardman, London, Macmillan, 1970
10 Godechot, J. *Les Révolutions (1770–1799)*, Paris, PUF, 1963. Trans. H. H. Rowan, as *France and the Atlantic Revolution 1770–1799*, New York, 1965
11 Lefebvre, G. *La Révolution française*, Paris, new edn 1951, reprinted PUF, 1963
12 Lefebvre, G. *Etudes sur la Révolution française*, Paris, 1954, reprinted PUF, 1963
13 Mousnier, R., Labrousse, E. and Bouloiseau, M. *Le XVIIIᵉ Siècle, Révolution intellectuelle, technique et politique (1715–1815)*, Paris, PUF, 1953
14 Soboul, A. *Précis d'histoire de la Révolution française*, Paris, Ed. Sociales,

1962. Trans. A. Forrest and C. Jones, as *The French Revolution 1787–1799*, London, 1974

15 Soboul, A. *La Révolution française*, 'Que sais-je?', Paris, PUF, 1965
16 Cobban, A. *The Social Interpretation of the French Revolution*, Cambridge, 1964
17 Furet, F. 'Le Catéchisme républicain', *Annales E.S.C.*, 1971
18 Mazauric, C. *Sur la Révolution française*, Paris, Ed. Sociales, 1970

2. *Certain Aspects of the Revolution*

19 Massin, J. *Almanach de la Révolution française*, Paris, Club du livre, 1963
20 Godechot, J. *Les Institutions de la France sous la Révolution et l'Empire*, Paris, PUF, 1951
21 Labrousse, E., Léon, P., Goubert, P. *et al.* *Histoire économique et sociale de la France (1660–1789)*, Paris, PUF, 1970
22 Guérin, D. *La Lutte des classes sous la première République: bourgeois et bras nus*, Paris, Gallimard, 1946, reprinted 1968
23 Mathiez, A. *La Vie chère et le mouvement social sous la Terreur*, Paris, A. Colin, 1927
24 Rudé, G. *The Crowd in the French Revolution*, Oxford, 1959
25 Barbier, P. and Vernillat, F. *L'Histoire de France par les chansons*, vol. 4 of *La Révolution et l'Empire*, Paris, Gallimard, 1957
26 Brunot, F. *Histoire de la langue française des origines à 1900*, vol. 9 of *La Révolution et l'Empire*, Paris, 1927
27 Jullian, M. *L'Art en France sous la Révolution et l'Empire* (duplicated lectures), Paris, CDU–SEDES, 1956
28 Godechot, J. *La Pensée révolutionnaire en France et en Europe (1789–99)*, Paris, A. Colin, 1964
29 Latreille, A. *L'Eglise catholique et la Révolution française*, Paris, Hachette, 1946–50, reprinted 1971
30 Leflon, J. *La Crise révolutionnaire (1789–1848)*, in *Histoire de l'Eglise*, ed. Fliche and Martin, vol. 20, Paris, Bloud et Gay, 1951
31 Plongeron, B. *Conscience religieuse en Révolution. Regards sur l'historiographie religieuse de la Révolution française*, Paris, Picard, 1969
32 Fugier, A. *La Révolution française et l'Empire napoléonien*, vol. 4 of *Histoire des relations internationales*, Paris, Hachette, 1954
33 Godechot, J. *La Grande Nation. L'expansion révolutionnaire de la France dans le monde, 1789–99*, Paris, PUF, 1956
34 Godechot, J. *La Contre-Révolution, doctrine et action (1789–1804)*, Paris, PUF, 1961. Trans. Salvator Attanasio, as *The Counter-Revolution: Doctrine and Action*, London, 1972
35 Vidalenc, J. *Les Emigrés français, 1789–1825*, Public. Faculté des Lettres de Caen, 1963

36 Bois, P. *Paysans de l'ouest. Des structures économiques et sociales aux options politiques depuis l'époque révolutionnaire dans la Sarthe*, Paris, Vilaire, 1960

37 Lefebvre, G. *Les Paysans du Nord pendant la Révolution française*, Paris, 1924, reprinted Bari, Laterza, 1959

38 Lefebvre, G. *Etudes orléanaises*, 2 vols., Paris, Imprimerie nationale, 1963

39 Ligou, D. *Montauban à la fin de l'Ancien Régime et au début de la Révolution (1787–1794)*, Paris, Rivière, 1958

40 Sentou, J. *Fortunes et groupes sociaux à Toulouse sous la Révolution: essai d'histoire statistique*, Toulouse, Privat, 1969

41 Trenard, L. *Lyon de l'Encyclopédie au préromantisme*, 2 vols., Paris, 1958

B. BIBLIOGRAPHY FOR SPECIFIC CHAPTERS

1. The 'ancien régime'

42 Chaunu, P. *La Civilisation des Lumières*, Paris, Arthaud, 1971

43 Goubert, P. *L'Ancien Régime*, Paris, A. Colin, 1969. Trans. S. Cox, London, 1973

44 Soboul, A. *La France à la veille de la Révolution*, Paris, SEDES, 1966

45 Soboul, A. *La Civilisation et la Révolution française*, Paris, Arthaud, 1971

46 Centre d'études et de recherches marxistes *Sur le féodalisme*, Paris, Ed. Sociales, 1971

47 Labrousse, E. *Le Paysan français des physiocrates à nos jours* (duplicated lectures), CDU–SEDES, Paris, n.d.

48 Lefebvre, G. 'Répartition de la propriété et de l'exploitation foncières à la fin de l'Ancien Régime', reprinted in his *Etudes révolutionnaires* (see no. 12 above)

49 Lemarchand, G. 'Le féodalisme dans la France rurale dans les temps modernes, essai de caractérisation', *Annales Historiques de la Révolution française*, January 1969

50 Mousnier, R. *Les Hiérarchies sociales de 1450 à nos jours*, Paris, PUF, 1969. Trans. Peter Evans, as *Social Hierarchies*, New York, 1978

51 Mandrou, R. *La France aux XVIIe et XVIIIe siècles*, Paris, PUF, 1967

52 Méthivier, H. *L'Ancien Régime*, Paris, PUF, 1961

53 Mousnier, R. 'Réflexions critiques sur la notion d'absolutisme', *Bulletin de la Société d'Histoire Moderne et Contemporaine*, 1955

54 Mousnier, R. and Hartung, F. 'Quelques problèmes concernant la monarchie absolue', *Relazioni, International Congress of Historical Sciences*, 1955, vol. 4

2. Conflict and change

55 Ariès, P. *Histoire des populations françaises et de leurs attitudes devant la vie*, Paris, Seuil, 1948, reprinted 1971

56 Armengaud, A. and Reinhard, A. *Histoire générale de la population mondiale*, Paris, Monchrestien, 1961

57 Daumard, A. and Furet, F. *Structures et relations sociales à Paris au XVIIIe siècle*, Cahiers des Annales, Paris, A. Colin, 1961

58 Palmer, R. R. 'Sur le rôle de la bourgeoisie dans la Révolution française', *Annales Historiques de la Révolution Française*, 1967

59 Robin, R. *La Société française en 1789: Semur-en-Auxois*, Paris, Plon, 1970

60 Dupront, A. (ed.). *Livre et société dans la France du XVIIIe siècle*, vol. 2, Paris, Mouton, 1970

61 Mandrou, R. *De la culture populaire en France aux XVIIe et XVIIIe siècles*, Paris, Stock, 1964

62 Mornet, D. *Les Origines intellectuelles de la Révolution*, Paris, A. Colin, 1933

63 Richet, D. 'Autour des origines idéologiques lointaines de la Révolution française', *Annales E.S.C.*, 1969

64 Reinhard, M. 'Elite et noblesse dans la seconde moitié du XVIIIe siècle', *Revue d'Histoire moderne et contemporaine*, 1956

3. Birth of a Revolution

65 Egret, J. *La Prérévolution française, 1787–88*, Paris, PUF, 1962. Trans. W. D. Camp, as *The French Pre-Revolution, 1787–1788*, Chicago, 1977

66 Labrousse, E. *La Crise de l'économie française à la fin de l'Ancien Régime et au début de la Révolution*, Paris, PUF, 1943

67 Goubert, P. and Denis, M. (eds.). *1789, les Français ont la parole*, Paris, Julliard, 1964

4. The constitutional Revolution

68 Egret, J. *La Révolution des notables, Mounier et les monarchiens*, Paris, A. Colin, 1950

69 Godechot, J. *La Prise de la Bastille*, Paris, Gallimard, 1965. Trans. Jean Stewart, as *The Taking of the Bastille*, London, 1970

70 Lefebvre, G. *1789*, Paris, 1939. Trans. R. R. Palmer, as *The Coming of the French Revolution*, Princeton, 1947

71 Lefebvre, G. *La Grande Peur*, Paris, 1932. Trans. Joan White, as *The Great Fear of 1789: Rural Panic in Revolutionary France*, London, 1973

5. *Revolutionary France*

72 Bertaud, J. P. *Valmy, la démocratie en armes*, Paris, PUF, 1970

73 Lefebvre, G. 'La Vente des biens nationaux', reprinted in his *Etudes* (see no. 12 above)

74 Lefebvre, G. 'La Révolution française et les paysans', reprinted in his *Etudes* (see no. 12 above)

75 Godechot, J. 'La Société française pendant la Révolution', in L. Halphen and R. Doucet (eds.), *Histoire de la société française*, Paris, Nathan, 1953

76 Robiquet, J. *La Vie quotidienne au temps de la Révolution*, Paris, Hachette, 1938

77 Reinhard, M. *et al. Contributions à l'histoire démographique de la Révolution française*, 1st series, Paris, 1962; 2nd series, Paris, 1965; 3rd series, Paris, 1970 (Commission d'histoire économique et sociale de la Révolution française, *Mémoires et documents*, vols. 14, 18, 25)

78 Lefebvre, G. 'Foules révolutionnaires', reprinted in his *Etudes* (see no. 12 above)

79 Cardenal, L. de. *La Province pendant la Révolution: histoire des clubs jacobins*, Paris, Payot, 1929

80 Gaston-Martin. *Les Jacobins*, Paris, PUF, 1945

81 Bellanger, C. *et al. Histoire générale de la presse française*, part 1, Paris, PUF, 1968

6. *The second Revolution*

82 Walter, G. *La Révolution française vue par ses journaux*, Paris, 1948

83 Mathiez, A. *Le 10 août*, Paris, Gallimard, 1969

84 Reinhard, M. *La Chute de la royauté*, Paris, Gallimard, 1969

SUPPLEMENTARY BIBLIOGRAPHY

Bertaud, J.-P. *Les Origines de la Révolution française*, Paris, PUF, 1971

Bluche, F. *Les Magistrats du Parlement de Paris au XVIIIe siècle (1715–1771)*, Besançon, 1960

Bosher, J. F. *French Finances, 1770–1795*, Cambridge, 1970

Castan, N. *Les Criminels du Languedoc*, Université de Toulouse–Le Mirail, 1980

Chaussinand-Nogaret, G. *La Noblesse au XVIIIe siècle. De la féodalité aux Lumières*, Paris, Hachette, 1976

Darnton, R. *The Business of Enlightenment*, Cambridge, Mass., 1979

Doyle, W. *The Origins of the French Revolution*, Oxford, 1981

Duhet, P. M. *Les Femmes et la Révolution, 1789–1794*, Paris, Julliard, 1971

Dupâquier, J. *La Population française aux XVIIe et XVIIIe siècles*, Paris, PUF, 1979

Durand, Y. *Les Fermiers généraux au XVIIIe siècle*, Paris, PUF, 1971

Egret, J. *Necker, ministre de Louis XVI*, Paris, Champion, 1975

Furet, F. *Penser la Révolution française*, Paris, Gallimard, 1978. Trans. E. Forster, as *Interpreting the French Revolution*, Cambridge, 1981

Garden, M. *Lyon et les Lyonnais au XVIIIe siècle*, Paris, Université de Lyon, 1970

Godechot, J. *Un jury pour la Révolution*, Paris, Robert Laffont, 1974

Goubert, P. *L'Ancien Régime*, vol. 2, *Les Pouvoirs*, Paris, A. Colin, 1973

Higonnet, P. *Class, Ideology, and the Rights of Nobles during the French Revolution*, Oxford, 1981

Hincker, F. *Les Français devant l'impôt sous l'Ancien Régime*, Paris, Flammarion, 1971

Hufton, O. *The Poor of Eighteenth-century France*, Oxford, 1974

Johnson, D. (ed.). *French Society and the Revolution*, Cambridge, 1976

Kaplan, S. *Bread, Politics and Political Economy in the Reign of Louis XV*, 2 vols., The Hague, Martinus Nijhoff, 1976

McManners, J. *The French Revolution and the Church*, London, SPCK, 1969

Meyer, J. *La Noblesse bretonne au dix-huitième siècle*, Paris, Flammarion, 1972

Morineau, M. *Les Faux-semblants d'un démarrage économique: agriculture et démographie en France au XVIIIe siècle* (Cahiers des Annales, 30), Paris, A. Colin, 1971

Ozouf, M. *La Fête révolutionnaire, 1789–1799*, Paris, Gallimard, 1976

Roche, D. *Le Siècle des Lumières en province. Académies et académiciens provinciaux, 1680–1789*, 2 vols., Paris, Mouton, 1978

Scott, S. F. *The Response of the French Army to the French Revolution, 1787–1793*, Oxford, 1978

Sewell, W. *Work and Revolution in France*, Cambridge, 1980

Soboul, A. *Comprendre la Révolution: problèmes politiques de la Révolution française, 1789–1797*, Paris, Maspero, 1981

Starobinski, J. *1789, les emblèmes de la raison*, Paris, Flammarion, 1973

Suratteau, J. R. *La Révolution française, certitudes et controverses*, Paris, PUF, 1973

Vovelle, M. *Les Métamorphoses de la fête en Provence, 1750–1830*, Paris, Flammarion, 1976

Actes du colloque de Toulouse (1968), *L'Abolition de la féodalité dans le monde occidental*, 2 vols., Paris, CNRS, 1971

La Fête révolutionnaire, actes du colloque tenu à Clermont-Ferrand en 1974

Les Origines de la Révolution française, actes du colloque tenu à Göttingen en 1975

Index of names

Agout, Jean Antoine d', 132
Aiguillon, Armand, duc d', 74, 98, 112
Albert, François Hector d', 128
Allarde, Pierre Leroy d', 151
Amelot, Antoine Amelot de Chaillou, 91
Antoine or Anthoine, François, 144
Antraigues, Emmanuel de Launay, comte
 d', 126, 206
Artois, Charles, comte d', 74, 76, 105,
 110, 126, 139, 140, 145, 164
Augeard, Jacques, 125

Babeuf, François Noël, 106
Bailly, Jean Sylvain, 98, 101, 102, 105,
 121, 143, 144, 183
Barentin, Charles de, 100
Barnave, Antoine, 25, 49, 81, 98, 106,
 115, 119, 120, 121, 133, 142, 147, 212,
 213
Barruel, Augustin, abbé, 59, 68, 206
Basire, Claude, 212
Beauvais, Jean-Baptiste de, 18
Belle-Ile, Charles Fouquet, maréchal de,
 18
Bernard, Samuel, 52
Bernis, François, cardinal de, 131
Bertier de Sauvigny, Louis, 106, 179, 180
Bertin, 23
Bertrand de Molleville, Antoine, 222
Billaud-Varenne, Jacques Nicolas, 230
Blake, William, 137
Boisgelin de Cucé, Jean, cardinal de, 98,
 120, 129, 131
Bonneville, Nicolas, 135
Boscary de Romaine, Jean Marie, 104
Boucher, François, 71
Bouillé, François, marquis de, 128, 140,
 141, 143, 229
Boulainvilliers, Henri, comte de, 25
Boullée, 71, 197

Breteuil, Louis le Tonnelier de, 104, 132,
 140
Brienne see Loménie de
Brissot, 91, 186, 193, 198, 211, 212, 217,
 220, 221, 225, 227, 229
Broglie, Victor, duc de, 104
Brosses, Charles de, 16
Brunswick, Charles Guillaume, duc de,
 180, 193, 230
Burke, Edmund, 138, 206
Buzot, François, 121, 209, 218

Calonne, Charles Alexandre de, 75, 76,
 77, 78, 90, 126, 140
Carnot, Lazarre, 212
Carra, Jean-Louis, 193
Castellane, Jean Antoine, Jean Arnaud,
 Elléon (bishops all three), 20
Catherine II, 2, 138
Cazalès, Jacques Antoine de, 98, 120, 206
Cernay, marquis de, 53
Chabot, François, 212
Champion de Cicé, Jérôme, marquis de,
 119, 120
Charles III, king of Spain, 138
Chénier, Marie Joseph, 197
Clavière, Etienne, 220, 223, 226
Clermont-Tonnerre, Stanislas, comte de,
 120, 183
Cloots, Anacharsis, 138
Coleridge, Samuel Taylor, 137
Condé, Louis Henri, prince de, 140
Condorcet, Marie de Caritat, marquis de,
 72, 91, 142, 212, 220
Conti, Louis, prince de, 16
Coroller, Louis, 144
Couthon, Georges, 167, 212, 217
Croy, Anne Emmanuel de Croy-Solre,
 prince de, 53

Danjou, Jean Pierre, 134
Dansart, Claude, 185
Danton, Georges, 132, 142, 144, 185
David, Louis, 71, 149, 195, 197
Delessart, Antoine de Waldec de, 119, 132, 222
Delessert, Jules, 52, 104
Desilles, lieutenant, 196
Desmoulins, Camille, 104, 116, 146, 185, 193, 198
Diderot, Denis, 36
Dillon, Théobald de, general, 224
Dodun, Madame, 212
Dolivier, abbé, 208, 218
Dreux-Brézé, Henri, marquis de, 102
Drouet, Jean Baptiste, 141
Dubois-Crancé, Edmond de, 158
Duhamel du Monceau, Henri, 11
Dumouriez, Charles, 223, 226
Duplay, Maurice, 53
Dupont de Nemours, Pierre, 98
Duport, Adrien, 91, 115, 119, 121, 132, 133
Duportail, Louis le Bègue, 119, 132

Eprémesnil, Jean Jacques Duval d', 79

Fauchet, Claude, 147
Favras, Thomas de Mahy, marquis de, 125
Ferrand, Antoine, comte, 206
Fersen, Axel de, 74, 140, 213, 221
Fichte, Johann, 137
Flesselles, Jacques de, 180
Florida Blanca, François Moñino, marquis de, 138
Forster, Johann, 137
Foulon de Doué, Joseph, 106, 179, 180
Fox, Charles, 137
Fragonard, Honoré, 71
Fréron, Louis-Marie, 193
Froment, 126

Gensonné, Armand, 212, 227
Gerle, Dom Christophe, 149
Gorsas, Antoine, 193
Gossec, François, 195, 199
Gournay, Vincent de, 23
Grégoire, Henri, abbé, 98, 121, 133, 149
Greuze, Jean-Baptiste, 71
Gribeauval, J. B. Vaquette de, 29
Guadet, Marguerite-Elie, 212, 220, 227
Guibert, Hippolyte, comte de, 29

Guillotin, Dr Joseph, 149
Gustavus III, king of Sweden, 138, 223

Hamel, Madame, 200
Hanriot, François, 182, 208
Hébert, Jacques René, 185, 191, 193
Helman (engraver), 198
Hottinguer, Jean-Conrad, 52
Huguenin, Sulpice, 182
Hugues, Joseph, 52

Imbert-Colomès, Jacques, 127
Isnard, Maximin, 208

Joseph II, emperor, 138
Jourdan, Mathieu Jouve (the 'butcher'), 214

Kant, Immanuel, 137
Klopstock, Friedrich, 137

Laclos, Pierre Choderlos de, 92
Lacombe, Claire, 204
La Fayette, Marie-Joseph du Motier, marquis de, 78, 80, 91, 98, 116, 117, 119, 120, 121, 122, 123, 124, 128, 132, 133, 135, 137, 143, 144, 173, 183, 187, 192, 212, 221, 223, 224, 225, 226, 227
Lally-Tollendal, Trophime, marquis de, 115, 120
La Luzerne, César, duc de (cardinal), 119
Lambesc, Charles de Lorraine, prince de, 104
Lameth, Alexander and Charles de, 115, 120, 121, 133, 223
Lamoignon, Charles François II de, 79, 80, 83, 89
Lange, 218
Lanjuinais, Jean Denis, 101, 121
La Rochefoucauld, François de, 20, 91, 98, 120
La Rouairie, Charles de Sapinaud de, 215
La Tour du Pin, Jean de Paulin, comte de, 119, 128
Launay, Bernard Jourdan, marquis de, 105, 180
Le Chapelier, Isaac, 98, 101, 121, 151, 165, 183
Lecoulteux de Canteleu, Jean-Barthélemy, 120
Lécuyer or Lescuyer (Avignon 'patriot'), 214
Ledoux, Claude Nicolas, 71

Legendre, Louis, 182, 226
Leopold II, emperor, 138, 140, 221, 222
Lieutaud (mayor of Marseilles), 122
Limon, marquis de, 230
Lindet, J. B. Robert, 212
Loménie de Brienne, Etienne Charles de, 20, 77, 78, 80, 83, 88, 93
Louis XIV, 17, 30
Louis XV, 24, 25, 73
Louis XVI, 25, 26, 27, 73, 74, 105, 114, 117, 131, 140, 153, 194, 213, 221, 223, 226, 227, 228, 231
Loustalot, or Loustallot, Elisée, 116, 135, 193
Lückner, Nicolas, baron de, 224

Machaut d'Arnouville, J. B., 37
'Madame Royale', 74
Maillard, Julien, 116, 182
Malbosc, 213
Malesherbes, Guillaume Chrétien de Lamoignon de, 36
Mallet (banker), 52
Mallet du Pan, Jacques, 183, 206, 230
Malouet, 115, 117, 183
Malseigne, 128
Marat, 72, 116, 119, 121, 122, 124, 125, 127, 135, 141, 142, 144, 147, 153, 175, 180, 185, 191, 192, 193, 198, 204, 208, 209, 218, 219, 224, 225
Marche, Jean-Paul de la, bishop, 20
Marie-Antoinette, 26, 73, 74, 143, 221, 227
Maupeou, René Nicolas de, 27, 37, 74, 79
Maury, Jean Siffrein, abbé, 98, 120, 129, 206
Mehul, Etienne, 199
Mercy Argentau, François de, 140, 213, 224
Merlin de Douai, Philippe, 121, 139
Merlin de Thionville, Antoine, 212
'Mesdames' (the king's aunts), 135, 140
Mirabeau, 16, 32, 75, 77, 88, 91, 98, 101, 102, 113, 114, 119, 120, 121, 122, 123, 132, 133, 155, 183, 191, 192, 193, 195, 197
Mirabeau (the 'Barrel'), André Boniface Riquetti, vicomte de, 120, 206
Monnet (engraver), 198
Monnier de la Quarrée, 135
Montesquieu, Charles de Secondat, baron de, 16, 25, 30, 37, 72, 150
Montlosier, 206

Montmorency-Laval, Mathieu, duc de, 53, 91, 120
Montmorin-Saint Hérem, Armand, comte de, 119, 141
Montsabert, Anne Louis Goislard, comte de, 79
Mounier, Jean-Joseph, 81, 82, 83, 98, 101, 114, 117, 120

Narbonne, Louis Marie, comte de, 222
Necker, Jacques, 74, 75, 77, 80, 83, 88, 89, 90, 98, 100, 104, 105, 106, 115, 129
Noailles, Louis, vicomte de, 98, 112
Normandie, duc de, 74

Oberkampf, Christophe, 40
Orléans, Louis-Philippe-Joseph, duc d', 16, 74, 79, 91, 92, 102, 142, 173

Paine, Thomas, 138
Périer, Claude, 52, 53, 81
Perrégaux, Jean, 52
Pétion de Villeneuve, Jérôme, 55, 98, 121, 133, 144, 209, 218, 221, 226, 227, 231
Pius VI, Pope, 131
Polignac, Yolande de Polastron, duchesse de, 74
Prieur, Pierre-Louis, 198
Provence, Louis, comte de, 74, 76, 125, 140, 219

Rabaut Saint-Etienne, Jean-Paul, 149
Réveillon, 87, 176, 181
Rivarol (Antoine Rivaroli), 192, 206
Robert, Pierre François, 144
Robespierre, Maximilien de, 53, 91, 98, 101, 120, 121, 133, 142, 144, 145, 147, 148, 153, 186, 198, 208, 209, 211, 212, 215, 218, 219, 221, 222, 223, 224, 225, 226, 230
Rochambeau, Jean-Baptiste, comte de, 224
Roederer, Pierre Louis, 229, 231
Rohan, Louis René, cardinal de, 20
Roland, Jean Marie Roland de la Platière, 223, 225, 226
Roland, Madame, née Manon Phlipon, 212
Rouget de l'Isle, Claude, 199, 229
Rousseau, Jean-Jacques, 59, 66, 70, 71, 148
Roux, Jacques, 182, 218

Sade, Donatien Alphonse François, marquis de, 16
Saint-Priest, François, comte de, 119
Saint-Simon, Claude Henri de Rouvroy, comte de, 17, 25
Santerre, Antoine, 182, 226
Sauce, 141
Savary, Jacques (businessman), 52, 70
Ségur, Philippe, marquis de, 18, 29, 53
Sénac de Meilhan, Gabriel, 206
Servan, Joseph Servan de Gerbey, 225, 226
Sieyès, Emmanuel, 50, 91, 98, 101, 113, 115, 120, 146, 155, 183
Simonneau (mayor of Etampes), 196, 217
Solages, chevalier de, 53
Staël, Germaine Necker de, 212

Talleyrand, Charles de Talleyrand-Périgord, 20, 91, 98, 120, 129, 136, 161, 223
Target, Guy, 91, 121

Terray, Joseph-Marie, abbé, 37, 44, 74
Thouret, Jacques, 91, 94, 98, 121, 155
Trier (elector of), 219, 221, 222
Tronchet, François, 121
Turgot, Anne-Robert, 23, 28, 37, 74

Varlet, Jean, 182
Vauban, Sébastien Leprestre de, 44
Vergniaud, Pierre, 147, 197, 209, 212, 225, 227
Victor-Amadeus, king of Sardinia, 126, 138
Virieu, François-Henri, comte de, 115, 120
Volney, Constantin, 98
Voltaire, François-Marie Arouet de, 16, 59, 69, 70, 195, 199

Wendel, de, 53
Wilberforce, William, 137
Wordsworth, William, 137